WELCOM

Leaders of men in wartime are a breed apart. Training, dedication, discernment and risk versus reward dictate the course of a battle – and subsequently a conflict. It follows then that the future of nations, the lives of generations to come and the fate of the globe are at times bound up in military conflict.

Nowhere else in the human experience are the stakes so high. And the men who prosecuted World War Two, Allied and Axis, profoundly influenced the outcome of that conflict, liberation and self-determination versus the imposition of a new, cruel Dark Age, charting the strategic and tactical course of events that determined the victor and the vanquished. Their decisions meant life and death for those who followed their orders. Their perspectives on the battlefield, the grand design, the political landscape and the post-war world made a lasting impact.

Where, then, did their competence – or incompetence – originate? How were they prepared to execute some of the most significant operations in history? Eisenhower teetering on the brink of D-Day triumph or disaster, Montgomery and Rommel grappling in the desert, Yamamoto sending waves of planes to attack Pearl Harbor, Zhukov and the Soviet sledgehammer bludgeoning Berlin, the capital and black heart of Nazi Germany – each of these had reached a crossroads, a moment for command decision. And then, they acted.

Author George Orwell once observed: "People sleep peaceably in their beds at night only because rough men stand ready to do violence on their behalf." In this statement lies the essence of military preparedness, command presence and execution. A vigilant people will guard their civilisation through the presence of a strong, armed force – or their freedom and national survival will be in peril. In their preparedness, they rely on the soldier, sailor and airman sworn to do their duty.

That duty is defined by the military acumen of their leaders. And so, the proverbial hinge of fate swings forwards or backwards, based upon the command decisions made by military leaders in time of war. During World War Two, great commanders on land, sea and air sent men into battle and the soundness of their decisions was borne out in the casualty rolls, the territorial gains and losses, control of the great oceans, mastery of the skies and eventual Allied victory.

Commanders of World War Two explores the lives, times, successes and failures of the great military leaders who conducted the largest, most consequential military conflict in the history of mankind.

Consider their situations, their initiatives and their responses in moments of seismic magnitude. The lives and times of the great commanders come into sharp focus and offer insight into the course of the war, its triumphs, tragedies and depth of human experience and survival amid extraordinary circumstances. Engage in the discourse, consider these military men and their moments.

Michael E Haskew
Editor

ISBN: 978 1 80282 571 8
Editor: Michael E Haskew
Senior editor, specials: Carol Randall
Email: carol.randall@keypublishing.com
Design: SJmagic DESIGN SERVICES, India
Cover design: Daniel Hilliard
Cover images: Getty Images
Colourisation: Richard Molloy

Advertising Sales Manager: Brodie Baxter
Email: brodie.baxter@keypublishing.com
Tel: 01780 755131
Advertising Production: Debi McGowan
Email: debi.mcgowan@keypublishing.com

SUBSCRIPTION/MAIL ORDER
Key Publishing Ltd, PO Box 300, Stamford, Lincs, PE9 1NA
Tel: 01780 480404
Subscriptions email: subs@keypublishing.com

Mail Order email: orders@keypublishing.com
Website: www.keypublishing.com/shop

PUBLISHING
Group CEO: Adrian Cox
Publisher, Books and Bookazines: Jonathan Jackson
Head of Marketing: Shaun Binnington
Published by
Key Publishing Ltd, PO Box 100, Stamford, Lincs, PE9 1XQ
Tel: 01780 755131 **Website:** www.keypublishing.com

PRINTING
Precision Colour Printing Ltd, Haldane,
Halesfield 1, Telford, Shropshire. TF7 4QQ

DISTRIBUTION
Seymour Distribution Ltd, 2 Poultry Avenue, London,
EC1A 9PU
Enquiries Line: 02074 294000.

Below: General Dwight D Eisenhower, supreme commander allied expeditionary force, meets with his deputies in London on February 1, 1944. Seated from left: Air Chief Marshal Sir Arthur Tedder, Eisenhower and General Sir Bernard Law Montgomery. Standing, from left, are: General Omar N Bradley, Admiral Sir Bertram Ramsay, Air Marshal Sir Trafford Leigh-Mallory and General Walter Bedell Smith. (Public Domain)

CONTENTS

During the campaign in Western Europe, General Courtney Hodges, Harry Crerar, Bernard Montgomery, Omar Bradley and Miles Dempsey pose during a conference in 1944. (Public Domain)

Admirals Chester Nimitz (centre) and William F 'Bull' Halsey, are sworn in as permanent officers of fleet admiral rank in May 1946. (Public Domain)

Admiral Karl Dönitz, centre, stands with Reich Armaments Minister Albert Speer (left) and Colonel General Alfred Jodl (right) after their arrest in 1945. (Public Domain)

German prisoners captured during the opening hours of Operation Overlord, the D-Day invasion, are marched to the rear in Normandy.
(Public Domain)

The ashes of Japanese Admiral Isoroku Yamamoto are carried aboard the battleship *Musashi* in 1943. (Public Domain)

Marshal Georgi Zhukov, victor of the Battle of Berlin, greets officers of the British Army in 1945.
(Public Domain)

GENERAL DWIGHT D EISENHOWER

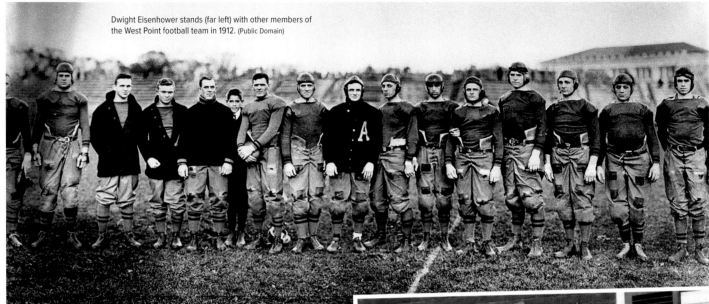

Dwight Eisenhower stands (far left) with other members of the West Point football team in 1912. (Public Domain)

As chief of staff to General Walter Kreuger, commander of the US Third Army, Dwight D Eisenhower planned the massive Louisiana Manoeuvres of 1941, which involved around 270,000 soldiers. His key role, however, barely gained acknowledgment from the media. In fact, in newspapers, Eisenhower was identified as Lieutenant Colonel D D Ersenbeing.

Three years later, however, General Dwight D Eisenhower's name would be known worldwide. As supreme commander allied expeditionary Fforce, it was Eisenhower who led the great Allied D-Day invasion of Hitler's Fortress Europe, committing 150,000 troops, more than 5,000 ships of every description and countless aircraft to the effort of liberating Western Europe from Nazi occupation in World War Two.

Eisenhower's rise to the highest echelon of military command was nothing short of remarkable. When he set D-Day in motion, he had never experienced combat and had never fired a shot in anger. However, his abilities as an administrator, team builder and organiser had already come sharply into focus. The military, though, had seemed an unlikely career option for a boy of the American Midwest, born on October 14, 1890, in the small town of Denison, Texas. The third of seven sons, Dwight grew up in the dusty cow town of Abilene, Kansas, the terminus of the great Chisholm Trail. He was a natural athlete and enjoyed American football and other sports, as well as getting into a few minor scrapes with other boys.

A wider world

The Eisenhower brothers did not lack ambition and college was perhaps a way to see the world, broaden horizons and find a vocation. Since the family's financial resources were quite limited, Dwight made a pact with his brother Edgar. One would go to college while the other worked and sent money to help pay for the schooling. When the first graduated, the other would reciprocate.

Edgar packed off to the University of Michigan, while Dwight remained in Abilene, working long hours at the local Belle Springs Creamery. Two years passed slowly by and then, one evening, Dwight's close friend Edward 'Swede' Hazlett broached the topic of applying for admission to the US Naval Academy at Annapolis, Maryland. The

Eisenhower and three friends pause for a photograph prior to participating in a transcontinental military convoy in 1919. (Public Domain)

government would pay for the education, while the service academies were known for their prowess in sports.

The appeal was tremendous. Dwight dreamed of playing football and the drudgery of the creamery had become almost unbearable. He decided to sit for the competitive entrance examination and travelled to Jefferson Barracks in St Louis, Missouri. Soon enough, he learned that he was too old for admission to Annapolis. Instead, he focused on an appointment to the US Military Academy at West Point, New York, entering in the summer of 1911. A member of the class of 1915, the fabled 'Class the Stars Fell On', he stood 61st among 164 newly commissioned second lieutenants and gained the nickname Ike.

A year after graduation, he married socialite Mamie Dowd, of Denver, Colorado. The couple had two sons. Dwight 'Icky' Eisenhower was born in 1917 and died of scarlet fever at just three years old. The young couple were shaken by the tragedy and carried the sorrow with them for the rest of their lives. John Eisenhower was born in 1922, later attended West Point, rose to the rank of brigadier general, served

General Eisenhower sits in a vehicle along with President Franklin D. Roosevelt during a visit to Sicily in 1943. General George S Patton Jr is visible in the background. (Public Domain)

Wearing the two-star rank of major general, Eisenhower sat for this portrait in 1942, the year of his appointment as Allied commander in the European Theatre. (Public Domain)

as US ambassador to Belgium and became a well-known historian and author. John died at the age of 91 in 2013.

An officer's journey

Eisenhower regretted that he remained in the US during World War One and did not have the privilege of serving overseas. He believed that the lack of such experience would impede his military career and at times it appeared he was correct. Actually, his skill and capability as a staff officer and trainer of soldiers had been recognised and made him more valuable in preparing troops for service abroad. Holding several different posts around the United States, he was instrumental in the establishment of Camp Colt in Gettysburg, Pennsylvania, where men trained for the fledgling US Army's armoured corps. He had risen temporarily in rank during the Great War, but with its conclusion reverted to his permanent rank of captain. Promoted to major shortly afterward, he held that rank for the next 16 years.

Between the two world wars, Eisenhower served in the Panama Canal Zone under General Fox Connor and in Washington, DC and the Philippines under General Douglas MacArthur. Both were to have profound influence on his command perspective. He graduated the Command and General Staff College at Fort Leavenworth, Kansas, at the top of his class among 245 officers and commanded an infantry battalion at Fort Benning, Georgia. During the unrest in the capital surrounding the Bonus Marchers, World War One veterans clamouring for financial payments they believed were due, Eisenhower warned MacArthur, then army chief of staff, to stay away from the violence that ensued with the dispersal of the marchers.

However, MacArthur donned his dress uniform and went to observe the destruction of the Bonus Marchers' camp at Anacostia Flats, sparking a public relations disaster. Eisenhower was incensed. He never forgot the spectacle and came to regard MacArthur with disdain – not only for the Bonus March fiasco but also for being blamed in a spending scandal in the Philippines that involved a lavish parade that MacArthur favoured during austere financial times.

As an obscure lieutenant colonel, Eisenhower's future in the US Army seemed somewhat limited when he returned to the US from the Philippines in late 1939 to command a battalion of the 15th Infantry Division at Fort Lewis, Washington. However, the posting to Third Army and the success of the Louisiana Manoeuvres followed in mid-1941. After 26 years in the Army, Eisenhower was promoted to the rank of brigadier general. He had forged numerous

Dwight Eisenhower with his future wife, Mamie in San Antonio, Texas, in January 1916. (Public Domain)

friendships within the officer corps but still wondered whether his military career would advance any further.

Years of experience, some of them quite humbling, had brought him to the realisation that he had to control a volatile temper. He could be quite charming and co-operative, nurturing those traits in others. He flashed an incredible grin just at the right moment to seal a friendship and his administrative skills were widely known. Opportunity did come after US entry into World War Two.

During their days at West Point, Eisenhower had become friends with another officer, one whose star was on the rise as war clouds gathered in Europe. Mark Clark, a member of the academy class of 1917, was already a part of the inner circle of General George C. Marshall, who had assumed the duties of Army chief of staff in the summer of 1939. During a reorganisation of the war department, Marshall asked Clark to provide the names of 10 candidates to lead the newly created War Plans Division.

Clark responded without hesitation: "Ike Eisenhower. If you have to have ten names I'll just put nine ditto marks below."

A meteoric rise

Marshall summoned Eisenhower to Washington and asked for a frank assessment of the US military situation in the Pacific, which presented a complex array of issues and challenges. Marshall concurred with Eisenhower's conclusions and soon the war plans division officer was a trusted member of the cadre that charted the American strategy during the difficult days of World War Two, both in Europe and the Pacific. By the spring of 1942, Eisenhower was sent to Great Britain to gauge the level of preparedness for a major offensive that would return the Allies to the European continent.

When he returned to the US, Eisenhower delivered a frank and somewhat alarming report on the lack of progress being made. He was surprised to find himself heading back to Britain with the responsibility for making the preparations proceed properly. With the rank of lieutenant general, he was elevated to Allied commander in the European theatre of operations on June 25, 1942. Less than a year earlier, he had been an obscure lieutenant colonel planning war games in Louisiana. On the evening of his appointment, Ike and Mamie had gone to dinner.

He broke the news to his wife that he would again be leaving the country and confessed that he had no idea when he would see her again.

She asked: "What post are you going to have?" He grinned and replied: "I'm going to command the whole shebang!"

Operation Torch

Eisenhower also held command responsibility for the initial major Allied offensive against the Axis. As commander of Allied forces in the Mediterranean, he led Operation Torch, the landings of American and British troops on the shores of North Africa at Oran, Algiers and Casablanca on November 8, 1942. It was in North Africa that American soldiers first encountered the veteran troops of the German Wehrmacht – and those first encounters brought setbacks to be sure. Nevertheless, the Americans gained combat experience rapidly amid some scepticism from their British partners. As overall commander, Eisenhower not only confronted the Nazis and their Italian Fascist cohorts, but also dealt with the inevitable wrangling and rivalry that existed among senior Allied officers. He took on the job with his usual flair for the positive and became a master of coalition warfare.

During the North African campaign, Eisenhower faced a real crisis when the US Army's II Corps was roughly handled by enemy forces under the vaunted General Erwin Rommel at Kasserine Pass in February 1943. Soon after the fiasco at Kasserine, it was apparent that General Lloyd Fredendall had to be replaced. Eisenhower turned to Clark, his trusted friend who had brought him to Marshall's attention and then accompanied him to Britain a year earlier.

Clark, however, declined the command opportunity. He believed that leading II Corps would be a demotion from his position as deputy

US troops and M4 Sherman medium tanks are loaded aboard transport craft in England in preparation for the June 6, 1944, Normandy invasion. (Public Domain)

theatre commander and that such a move would be detrimental to his career. Eisenhower was bitterly disappointed and instead gave II Corps to another old friend, General George S. Patton Jr. Patton accepted the post with enthusiasm and went on to become a legendary field commander. Eisenhower never forgot Clark's decision and the fact that his deputy had placed his own career above the urgency of the mission at hand.

With the introduction of Allied troops in western North Africa, Rommel and Panzerarmee Afrika were forced to fight on two fronts. Six months after Operation Torch commenced, the Allied forces advancing eastward linked up with General Bernard Montgomery's Eighth Army, which had pursued Rommel westward across hundreds of miles of desert following the great victory at El Alamein in October 1942. In the spring of 1943, the Germans and Italians were pressed into a pocket along the Mediterranean coast of Tunisia, finally surrendering as thousands of Axis soldiers marched into captivity. In retrospect, lessons had been learned. There were some aspects of the conduct of the campaign that could have been carried off better. However, planning was already well underway for the next major military operation.

Operation Husky

In July 1943, American and British troops executed Operation Husky, landing on the shores of Sicily, and Eisenhower was again in command of a coalition that proceeded towards victory over the German and Italian forces on the island. However, he was further confronted with the inherent difficulties of maintaining the co-operation of British and American commanders. Two of his subordinates, Patton and Montgomery, were possessed of towering egos and had clashed even before their soldiers hit the Sicilian beaches.

Eisenhower regularly dealt with the squabbles between the two army commanders and struggled at times to keep their focus on the defeat of the enemy rather than a game of one-upmanship between themselves. Patton complicated matters mightily during a pair of unfortunate incidents when he visited field hospitals and slapped soldiers suffering from battle fatigue. Eisenhower was enraged at the behaviour of his old friend and had no choice other than to sideline one of his most capable field officers.

In the throes of the public relations catastrophe, Eisenhower wrote a pointed letter of reprimand to Patton. It read: "I clearly understand that firm and drastic measures were at times necessary in order to secure the desired objectives. But this does not excuse brutality, abuse of the sick, nor exhibition of uncontrollable temper in front of subordinates. I must so seriously question your good judgement and your self-discipline as to raise serious doubt in my mind as to your future usefulness."

This troubling episode with Patton illustrated Eisenhower's growth as a senior commander. He had not only tamed his own fiery temper but recognised that decisive action had to be taken in response to another's lack of control. He was willing to make tough decisions even when they involved close friends. Although Patton was benched, he did re-emerge later in the war to lead Third Army in Europe and

On June 5, 1944, just prior to D-Day, Eisenhower visits with paratroopers of the US 101st Airborne Division prior to their departure for France. (Public Domain)

Southwick House served as Eisenhower's headquarters in the days leading up to the launch of Operation Overlord. (Creative Commons via Wikipedia)

American soldiers wade ashore at embattled Omaha Beach on D-Day, June 6, 1944. Eisenhower's decision set the invasion of Western Europe in motion. (Public Domain)

Eisenhower, seated centre, posed for this portrait with senior American ground and air commanders in 1945. (Public Domain)

it was Eisenhower's adept handling of the situation – in the face of a caustic press that wanted Patton's head on a plate – which allowed such redemption to occur.

Following the weeks-long campaign in Sicily, the next major Allied offensive took place in September 1943, with Operation Avalanche, the invasion of the Italian mainland at Salerno. Clark took command of the Allied Fifth Army, while Montgomery maintained control of his Eighth Army and the two forces began a long, painful slog up the Italian boot, Clark from Salerno on the Tyrrhenian coast and Montgomery from Calabria and Taranto to the south. The Salerno landings faced fierce opposition and Clark was required to scramble all available troops and rely on heavy, accurate naval gunfire support to stem the German counterattacks. As World War Two in Europe ended in the spring of 1945, the fighting in Italy had not concluded.

Focus on Fortress Europe

While the war progressed in the Mediterranean, the prospect for an Allied invasion of Hitler's Fortress Europe (Festung Europa in German), somewhere in northwestern France, remained a principal focus for the Allied high command. President Franklin D Roosevelt was well aware that General Marshall had long desired the role of supreme Allied commander for the invasion. However, he also confessed that he could not sleep soundly if Marshall, his closest military adviser, was permanently detached from Washington, DC.

Given his recent experience and his recognised ability to manage the sometimes tenuous relationship between British and American generals, Eisenhower became the logical choice to lead the invasion of Nazi-occupied France. Codenamed Operation Overlord, the assault was slated for the coast of Normandy on June 5, 1944. The Normandy

invasion was fraught with risk and the planning was meticulous. Still, everyone involved at the highest levels of command realised that any military plan was likely to fracture when set in motion.

Three Allied airborne divisions, the American 82nd and 101st and the British 6th, were to reach Normandy by parachute and glider in the pre-dawn hours and seize key objectives, holding until relieved. Then, after preparatory aerial bombing and naval bombardment, Allied troops would hit the beaches, codenamed Gold, Juno, Sword, Omaha and Utah. After a lodgement was established, the Allied armies would proceed to destroy German opposition in Normandy, drive across France and the German frontier and eventually link up with the spearheads of the Soviet Red Army advancing from the east, ensuring the destruction of the Third Reich.

Of course, certain circumstances were completely beyond the control of Allied military planners. Chief among these was the weather – and the unpredictability of the elements across the English Channel and northern Europe exerted significant influence on the proceedings. The strongest gale to buffet the Channel in half a century arrived just in time to thwart the launch of Operation Overlord. Foul weather forced a 24-hour postponement and the landings were moved to June 6.

Still, there was an air of uncertainty as steady rain drummed on the rooftop of Southwick House, Eisenhower's headquarters just north of Portsmouth. Years of planning hung in the balance, while thousands of soldiers were loaded aboard troop transports for the cross-Channel attack. They could not be held aboard these ships indefinitely. If the weather did not sufficiently clear on the 6th, the next period of favourable moonlight and tides would not occur for another two weeks. Secrecy would no doubt be compromised. Such a postponement was anathema to Eisenhower. Fighting the defending Germans was bad enough and dealing with the terrible weather only compounded the problem.

At 4.15am on June 5, Eisenhower called his lieutenants together at Southwick House. He wanted their perspectives as the winds howled and sheets of rain continued to pour. RAF Group Captain James Martin Stagg delivered an update on the weather, offering a glimmer of hope as he predicted a slight improvement in conditions that might allow Overlord to move forward. When Stagg had finished his briefing, Eisenhower looked around the room. Regardless of what the other officers thought, the decision to unleash the Allied juggernaut belonged solely to him. The course of World War Two in Europe depended on his pronouncement alone.

General Montgomery, commander of Allied ground forces, spoke up, "I would say go!" As other officers voiced their concerns, Eisenhower paced the floor with his hands clutched behind his back, turned toward the other men, and firmly declared: "Okay, we'll go!"

Everyone sprang into action, hurriedly dispatching the necessary orders that would bring about the liberation of Western Europe and the defeat of Nazi Germany 11 months later. Perhaps no other major military undertaking in history had been loosed with such grave concerns, unanswered questions and so many lives at stake.

Eisenhower was equal to the challenge, hoping for and expecting a positive outcome. But in case a serious reversal was experienced, he wanted no ambiguity as to who was responsible for it. Eisenhower never placed himself above the mission and as supreme commander he was willing to accept full responsibility for the

Pausing to smoke a cigarette, Eisenhower wears the rank of five-star General of the Army on his uniform in 1945. As supreme Allied commander in Europe, he was a master of coalition warfare. (Public Domain)

After the surrender proceedings in Reims that ended World War Two in Europe, Eisenhower and other senior Allied officers share a light moment. (Public Domain)

the great River Rhine, Eisenhower prosecuted a broad front strategy, continuing to press the enemy at multiple locations to divide their forces and thus wear them down through attrition while minimising the potential for a strong German counter-attack with concentrated troops and tanks. Only once did Eisenhower divert from the broad front strategy and the result was the failure of Operation Market Garden in September 1944.

Montgomery had lobbied for Market Garden, a combined airborne and ground offensive to seize key bridges over the Rhine and other rivers in the Netherlands. Once the bridges were taken and held by the American 101st and 82nd Airborne Divisions and the British 1st Airborne Division, the ground forces of XXX Corps would relieve them and open the way for a decisive drive into the Ruhr, the industrial heart of Germany. With successful execution, Market Garden would, asserted Montgomery, very possibly end the war in Europe by Christmas.

In the event, Market Garden was a valiant effort, but elements of the 1st Airborne Division were trapped and ravaged at Arnhem as they attempted to capture the bridge there over the Neder Rhine. The

success or failure of Operation Overlord. In the event of the latter, he hastily scribbled a statement for the clutch of reporters that would be waiting. He hoped that the sombre message would never be released.

It read: "Our landings in the Cherbourg-Havre area have failed to gain a satisfactory foothold and I have withdrawn the troops. My decision to attack at this time and place was based upon the best information available. The troops, the air and the Navy did all that bravery and devotion to duty could do. If any blame or fault attaches to the attempt, it is mine alone."

Such clarity and willingness to accept the heavy burden of command is sublime. Overlord succeeded despite tense moments through the day, particularly at Omaha Beach, where the stiffest German resistance occurred.

Beyond the beaches

The Normandy campaign proved an arduous affair as the Germans defended the hedgerow country with tenacity. Originally intended to mark the boundaries between adjacent farmsteads, these ancient mounds of dirt, trees and sod, known locally as the bocage, provided ideal defensive positions. The enemy posted machine guns and anti-tank weapons down virtually every farm lane, forcing the Allied troops to slug their way forward.

The communications and road nexus at the village of Caen was one of Montgomery's D-Day objectives. However, stiff German defences prevented its capture. A full month of fighting was required before Allied soldiers secured Caen, but in the meantime Montgomery brought the heaviest concentration of German armour to him and facilitated the success of Operation Cobra, the long anticipated breakout from the hedgerow country, launched on July 25, 1944. After carpet bombing of the front line to the south, US tanks and troops spearheaded by Patton's Third Army plunged through the gap and broke through the stubborn German defences in Normandy, executing a dazzling dash across France.

While their soldiers slugged it out with the Germans, Patton and Montgomery maintained an intense rivalry and Patton chafed when fuel and other resources were diverted to Montgomery's northern thrust, halting his own tanks in their rush toward the German frontier. Elsewhere, Allied forces executed a giant pincer movement that trapped thousands of German soldiers in an ever-tightening ring at Falaise. Although the destruction of the enemy forces inside the pocket was a significant victory, hundreds of German troops were allowed to escape the net because of slow movement compounded by Allied tactical indecisiveness.

As the Allies advanced towards the last natural barrier along the German border,

Eisenhower visited the devastated Polish capital of Warsaw after World War Two ended and observed the devastation first hand. (Public Domain)

failure led to the destruction of the 1st Airborne as an effective fighting force and Eisenhower reverted to the broad front strategy for the balance of the war in the West.

In the winter of 1944, Adolf Hitler launched his last desperate gamble for a decisive victory against the American and British armies poised to invade the Fatherland. He launched a major offensive in the Ardennes Forest, attacking the thin American line in the area with overwhelming strength. The Germans intended to drive a wedge between the Americans in the south and British forces in the north, cross the River Meuse and capture the deep water port of Antwerp in Belgium, a vital Allied centre of supply and logistics.

The German offensive was launched on December 16, 1944 and initial progress was substantial as the attackers scooped up thousands of American prisoners. However, pockets of resistance slowed the German advance, particularly at the vital crossroads town of Bastogne in Belgium, where the 101st Airborne Division and Combat Command B of the 10th Armoured Division held firm.

Eisenhower and his lieutenants had been caught flat-footed, but their rapid response blunted the German

This official portrait of Dwight Eisenhower was taken during his second term as President of the United States. (Public Domain)

British prime minister Winston Churchill, in his dressing gown while recovering from an illness, confers with General Dwight Eisenhower during a visit to the Mediterranean. General Harold Alexander stands behind. (Public Domain)

drive, which foundered due to stiffening Allied defences, clearing weather that allowed Allied air power to operate against exposed German troop and tank concentrations and the stabilisation of the northern and southern shoulders of the penetration. Patton disengaged from a fight to the south and sent Third Army northward to relieve the besieged garrison at Bastogne. The 4th Armoured Division made contact with the 101st Airborne on the day after Christmas and the so-called Battle of the Bulge entered a decisive phase as the Germans were compelled to retreat due to tremendous losses and lack of fuel to sustain their momentum.

Eisenhower was promoted to five-star General of the Army rank on January 20, 1945. However, there was plenty of criticism levelled at

senior commanders for the near catastrophe of the Battle of the Bulge. Nevertheless, the Germans had lost heavily in their desperate offensive and the Allied drive into the Fatherland was renewed with vigour. The British and Americans crossed the Rhine in the spring and US troops made contact with the Soviets at the town of Torgau on the River Elbe in April. The Third Reich's days were numbered.

Strategic decision on Berlin

As Allied armies were positioned to strike the Nazi capital of Berlin from both east and west, Eisenhower considered the strategic and tactical implications of sending his forces into the last major battle of World War Two in Europe. He was aware, to an extent, of post-war plans for the partition of Germany into occupation zones and he studied the positions of the Red Army in the vicinity of Berlin. Considering every aspect of the situation, he concluded that the best course of action was to allow the Soviets to fight, bleed and die in the capture of the city.

Although several of his subordinates were shocked at the decision that denied them the opportunity for a moment of supreme triumph, Eisenhower had discussed the situation with General Bradley in depth. In an unusual twist, he had also conversed with Soviet Premier Josef Stalin. Subsequently, Eisenhower's decision was vindicated.

The Red Army conquest of Berlin was a bloody, difficult affair and when it was over, it was only a matter of time before the Western Allies were given their own sectors of the former Nazi capital city. These were occupied without the loss of a single American or British soldier.

On May 7, 1945, Eisenhower and his senior commanders accepted the unconditional surrender of German military forces in a schoolhouse in Reims, France. The commanding general sent a succinct message to General Marshall in Washington, DC. It was the epitome of understatement but conveyed the business-like manner in which the entire campaign in the west had been conducted. "The mission of this Allied Force was fulfilled at 3am local time, May 7, 1945. Eisenhower."

Parade and politics

With the end of World War Two in Europe, General of the Army Dwight Eisenhower was a national hero in the US and a respected partner among his Allied peers. Through the lens of history, it has become apparent that few other leaders could have maintained the often-strained relations between the Allies and prosecuted the massive military campaign required to win the war with more effectiveness than Eisenhower.

In the immediate aftermath of the war, he served as the first military governor of the American zone in occupied Germany. When he returned to the US, a ticker tape parade was held in his honour in New York City. Soon, he succeeded Marshall as chief of staff of the army and both political parties, Democratic and Republican, sought his favour as their candidate in the 1948 election for President of the United States.

Eisenhower declined and told the American people that he was first and foremost a soldier. He accepted the post of president of Columbia University and served as an adviser to Secretary of Defence James Forrestal. He was a key participant in the formation of the US Joint

On June 19, 1944, two weeks after the invasion of Normandy, Eisenhower made the cover of *LIFE* magazine. (Public Domain)

Eisenhower grew up in this modest home in Abilene, Kansas, in the heart of the American Midwest. (Creative Commons CSvBibra via Wikipedia)

Union's territorial ambitions during the early days of the Cold War and the burgeoning nuclear age.

As Americans were generally prosperous during the 1950s amid a post-war economic resurgence, Eisenhower faced his sternest tests during the last years of his presidency. During the U-2 Incident in 1960, the US government denied that any espionage flights were taking place over Soviet territory. When the Soviet government of Premier Nikita Krushchev produced the wreckage of a U-2 spy plane that had been shot down and the captured pilot, Francis Gary Powers, the subsequent show trial embarrassed Eisenhower on the world stage.

At home, President Eisenhower was seen at times as unenthusiastic in his support for the Civil Rights movement. However, he maintained existing programmes and signed the landmark Civil Rights Act of 1957, later sending federal troops to Little Rock, Arkansas, where they enforced integration law at Central High School in a sentinel event of turbulent times for race relations in the US.

During his second term, Eisenhower's health began to significantly diminish. For most of his adult life, he had been a heavy smoker and he had survived heart attacks during the 1950s. He suffered from intestinal problems, underwent several operations and recovered from a mild stroke in 1957. But once his political career was over, he settled with Mamie on a beloved farm the couple had purchased and restored in Gettysburg, Pennsylvania. He pursued his passion for golf and took up painting.

The last year of Dwight Eisenhower's life was spent in a suite at Walter Reed Army Hospital in Washington, DC, as his health further deteriorated. He died of congestive heart failure at the age of 78 on March 28, 1969. Today, he is remembered as an influential soldier and political figure in the United States and around the world. He remains one of the most revered military leaders of the 20th century.

This statue of Eisenhower stands in the grounds of the US Military Academy at West Point. He was a member of the fabled class of 1915. (Creative Commons Kenneth Casper via Wikipedia)

Chiefs of Staff and became the first supreme military commander of NATO (North American Treaty Organisation).

By 1951, the Republican Party had convinced Eisenhower to accept their nomination for President of the United States. He won the 1952 election by a landslide and was also elected to a second term in 1956. The slogan 'I Like Ike' was known far and wide as he pursued a moderately conservative political policy at home and abroad. He urged an end to the fighting on the Korean peninsula and this was accomplished in the summer of 1953. While his administration supported the French during their war against the communist Viet Minh in Indochina, Eisenhower was deeply concerned with Soviet

Right: Pilot Francis Gary Powers was at the centre of the U-2 Incident, which embarrassed the Eisenhower administration in 1960. (Creative Commons Chernov via Wikipedia)

After retirement, Dwight and Mamie Eisenhower spent comfortable years at their farm in Gettysburg, Pennsylvania. (Public Domain)

GENERAL GEORGE C MARSHALL

The most influential American military officer of the 20th century, according to many historians, General George Catlett Marshall was the architect of the United States Army that contributed mightily to the victory over Axis forces during World War Two. Furthermore, when his days in uniform were over, Marshall continued in diplomatic service and laid the foundation of European economic recovery following the destruction wrought by the great conflict.

Marshall reached five-star General of the Army rank and became such a trusted adviser to President Franklin D Roosevelt that the chief executive remarked in the days leading up to the invasion of Normandy: "I don't feel I could sleep at ease if you were out of Washington." At the time, Marshall was serving as chief of staff of the Army and he had hoped to command the Allied forces going ashore on D-Day personally. However, he did not lobby for the post and acceded to Roosevelt's wishes. In his stead, the capable General Dwight D Eisenhower was chosen in December 1943 to lead the Allied cross-Channel invasion.

Throughout his military and political career, Marshall proved resourceful and creative, sometimes appearing aloof or detached, but always focused on the task at hand and achieving the desired results. He tamed a volcanic temper and though he might initially have seemed cold and detached, those who grew to know him respected the officer as a loyal, candid and warm individual. Born in Uniontown, Pennsylvania, on December 31, 1880, he was the son of a coke and coal merchant, settling early on a career in the military. He entered the Virginia Military Institute in Lexington in 1897, endured some rugged hazing while a cadet and graduated as first captain of the corps of cadets in 1901. Although his initial academic effort was lacklustre, he recommitted to excellence and found the personal drive and determination to complete the VMI course with honours.

General George C Marshall served as Army chief of staff during the crucial years of World War Two. (Public Domain)

Successful staff officer

Marshall was commissioned a 2nd lieutenant in the US Army and served in the Philippines for 18 months. Just prior to his departure, he married Elizabeth Carter Coles and the couple were happy together until her death in 1927. As a young officer, Marshall graduated the Infantry-Cavalry School at Fort Leavenworth, Kansas, in 1907 and the following year completed the Army Staff College. Soon after the US entered World War One in 1917, he was among the first American soldiers to reach France, serving as operations officer with the 1st Infantry Division. His administrative skills soon led to his elevation to chief of operations for the First Army, directly under General John J 'Black Jack' Pershing, commander of the American expeditionary force.

Marshall impressed Pershing with his willingness to express his own opinion, regardless of the political fallout that might result. On one memorable occasion, he bluntly told Pershing that his decision to scold the commander of the 1st Division in front of the assembled troops due to training inadequacies had actually emanated from shortcomings in Pershing's own headquarters. The young major had remained true to his convictions and spoken truth to power. Pershing became a mentor and handed Marshall the responsibility for planning major operations involving nearly two million American soldiers. His core planning

charted the conduct of American combat during the battles at Catigny, Aisne-Marne, St Mihiel and the Meuse-Argonne offensive, the largest in the history of US ground forces.

After World War One, Marshall continued to serve under Pershing during the latter's tenure as chief of staff of the Army. He was stationed in China from 1924 to 1927 as executive officer of an infantry regiment at Tientsin. Enduring the grief that followed his wife's death, Lieutenant Colonel Marshall became an instructor at the Army War College and was soon detailed as assistant commander of the Infantry School at Fort Benning, Georgia. This position placed Marshall over training and instruction, providing an opportunity for the officer to shine. For the next five years, he reshaped the training methodology of the US Army, instilling in the young officers who passed through the school a perspective of self-reliance and an ability to think on their feet. They came to understand that planned operations might swiftly go awry and that their ability to adapt to current battlefield conditions meant the difference between victory and defeat.

During World War One, while serving as a staff officer in France, Marshall proved adept at planning major military operations. (Public Domain)

During World War Two, Marshall (left) and secretary of war Henry L Stimson discuss strategy and review positions on a map.
(Public Domain)

General Malin Craig and thoroughly analysed the needs of the army as it approached a war footing.

When Craig retired in the summer of 1939, several civilian and military colleagues, including trusted Roosevelt adviser Harry Hopkins, believed Marshall was the logical choice as his successor. However, Marshall was junior to 33 other generals and seniority had always been revered in the ranks of the American military. Nevertheless, Roosevelt called upon Marshall, who was named Army chief of staff with four-star rank and sworn in on September 1, 1939, the day the Nazis invaded Poland and ignited World War Two in Europe.

Marshall recognised quickly that the cumbersome command structure of the war department was unsustainable, particularly during wartime. More than 60 officers reported directly to Marshall, while at least 30 major and 350 minor army commands were beneath him. The new chief of staff set about reorganising the war department, eliminating redundant or outmoded elements.

Many of the American officers who commanded troops during World War Two were influenced by Marshall's methods, equipping them to deal with the unexpected and contributing greatly to the fighting effectiveness of the American soldier. During these years, Marshall also took note of talented officers who might one day serve in senior roles in wartime. Marshall was also a key proponent of the efficiency of US Army combat formations. He was instrumental in the reallocation of troops in formations such as the 850-man infantry battalion, armed and equipped sufficiently to operate. The infantry division was ultimately reorganised to its familiar 'triangular' composition, while tactics were refined and modernised with the introduction of 'fire and manoeuvre' at the squad level. He further encouraged his infantry school charges to read consistently, building their knowledge of history and gleaning practical lessons from earlier military campaigns.

Marshall remarried in 1930 and General Pershing stood as his best man. His second wife, Katherine Tupper Brown, was a widow with three children.

Marshall commanded the Eighth Infantry Regiment and then became a senior instructor with the 33rd Division of the Illinois National Guard. At first, the National Guard appointment appeared to be a path to nowhere, an exit from the regular army for the colonel who had spent more than three decades in the service. On the contrary, Marshall was told to raise the division's level of performance to acceptable standards. He also oversaw the construction of more than 30 camps built by the government's civilian conservation corps and this housing proved to be much needed during the army's rapid growth in the late 1930s. From 1936 to 1938, Marshall commanded the Fifth Infantry Brigade and at long last, he was promoted brigadier general in October 1936. He was 55 years old.

Rapid rise and Roosevelt

In July 1938, Marshall was summoned to Washington DC to lead the army war plans division. Rapidly, he displayed a keen ability to distil organisational and operational issues to the basic level and offer solutions. During one meeting that included President Roosevelt, he had dared to express his disagreement with one of the chief executive's conclusions. He became the deputy to chief of staff Major

Further, in 1939 the US Army numbered fewer than 200,000 men in uniform and was slightly smaller than that of Portugal. Marshall's prescience set the stage for an unprecedented growth of the army to more than eight million troops during the war years.

As the tide of the conflict turned in favour of the Allies, Marshall became an early proponent of an invasion of Western Europe. However, differences of opinion among the Allied leaders led to vigorous discussion of the best course of strategic action. While the British advocated a primary thrust through Italy, Marshall eventually prevailed and Operation Overlord began to take shape with American military resources building up to sufficient levels in England.

Meanwhile, Marshall managed the war in the Pacific as the tenuous co-operation between the army and navy under theatre commanders General Douglas MacArthur and Admiral Chester Nimitz was at times strained. At home, there was the continuing necessity to maintain good

During a visit to Britain, Marshall (left) and Army Air Forces General Henry 'Hap' Arnold pass an honour guard.
(Public Domain)

Marshall addresses the appropriations committee of the US House of Representatives in 1948.
(Creative Commons US National Archives via Wikipedia)

relations with Congress, the public and the press. By 1943, rumours that Marshall was headed to Britain to command Operation Overlord began to circulate around Washington DC. When concerns developed among members of Congress and Roosevelt expressed his wishes for Marshall to remain as chief of staff he agreed, although a concerted push for the Overlord command might have led to his appointment.

Marshall's willingness to remain in the capital at Roosevelt's side demonstrates his selfless attitude and devotion to duty above personal recognition. Eisenhower went on to lead the Western Allied armies to victory, earned great fame and served two terms as President of the United States. Despite their differing perspectives on the conduct of the war in Europe, British Winston Churchill called Marshall the 'organiser of victory'.

Diplomacy and the Marshall Plan

After the war, President Harry Truman sent Marshall to China in an attempt to mediate a settlement between the communist and nationalist forces, which were then engaged in a civil war. The effort showed early promise but eventually failed and China fell under the rule of the Mao Tse-Tung and the communists. It was a rare setback for Marshall despite his best effort.

Meanwhile, Marshall served as Truman's Secretary of State and later Secretary of Defense and led the initiative that produced the European Recovery Programme. The immense blueprint for the economic revitalisation of Europe, ravaged by war, came to be known as the Marshall Plan. The general commented: "It is logical that the United States should do whatever it is able to do to assist in the return of normal economic health to the world, without which there can be no political stability and no assured peace." More than $12 billion in economic aid flowed to 16 European countries and Marshall received the Nobel Peace Prize in 1953. He was instrumental in the creation of the North Atlantic Treaty Organisation (NATO), which was established in 1949 and buttressed the west and the free world against Soviet expansionism during the burgeoning Cold War.

In the autumn of 1951, Marshall retired after half a century of military and civilian public service. He resided in Leesburg, Virginia and enjoyed

gardening. After suffering several strokes, he died at the age of 78 on October 16, 1959 and was buried in Arlington National Cemetery.

General George C Marshall left a legacy of leadership and skill in interpersonal and international relations seldom seen in the modern world. His contribution to victory in World War Two cannot be overestimated and for many he was simply, during that time, the 'indispensable man'.

Artist Thomas Edgar Stephens painted this portrait of General of George C Marshall in 1949.
(Public Domain)

FIELD MARSHAL SIR HAROLD ALEXANDER

During his command in the Mediterranean theatre, Alexander surveys the front line while standing in an open car. (Public Domain)

"We are masters of the North African shores," General Harold Alexander cabled prime minister Winston Churchill at 1.16pm on May 13, 1943. Axis forces on the continent had been defeated and more than 230,000 enemy soldiers taken prisoner. At the time, Alexander served as commander of the Allied 18th Army Group, formed four months earlier to play a key role in the successful conclusion of the fighting in North Africa.

He went on to command 15th Army Group during operations in Sicily and Italy and Allied Force headquarters, responsible for operations in the Mediterranean theatre. He was promoted to field marshal in 1944 and accepted the surrender of the German forces fighting in Italy the following spring.

A hero in combat

Born December 10, 1891, Alexander, like Winston Churchill, was educated at Harrow and attended the Royal Military College at Sandhurst. He served with distinction during World War One, receiving the Military Cross, Distinguished Service Order and the French Légion d'honneur. He was wounded during the fighting at Passchendaele but returned to action to lead the 4th Guards Brigade in 1918. Between the world wars, Alexander served in Poland, Turkey and India and was appointed aide-de-camp to King George VI. Promoted brigadier general in October 1937 aged 45, he was the youngest officer of the British Army to achieve such high rank.

With the outbreak of World War Two, he commanded the 1st Division in France. As the British expeditionary force withdrew from the European continent under tremendous German pressure in 1940, Alexander led a rear-guard action that bought precious time to facilitate the evacuation of troops at Dunkirk. He was one of the last British soldiers to leave France and subsequently took charge of southern command in Britain. Detailed to India with the rank of full general, he led the fighting withdrawal

Field Marshal Sir Harold Alexander was a highly decorated commander of Allied troops in the Mediterranean Theatre of Operations. (Public Domain)

from Burma before the advancing Japanese. He was then appointed commander-in-chief, Middle East, based in Cairo, serving in the post as General Bernard Montgomery's Eighth Army won the decisive victory in the theatre at El Alamein in October 1942.

Courtesy and conflict

Throughout the course of World War Two, Alexander demonstrated an ability to work with Britain's American allies. He shunned the spotlight and did not seek fame or glory. He managed to forge working relationships with Montgomery and the mercurial American General George S Patton Jr, even as these two subordinate commanders were continually at odds. His diplomacy, charm and unpretentious nature were appreciated by Churchill and General Dwight Eisenhower, his superior during much of his tenure in the Mediterranean, but these traits were discounted by others. Some contemporaries, including Field Marshal Sir Alan Brooke, chief of the imperial general staff, considered him 'average at best and lacking intelligence'.

Nevertheless, Alexander's conduct of the campaign in Italy displayed flashes of brilliance. His execution of Operation Diadem in 1944 broke a lengthy stalemate at Monte Cassino, cracking the formidable defences of the Gustav Line. However, he has been criticised for failing to rein in such subordinates as Montgomery, Patton and Fifth Army commander General Mark Clark. This is evidenced at times by the willingness of these officers to ignore their superior's orders. During Diadem, for example, General Clark was directed to cut the line of retreat of enemy forces to the south, thereby trapping the entire German Tenth Army in southern Italy. Instead, Clark ordered the vanguard of his Fifth Army to turn northwest to capture Rome on June 4, 1944. Although Alexander was livid, there was little he could do.

In March 1946, Alexander was elevated to the peerage as Viscount Alexander of Tunis and Errigal. After World War Two, he was appointed the last British Governor General of Canada, serving from 1946 to 1952. His term was tremendously successful and after his return to Britain Churchill called once again. When asked to assume the post of minister of defence, Alexander responded: "I simply can't refuse Winston." True to form, though, Alexander had no interest in politics and resigned from the position in the autumn of 1954, retiring from public service.

During the last years of his life, Alexander made several visits to Canada. He edited wartime military dispatches and returned to his long time hobby of painting. He died suddenly of a heart attack on July 16, 1969 at the age of 78 and was buried near his family's Hertfordshire home following a funeral at St. George's Chapel, Windsor Castle.

KEY Books MAIL ORDER KEY Books

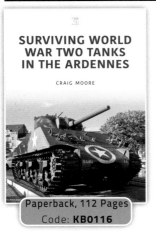
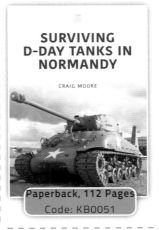

FIELD MARSHAL BERNARD LAW MONTGOMERY

Above left: General Bernard Law Montgomery wears his trademark black beret with the badge of the Royal Tank Regiment in this 1943 image. (Public Domain)

Above right: Montgomery stands at right with General J W Sandilands of the 104th Infantry Brigade in World War One. He was seriously wounded and received the DSO for gallantry. (Public Domain)

The best-known British senior military commander to emerge from World War Two, Field Marshal Bernard Law Montgomery is further the most successful and controversial of the period. He led the Eighth Army to victory at the pivotal Battle of El Alamein in North Africa in October 1942, commanded Allied ground forces and 21st Army group during the campaigns in Normandy and Western Europe and was the principal proponent of the ill-fated Operation Market Garden, the combined airborne/ground offensive into the Netherlands that ended in defeat in the autumn of 1944.

Montgomery was possessed of a monumental ego and prime minister Winston Churchill once commented that he was 'in defeat, unbeatable: in victory, unbearable'. His ability to motivate men and organise troops cannot be discounted and his vital contribution to the ultimate Allied victory is undisputable. Montgomery was direct and quick-witted, resolute and committed to the task at hand, even in the face of tremendous adversity. He did not hesitate to speak his mind and frequently alienated himself from his American counterparts. Even his fellow British officers, including Air Chief Marshal Sir Arthur Tedder, deputy commander for Operation Overlord, the Allied landings in Normandy on June 6, 1944, found him insufferable at times. His rivalry with American General George S Patton Jr is legendary.

Born in St. Mark's Vicarage, Kennington Oval, London, on November 17, 1887, Montgomery was the son of Henry Montgomery, a minister of the Church of Ireland and Maud Farrar Montgomery, who was many years younger than her husband. Montgomery's perspective on the world was undoubtedly shaped by his relationship with his domineering mother, who regularly beat her children and participated only on a limited basis in their education. When she died in 1949, Montgomery declined to attend her funeral and he forbade his own son David from any association with her.

Towards the military

Following several years in the British colony of Tasmania, the family returned to England in 1897. Montgomery completed his education

Carrying a swagger stick, Montgomery reviews troops preparing to defend Britain against a German invasion in the spring of 1941. (Public Domain)

at King's College, Canterbury and St. Paul's School in London. He entered the Royal Military College, Sandhurst, and found himself frequently in hot water for disciplinary infractions. One episode stands out as particularly serious. A leader among a group of cadets that set fire to the shirt tail of an unpopular fellow, he was stripped of his corporal stripes and set back six months. The victim suffered serious burns and spent some time in hospital.

After graduation in 1908, Montgomery was disappointed. His aspirations for the Indian Army were quashed because his academic marks were too low, even though he ranked 30th of 150 cadets. He then chose the Royal Warwickshire Regiment, was commissioned 2nd lieutenant and shipped off to India anyway to serve with its 1st battalion at Peshawar. By the time the unit returned to Britain, he was its adjutant with the rank of lieutenant.

With the outbreak of World War One, the 1st battalion moved to France in the late summer of 1914. In October, Montgomery was shot in the chest during action near the Belgian border. While attacking towards the village of Mérteren he led his men forward. "The bullet entered at the back which was toward the enemy and came out in front, having gone through my right lung," he remembered years later. "A soldier from my platoon ran forward and plugged the wound with my field service dressing. While doing so, the sniper shot him through the head and he collapsed on top of me. I lay there all afternoon. The sniper kept firing at me and I received one more bullet in the left knee. The man lying on me took all the bullets and saved my life."

Captain Montgomery received the Distinguished Service Order for gallantry and the citation read: "Conspicuous gallant leading on October 13 when he turned the enemy out of their trenches with the bayonet. He was severely wounded."

After a recovery of four months, Montgomery was promoted to brigade major, with units then training in Lancashire. In 1916, he returned to the Western Front and narrowly missed the dreadful bloodletting of the Somme. He was promoted to the staff of the 33rd Division and fought at Arras in the spring of 1917. Subsequently, he was elevated to the staff of the IX Corps, which held a key position at Kemmel Ridge, suffering 27,000 casualties, during the great German offensive in the spring of 1918. As the Great War concluded, Montgomery was a 30-year-old lieutenant colonel and chief of staff of the 47th Division.

Focus forward

Montgomery's single-mindedness and his affinity for the military led superior officers to recommend him steadily for greater responsibility, if grudgingly at times. He was prone to speak frankly and known as somewhat erratic. Regardless, he acknowledged these personality traits and even embraced them. "One has to be a bit of a cad to succeed in the army," he once said as a young officer, "and I am a bit of a cad."

Indeed, he wangled a spot at the prestigious staff college in Camberley, after a conversation with General Sir 'Wully' Robertson, former chief of the imperial general staff, during a tennis party. He had otherwise been passed over, which might have dealt a blow to his career that would prevent a rise to senior command. He completed the course but bore the brunt of some criticism as the staff college magazine asked rhetorically in December 1920 just what type of weapon would be needed to prevent him from 'babbling at breakfast'.

Montgomery once said that service in the professional army was 'a life study and few officers seem to realise that'. He became friends with innovative military theorist Basil Liddell Hart, who appreciated his perspective and commented: "He was already one of the most thoroughly professional soldiers in the army. I was the more impressed because by then I had come to realise, through widening experience, how amateurish most 'professional soldiers' still were."

After service in Ireland, Montgomery assumed numerous staff positions for more than a decade. He served as deputy assistant adjutant general at the staff college and meanwhile married Elizabeth (Betty) Carver, a widow with two teenage sons, in 1927. Their son David was born in 1928. In 1931, he returned to his old 1st battalion, Royal Warwickshire Regiment, as its commanding officer in Egypt and three years later he was named senior instructor at the military staff college in Quetta, India. After six years abroad, he returned to Britain in the summer of 1937, received promotion to brigadier and took command of the 9th Infantry Brigade at Portsmouth.

Betty died tragically in 1937, but her influence may well have helped to curb Montgomery's more irascible personality traits and contributed to his opportunity to reach senior command during World War Two. Suffering such a great loss, Montgomery discharged his duties but lived otherwise as a recluse for the next five months. He was heartbroken but redoubled his commitment to professional soldiery. Along with this rededication came the convergence of war clouds in Europe.

Dunkirk and destiny

Promoted to major general, Montgomery was given command of the 3rd Infantry Division in 1938 and he led these troops to France in

Shortly after his appointment to command Eighth Army in August 1942, Montgomery confers with subordinates in the Egyptian desert. (Public Domain)

the opening days of World War Two. During the debacle of the spring of 1940, his command fought gallantly and Montgomery displayed his ability to conduct a large unit in battle. During a raging night engagement with the Germans, he reoriented elements of the 3rd Division to prevent being outflanked as neighbouring Belgian troops collapsed. The manoeuvre did not go unnoticed and helped establish Montgomery as a capable field commander.

General Alan Brooke, commander of the II Corps of the British expeditionary force and future chief of the imperial general staff remarked: "There is no doubt that one of Monty's strong points is his boundless confidence in himself. He was priceless on this occasion and I thanked heaven to have a commander of his calibre to undertake this march."

Brooke was ordered back to Britain and Montgomery temporarily assumed corps command after his departure. Subsequently, Montgomery took command of V and then XII corps and then southeastern command as defences were prepared against a potential German invasion of the British Isles. For his bravery in France, Brigadier Montgomery was made Companion of the Order of the Bath.

Still, along with his apparent command ability, Montgomery managed to maintain an air of abruptness and disdain for those perceived to be inadequate, particularly others of senior rank. Brooke wrote to him during the early months of the war and candidly noted: "I know you well enough also, Monty, to give you a word of warning

Montgomery peers from the turret of his Grant command tank during the Desert War, November 1942. (Public Domain)

Montgomery plays with his dogs, named Hitler and Rommel, at his headquarters in France, 1944. A cage of canaries is visible in the background. (Public Domain)

Soldiers of the Australian 9th Infantry Division surge forward in this posed photograph following the Battle of El Alamein. (Public Domain)

Montgomery shakes hands with General George S Patton Jr, his principal American rival, during a visit to Palermo, Sicily, in July 1943. (Public Domain)

against doing wild things. You have a name for annoying people at times with your ways and I have found difficulties in backing you at times against this reputation."

Into the desert

Nevertheless, there was no denying that Montgomery was an inspiring commander, positive and jaunty in the presence of the troops, optimistic and lively with energy that buoyed the spirits of the common soldier. In August 1942, he received his opportunity to take centre stage. The gruelling war in North Africa had raged for nearly three years and finally, Axis forces under General Erwin Rommel had been stopped, the defensive line of the Eighth Army drawn at El Alamein from the impassable Qattara Depression in the south to the coast of the Mediterranean Sea in the north.

Under General Claude Auchinleck, British forces were gaining strength in preparation for the launch of a decisive offensive, but Churchill had decided that a change of command was needed. Auchinleck was relieved from the post of commander-in-chief, Middle

East, in favour of General Harold Alexander and command of Eighth Army was given to Montgomery, who had not been first choice. He took charge of the desert force only after General William 'Strafer' Gott was killed when his transport plane was shot down en route to take the post.

Montgomery arrived in Cairo on August 12, 1942 and began immediately to reinforce ongoing training of the troops while weapons and supplies made their way to the front. The troops of the Eighth Army were tired and battle-worn, but Monty's spirit and optimism were infectious. He visited the front lines often, waving to soldiers rather than saluting them and tossing them packs of cigarettes. His small, wiry frame was easily recognisable wearing a pullover, crisply creased khaki trousers and a black beret adorned with the badge of the Royal Tank Regiment and his general (later field marshal) rank insignia.

The new army commander told his subordinates: "I want to impress on everyone that the bad times are over." He stressed that there would be no more 'bellyaching' and 'doubters in this party would no longer be tolerated'.

Decision at El Alamein

Auchinleck and his deputy chief of staff General Eric Dorman-Smith had pursued a strategy of attrition, which resulted in the repulse of a German attack at Alam Halfa in early September and set the stage for Montgomery's launching of the offensive at El Alamein on October 23.

In the predawn darkness, 900 British guns bombarded the German front line and Operation Lightfoot lurched forward. The enemy gave ground grudgingly and then counter-attacked, threatening to stall the offensive. However, Monty would have none of it and renewed the offensive effort with Operation Supercharge. By early November Rommel, who had been on sick leave when the fighting began, decided that he no longer had the resources to stand fast. The German and Italian forces of Panzerarmee Afrika began a retreat across hundreds of miles of desert.

By November 10, the victorious commander had confidently written to his son: "This battle is really over and I have smashed Rommel and his army. It has been great fun and I have enjoyed it. Someday I will tell you all about it. I expect the papers in England are full of it and contain a good deal about me." When the Allies executed Operation Torch on November 8, Rommel was forced to fight on two fronts. The campaigns in North Africa ended with a massive Axis surrender in May 1943 and Montgomery was hailed a hero.

Montgomery stands before his Miles Messenger liaison aircraft, sometimes used to travel. He was popular with the common soldier, exuding a positive, winning attitude. (Public Domain)

Sicily and Italy

Operation Husky, the Allied invasion of Sicily, was scheduled for July 10, 1943, but the plan was initially unsatisfactory to Montgomery. He managed to have it reworked with greater concentration of force, the Eighth Army landing at Syracuse and the American Seventh Army, under Patton, in support coming ashore at the Gulf of Gela. The seeds of rivalry were sewn and Monty had already begun to burnish with the Americans the prickly reputation for which he was known among some British peers.

Montgomery reviews kilted soldiers of the Gordon Highlanders at Beaconsfield in February 1944. (Public Domain)

While Eighth Army slugged its way northward through rugged country toward the city of Messina, German opposition was stiff. Patton ordered Seventh Army northwest, took the city of Palermo on July 22 and then captured Messina., All the while, the flamboyant commander yearned to spite Montgomery in the process. The campaign concluded in about five weeks but thousands of German and Italian troops were evacuated across the Strait of Messina to fight another day on the Italian mainland.

In September, the Eighth Army landed in southern Italy at Reggio and Taranto, while the Fifth Army, under General Mark Clark, came ashore at Salerno. While the fighting at the Salerno beachhead was severe and the landings were in jeopardy for a time, the Fifth Army clung to its foothold. Early progress was slow but by late 1943, Naples had fallen to Clark while Montgomery had captured Foggia and its complex of airfields.

In December, Montgomery was informed that he was to return to England to engage in planning for Operation Overlord and to command Allied ground troops committed to the effort.

Overlord and victory

When foul weather forced a 24-hour postponement of Operation Overlord and General Dwight Eisenhower, supreme commander allied expeditionary force, called his subordinates together at Southwick House to solicit their views for unleashing the offensive on June 6, 1944, Montgomery was the first to raise his voice in favour of moving forward. "I would say go!" he chirped. Eisenhower was, no doubt, appreciative of Monty's can-do approach and set the landings in motion.

On D-Day, Allied forces landed at five beaches along the Normandy coast of France. Montgomery had fully expected his drive inland to capture the vital communications and crossroads town of Caen within 24 hours. However, the expectation proved too ambitious and a month of hard fighting was required to finally wrest control of the city from the Germans. Although the Allied timetable had been upset by the vigorous enemy resistance, Montgomery continued to hammer away in the north and brought the bulk of the German panzer divisions to his own front.

Meanwhile, the American forces to the south unleashed Operation Cobra, a drive to break out of the hedgerow country of Normandy on July 25, 1944. Following a devastating saturation bombing of the front lines, the Americans charged through the breach. Patton's Third Army began a hell-for-leather dash across France and by August, Montgomery and General Omar Bradley had directed their forces to trap thousands of German troops in the Falaise Pocket.

Criticism that the movement to Falaise occurred too slowly and might have led to an even greater destruction of the enemy's resources was sloughed off and Montgomery wrote later of the key role played by Allied air superiority during the thrust to Falaise. He said: "Allied fighter-bombers were presented with targets probably unparalleled in this war. Aircraft formations were engaging endless columns of enemy transport packed bumper to bumper and rendered immobile by the appalling congestion."

In a previously agreed command restructure on September 1, 1944, General Eisenhower assumed direct overall command of ground

Soldiers gather around the car of Allied ground forces commander Montgomery on July 11, 1944. At the time, the troops had been engaged in the battle for the French city of Caen. (Public Domain)

At 21st Army group headquarters on July 7, 1944, General Montgomery chats with American general George S Patton Jr (left) and Omar Bradley (centre). (Public Domain)

Montgomery discusses ground strategy in his mobile headquarters with visiting King George VI in October 1944. (Public Domain)

In this post-war photo, Montgomery is seated with Field Marshals Archibald Wavell (centre) and Claude Auchinleck (right). (Public Domain)

forces in western Europe, while Montgomery reverted to command of 21st Army group – primarily British and Canadian troops – and General Omar Bradley retained command of the American 12th Army group. Although the change had been forthcoming, Montgomery resented the move and believed that his contribution to the success thus far had been underappreciated. As a balm for his bruise, Churchill pushed through Monty's promotion to field marshal.

Concurrently, the rivalry between Patton and Montgomery was rekindled as resources were limited and the further eastward the Allied spearheads advanced, the longer their supply lines extended. To address the issue of resupply, Montgomery conducted operations to capture French ports on the English Channel coast, as well as the deep water port at Antwerp in Belgium, a considerable distance up the estuary of the River Scheldt from the open sea. Before Antwerp could be put to use, the German defenders had to be cleared from the estuary. These operations were completed, largely by Canadian forces, in early November.

Setback at Market Garden

For the vast majority of the campaign in the west, General Eisenhower pursued a broad front strategy, pressing the Germans continually and impeding their ability to concentrate forces to execute a major counter-attack. Only once on a large scale did Eisenhower depart from the broad front – and that was primarily at the urging of Montgomery.

Well known for his desire to fight well-planned set piece battles when every element that could be controlled was in his favour, Montgomery surprisingly advocated an audacious offensive into Holland, one fraught with risk but that, if successful, might end World War Two in Europe by Christmas 1944. The British field marshal envisioned a combined air/ground operation, dubbed Market Garden, in which three Allied airborne divisions, the US 82nd and

Montgomery's M3 Grant command tank, used during the Desert War, is on display at the Imperial War Museum in London. (Creative Commons via Wikipedia)

Montgomery strolls in Berlin in 1945 with high-ranking Soviet Red Army officers. Marshal Georgi Zhukov is to Montgomery's immediate right and the Brandenburg Gate looms in the background. (Public Domain)

Montgomery greets dignitaries during a visit to New Zealand in 1947. (Creative Commons via Wikipedia)

101st and the British 1st would seize key bridges across the rivers of southern Holland, holding them until the ground spearheads of XXX Corps could link up successively with each division, cross the bridges and then pivot to plunge deeply into the Ruhr, the industrial heart of Germany. Deprived of their ability to produce weapons and war materiel, the Nazis would be compelled to surrender.

The most difficult assignment of Market Garden fell to General Roy Urquhart and the British 6th Airborne, which was to parachute furthest forward and capture the bridge across the Neder Rhine at Arnhem. Intelligence reports that two SS panzer divisions, the 9th Hohenstaufen and the 10th Frundsberg, had been moved to the area for refit after being mauled in Normandy were discounted. In the event, the Germans battled XXX Corps along a single narrow road and progress on the ground was painfully slow. The lightly armed paras fought bravely against the German armour but were overwhelmed. Urquhart had parachuted into the Arnhem area with 10,000 men and fewer than 2,000 were extricated from the debacle.

British commandos prepare to disembark from their landing craft as it approaches Sword Beach on D-Day, June 6, 1944. (Public Domain)

A statue of Montgomery stands in Montgomery Square in Brussels. (Creative Commons Benjamin Decraene via Wikipedia)

Montgomery defended the merits of Market Garden and commented in his 1958 memoirs: "It was a bad mistake on my part – I underestimated the difficulties of opening up the approaches to Antwerp. I reckoned the Canadian Army could do it while we were going for the Ruhr. I was wrong. In my – prejudiced – view, if the operation had been properly backed from its inception and given the aircraft, ground forces and administrative resources necessary for the job, it would have succeeded in spite of my mistakes, or the adverse weather, or the presence of the 2nd SS Panzer Corps in the Arnhem area. I remain Market Garden's unrepentant advocate."

Endgame in the west

British forces retained control of the salients established during Market Garden, beating back German attempts to eject them. Meanwhile, in the winter of 1944, Hitler launched his last desperate gamble for a reversal of fortune in the west, a bold offensive called 'Watch on the Rhine,' aimed at driving a wedge between the British in the north and the Americans in the south as German armoured columns rushed toward Antwerp. Seizure of the port would compel the western Allies to cancel their drive into Germany set for early 1945 and perhaps even bring them to the negotiating table without their Soviet allies.

The German offensive was launched on December 16, 1944, in the lightly defended Ardennes Forest, where inexperienced American troops were thinly spread. Initial German successes were inevitably slowed, their timetable disrupted and their fuel supplies exhausted. For a time, Montgomery assumed operational command of American forces along the northern shoulder of the enemy penetration due to the exigencies of the situation. Within days, the tide of the so-called Battle of the Bulge had turned and the Germans retreated, sustaining heavy and irreplaceable losses.

As the threat subsided, Montgomery made comments to the press that insinuated his command and tactical decision making had been primarily responsible for the defeat of the Nazi offensive. When senior American soldiers, Bradley among them, read such remarks in the press, they were livid. The controversy was a distraction and, no doubt, caused Eisenhower some tense moments – only exacerbating his difficulties in prosecuting a coalition war. The supreme commander had enough trouble managing his fellow American commanders, particularly Patton who had howled his disapproval when fuel and supplies were diverted to Montgomery and caused his dash across France to come to a halt the previous summer.

Nevertheless, with the crisis of December overcome, the spring of 1945 ushered in the last operations in the west. Montgomery led his troops in Operations Veritable and Grenade, approaching the River Rhine, and executed a crossing of the last natural barrier on the German frontier with Operation Plunder in late March. Afterwards, 21st Army group executed the encirclement of the Ruhr Pocket, cutting off more than 350,000 German troops. On May 4, 1945, Montgomery accepted the surrender of all German forces in the north of the country, the Netherlands and Denmark.

Twilight of the warrior

After World War Two, Montgomery was chosen to succeed Brooke as chief of the imperial general staff. The decision to elevate Monty, also called the 'Spartan General', was not taken lightly. General Hastings Ismay, principal adviser to Churchill during the war years, acidly remarked on Monty: "I have come to the conclusion that his love of publicity is a disease, like alcoholism or taking drugs, and that it sends him equally mad."

Still, Montgomery was a national hero and without question he was due ample credit for leading the Allies to victory in North Africa, the Mediterranean and in northwest Europe. Always, though, he carried the stigma of the brash, temperamental prima donna. In 1946, he was raised to the peerage as the Viscount Montgomery of Alamein. He served as commander of the British Army of the Rhine and as Eisenhower's deputy in the early days of the NATO alliance, later working in the same capacity with Eisenhower's successors until retirement from the military in 1958 at the age of 71. When the field marshal's memoirs were released in the late 1950s, his commentary and criticism of fellow Allied officers, including Eisenhower and Auchinleck, generated significant controversy.

In a BBC interview after the war, Monty said: "The supreme commander had not the experience, the knowledge, the organisation, or the time. He should have been devoting himself to questions of overall strategy, to political problems and to problems of inter-Allied relations and military government. Instead, he insisted on trying to run the land battle himself. Here he was out of his depth and in trying to do this, he neglected his real job at the highest level."

Further, Monty's comments on Auchinleck's posture prior to the Battle of El Alamein resulted in the threat of a lawsuit by the latter and a public 'walk back'. The text of the memoir had suggested that Auchinleck was prepared to withdraw from the Alamein front if the Germans attacked again after Alam Halfa. In the wake of the public disagreement, Monty praised Auchinleck for stabilising the North African front and having the presence of mind to stand at El Alamein, a highly defensible position from which Eighth Army could be strengthened and the success of the October 1942 turning point of the war in the desert could be assured.

In his later years, Montgomery continued to freely express opinions on controversial political, social and military issues. He visited the El Alamein battlefield in 1967, a quarter of a century after the triumph that changed both his life and the course of World War Two. Throughout his lifetime, he had maintained his Christian faith, never smoked or partaken of alcohol and adhered to a strict vegetarian diet. Montgomery died at the age of 88 on March 24, 1976, in Isington, Hampshire.

One of the towering figures of World War Two, the viscount was buried in the Holy Cross churchyard in Binsted, Hampshire, following a funeral at St. George's Chapel at Windsor Castle.

Field Marshal Sir Alan Brooke and Winston Churchill visit Montgomery at his field headquarters in Normandy in 1944. (Public Domain)

FIELD MARSHAL CLAUDE AUCHINLECK

The verdict of history regarding the command performance of Field Marshal Claude Auchinleck in World War Two is ambiguous at best – and hypercritical at worst. Auchinleck was handed a no-win prospect during the abysmal campaign in Norway in 1940 and commanded British and Commonwealth forces in the Middle East during some of the most perilous days of the Desert War.

Auchinleck did manage to halt the last offensive drive of the Axis Panzerarmee Afrika, drawing the line in the Egyptian sand at El Alamein, a railroad whistlestop a scant 69 miles from the great port of Alexandria, and anchoring his defences against the impassable Qattara Depression to the south and the shores of the Mediterranean Sea in the north. While he accumulated supplies and weapons, including 300 new American-built M4 Sherman medium tanks, he prepared to launch the counterstroke that would defeat Rommel and the German and Italian forces in North Africa for good.

Field Marshal Claude Auchinleck, a key figure in the Desert War, posed for this portrait in 1945. (Public Domain)

But it was not to be. As preparations were underway, prime minister Winston Churchill had become convinced that a change of command was necessary. He relieved Auchinleck of command in the Middle East and gave the post to General Harold Alexander, while command of Eighth Army went to the energetic but petulant General Bernard Montgomery. In the midst of the change, Churchill did appear to grudgingly acknowledge Auchinleck's contribution to the eventual victory and compared his firing to 'killing a great stag'.

The prime minister offered Auchinleck the newly created post of commander-in-chief Persia and Iraq command, but 'the Auk' as he was affectionately known, declined. He chose to remain idle for some months, pondering his future in the British Army. As fate would prove, his active participation had not reached its conclusion.

Scion of the Raj

Claude Auchinleck was born on June 21, 1884, at the family home in Aldershot, Hampshire. He was the eldest of four children and the son of a career soldier, Lieutenant Colonel John Claud Alexander Auchinleck of the Royal Horse Artillery, and Mary Eleanor Eyre. When Claude was a child, the family relocated to India as his father commanded the batteries at Bangalore. The colonel retired in 1890 and the family returned to Britain, residing by the shore at Langstone, Hampshire. He died two years later of pernicious anaemia, leaving his widow and children in a financial pinch.

Claude was eight years old and the ensuing years of money problems left their mark on him for the rest of his life. He attended Mr Spurling's preparatory school on the grounds of Wellington College, an institution that had been founded 40 years earlier to provide subsidised education for the children of deceased officers of the British and Indian armies. Students who received financial benefit were referred to as 'Foundationers' and Claude remembered years later that his education had been made possible by the generosity of others.

"My mother was left a widow when I was quite young," he recalled, "But I was lucky because I was able to go to Wellington on a foundation. Wellington is really a school founded for the sons of officers whose widows can't afford to send them to other schools. Otherwise, I should never have gone to a public school. Quite impossible."

Auchinleck entered the Royal Military College at Sandhurst and he aspired to join the Indian Army upon graduation in December 1902. Since he had always been financially strapped, India was attractive because of his earlier years there and substantially better pay than the British Army at the time. Although his academic performance was unremarkable, fate smiled on him. Forty-five slots had been allocated to the Indian Army and he stood 45th. After two months' leave, he boarded a ship bound for India as a subaltern with the King's Shropshire Light Infantry, gaining knowledge with the British Army unit prior to joining the 62nd Punjabis. He participated in expeditions against Russian-backed Tibetan fighters in the north and then served as a recruiter in northern Punjab.

Auchinleck later recalled that these were among the happiest times of his life and he gained quite an affinity for the customs and languages of the Indian people. When he returned to Britain in 1911 for the first time in six years, he realised that he had a greater affinity for India than for his native country.

Auchinleck is shown standing at far right with officers of the 62nd Punjabis. He spent years with the Indian Army and had a great affinity for the Indian people. (Public Domain)

During the Great War, the 62nd Punjabis fought the Ottoman Turks in several sharp clashes. Auchinleck remembered the exhilaration of his first hours in combat offering. He said: "That was most exciting. I had the machine guns of the regiment. I was across from the Turkish side of the canal in a sort of fort. And I remember going into action for the first time with them. I remember the first bullet going over my head, which made me duck damn quickly. But, after all, one got used to it very quickly."

Continued campaigning in the Middle East provided combat experience that shaped Captain Auchinleck's career in the army. He participated in the failed effort to relieve the besieged garrison at Kut in modern day Iraq and learned that his younger brother, Leslie, had been killed in action on the Somme.

For his outstanding service in Mesopotamia, Auchinleck was mentioned in despatches and awarded the Distinguished Service Order (DSO). He was promoted to the permanent rank of major in January 1918 and elevated to brigade major of the 52nd Indian Infantry Brigade. Just as preparations were under way for an offensive into Kurdistan, the Great War ended. In January 1919, Auchinleck was named an Officer of the Order of the British Empire (OBE).

By the summer of 1921, the young officer had completed the staff college at Quetta in India and placed in the top 10 of his class. He married 21-year-old Jessie Stewart, an American-born beauty 16 years his junior. The couple had no children and the marriage ended in divorce years later following Jessie's affair with Air Chief Marshal Sir Richard Peirse that had begun when the latter commanded Allied air forces in southeast Asia from his base in India. Auchinleck was devastated and continued to carry her photograph in his wallet.

In the spring of 1933, Auchinleck had commanded Punjabi troops once again, completed the imperial defence college and served as an instructor at Quetta for three years. He was promoted to temporary brigadier and given command of the Peshawar brigade, then engaged in suppressing an uprising in upper Mohmand. He was mentioned in despatches for the third time in his career and earned honours as Companion of the Order of the Bath and Companion of the Star of India. In November 1935, he was promoted major general.

War and destiny

With the coming of World War Two, Auchinleck was given command of the Indian 3rd Infantry Division and then the British VI corps. This was a historic move, the only occasion in the entire war that an officer of the Indian Army was placed in charge of a British corps. He was promoted to lieutenant general in March 1940 and handed the virtually impossible task of holding the port of Narvik in Norway during the expedition against the occupying Germans. Returning to England in July, he took command of V Corps and then southern command a month later. One of his subordinates was the

Right: Auchinleck (left) and General Archibald Wavell discuss British strategy in the Middle East in September 1941. (Public Domain)

Below: A British Crusader tank passes a flaming German PzKpfw. IV tank during Operation Crusader on November 27, 1941. (Public Domain)

new V Corps commander, General Bernard Montgomery. The two had a long-standing adversarial relationship and Montgomery once commented: "I cannot recall that we ever agreed on anything."

Auchinleck returned to India in 1941 and became commander-in-chief of the Indian Army, bolstering key defences in Iraq to stem Axis inroads there. In the spring, Churchill appointed the Auk to succeed General Archibald Wavell as C-in-C Middle East, while Wavell took the Indian Army and the two essentially swapped commands. Wavell's Operation Battleaxe offensive had failed to stop the resurgence of Axis forces under Rommel and with the installation of Auchinleck, the prime minister began to clamour for a renewed effort against Rommel, the enemy's 'Desert Fox'.

Auchinleck managed the situation delicately and did not buckle under the pressure. When he felt an offensive had a reasonable chance of success, he launched Operation Crusader on November 18, 1941. Attack and counter-attack left the issue temporarily in doubt, but Auchinleck had given great latitude to his subordinates, particularly General Alan Cunningham and subsequently General Neal Ritchie, successive commanders of Eighth Army. Auchinleck faced the unenviable task of flying to the front and directing operations personally for 10 days. As Rommel faced a stiffening Eighth Army and supplies dwindled, he halted his own attacks. The British succeeded in lifting the siege of Tobruk, a major aim of Crusader, on December 10.

Auchinleck served as commander of the Indian Army during critical operation against the Japanese in Burma. (Creative Commons CR Guru PK via Wikipedia)

A desert crisis

Within days, however, intelligence reports began to filter into Auchinleck's headquarters that Rommel was again receiving supplies and reinforcements. Panzerarmee Afrika struck in May 1942, driving the Eighth Army back to the Gazala Line and the vicinity of Tobruk, which fell quickly to the Germans on June 21. Churchill demanded Auchinleck to take decisive action. The Auk fired Ritchie and again assumed direct tactical command of Eighth Army.

Early plans to stem the Axis tide had indicated a British and Commonwealth stand at Mersa Matruh, but as Auchinleck overcame serious self-doubts, he determined another course of action. The great, decisive stand of the Eighth Army would occur at El Alamein, on an 80-mile front that would have secure flanks on the Mediterranean and the Qattara Depression. Badly needed reinforcements began arriving to augment the Allied strength, while Rommel's supply lines were constantly harassed by RAF planes and Royal Navy submarines at sea. Auchinleck and his chief of staff, the prickly General Eric Dorman-Smith, laid the foundation for a successful offensive set for the autumn of 1942. In July, Rommel's drive toward Alexandria, Cairo and the Suez Canal was rebuffed with at least five counter-attacks that were collectively dubbed the First Battle of El Alamein. Grudgingly, Rommel wrote to his wife that his opponent was 'handling his forces with very considerable skill. He took the initiative himself and executed his operations with deliberation and noteworthy courage'.

Relief and redemption

Even as Rommel had stalled before the El Alamein defences, Auchinleck was relieved by Churchill. And the rest, as they say, is history. Montgomery went on to glory as the victor at the 'second' Battle of El Alamein in October 1942. Meanwhile, Auchinleck remained side-lined until June 1943, when he was again named commander of the Indian Army.

In this role, he acted decisively in support of the 14th Army, under General William Slim, then fighting the Japanese in Burma. Slim wrote in 1956: "It was a good day for us when he took command of India, our main base, recruiting area and training ground. The 14th Army, from its birth to its final victory, owed much to his unselfish

support and never-failing understanding. Without him and what he and the Army of India did for us, we could not have existed, let alone conquered."

While Montgomery grabbed headlines in North Africa, Auchinleck maintained a quiet dignity and provided the means necessary to assist Slim in his eventual victory in Burma. The Auk was rewarded with the Knight Grand Cross of the Order of the Bath and then promotion to field marshal on June 1, 1946. He remained in command of the Indian Army and presided over its post-war division into the new Indian and Pakistani armies. He resigned over disputes with Earl Mountbatten, then Governor of India, and refused a peerage.

Auchinleck lived quietly in Beccles in Suffolk, and later Marrakesh in Morocco and enjoyed painting watercolours. He died of influenza at the age of 96 on March 23, 1981. In the years that followed, his contribution to victory in the desert has undergone re-evaluation. No doubt, he does bear responsibility for some shortcomings as a theatre commander. However, he deserves acknowledgment for the successes as well.

This statue of Field Marshal Claude Auchinleck stands in Birmingham. (Creative Commons Elliott Brown via Wikipedia)

Future General Patton during the fencing portion of the modern pentathlon competition during the 1912 Olympic Games in Stockholm, Sweden. (Public Domain)

GENERAL GEORGE S PATTON JR

During the last days of World War Two in Europe, Allied armies advanced from both east and west, dooming the Third Reich to defeat. In the process, General George S Patton Jr's US Third Army gained a reputation as a formidable fighting force, while its flamboyant commander relentlessly drove his troops to press and destroy the enemy.

On March 1, 1945 German forces were still mounting substantial resistance in some areas and the Third Army received orders to bypass the German city of Trier on the banks of the River Moselle. The communiqué asserted that Trier was too well defended to risk an attack, while an estimated strength of four infantry divisions and accompanying armour would be required to complete the task.

General Patton had never shied away from an opportunity to fight and his approach to Trier had been no different. He relished the opportunity to respond to the higher echelon directive and dashed off an epic reply: "Have taken Trier with two divisions. Do you want me to give it back?"

The humorous riposte was typical of Patton, a mercurial and controversial officer who was possessed of a tremendous ego and sought the

glory and praise associated with military conquest. Since American involvement in World War Two had begun, Patton had been a central figure in the US Army, a polarising presence that confounded superiors and engendered both devotion and scorn among subordinates. Patton was, in the truest sense, a lightning rod. His conduct was both praiseworthy and reprehensible and the story of his life is simply remarkable.

Commander for the ages

Since taking command of the newly activated Third Army in France on August 1, 1944, Patton had orchestrated a lightning dash across the country following the Allied breakout from the Normandy beachhead. Third Army then plunged into Germany, killing and capturing thousands of enemy soldiers. Just 10 days after the message regarding Trier had been received, Third Army cleared the area north of the Moselle and linked up with the US Seventh Army to the south. Together, these armies executed a rapid sweep through the Saarland and Palatinate, scooping up another 100,000 German prisoners.

General George S Patton Jr, although controversial, emerged as one of the great American battlefield commanders of World War Two. (Public Domain)

Patton stands in front of a French Renault FT light tank in 1918. He was a pioneer of armoured warfare in the US Army. (Public Domain)

Right: Patton photographed while he was a colonel stationed at Camp Meade, Maryland, in 1919. He had been seriously wounded during World War One and decorated for bravery. (Public Domain)

of General Fox Connor, he became interested in the fledgling Tank Corps of the US Army. Transferring from the cavalry, Patton received French tanks and trained his soldiers in their tactical deployment. He commanded the armoured vehicles in their first combat at Saint-Mihiel. During the Meuse-Argonne offensive, he was seriously wounded while leading six soldiers and a single tank in an attack on a German machine gun position. He received the Distinguished Service Cross, Distinguished Service Medal and later the Purple Heart.

By the end of the Great War, he was among the foremost experts on armoured warfare in the US Army. He befriended future military leaders such as Dwight D Eisenhower, who later played a pivotal role in his career. He held various posts in Maryland, Washington DC and Hawaii, while receiving promotion to colonel in 1938. With the outbreak of war in Europe, the US military began to mobilise and Patton was a strong advocate for the development of an armoured corps within the army. He led demonstrations of armoured deployment and participated in large scale manoeuvres in Tennessee and Louisiana, receiving command of the 1st armoured corps in January 1942. A month later, he established the Desert Training Centre in California, emphasising armoured doctrine.

Within months of the US entry into World War Two, Allied commanders planned Operation Torch, an invasion of North Africa

With the end of World War Two in Europe, Patton had burnished his reputation as a hard-driving field commander who expected only the finest effort from his soldiers, scorned lackadaisical conduct and revered bravery and determination in the face of the enemy. Exhorting his troops relentlessly, he had been criticised for harshness, but in fact the stern discipline he imposed had prepared the troops for the privations of war, the hardships of lengthy combat that they were bound to encounter. His theory had been put to the test and largely vindicated in terms of casualties lost and inflicted on the enemy, territory gained and victories won.

Indeed, Patton had forged a combat record second to none among his Allied peers in World War Two. However, his legacy has been highly scrutinised in the decades following the end of the conflict and it remains one of poignant paradox. Patton was an enigmatic figure, a devout Christian prone to outbursts of anger, easily moved to tears, vain and arrogant. He proved himself an exceptional leader of men and a perceptive tactician willing to take risks on the battlefield and determined to keep advancing. Even so, his character flaws were daunting and nearly cost him his military career while on the cusp of greatness.

Development and destiny

George S Patton Jr was the scion of an aristocratic and wealthy family, born November 11, 1885, in San Gabriel, California, in suburban Los Angeles. His father was a successful attorney, businessman and local politician, His grandfather, commander of a Virginia regiment of the Confederate Army during the American Civil War, had been killed in action at the Third Battle of Winchester. His early academic progress was impeded by dyslexia, but he worked to overcome the disability.

Patton was a 1909 graduate of the US Military Academy at West Point, finishing 46th among 103 cadets. He was commissioned a 2nd lieutenant in the cavalry and posted to Illinois at Fort Sheridan and Fort Myer, Virginia. He was athletic and competed in the 1912 Summer Olympic Games, finishing fifth in the modern pentathlon.

As a young officer, Patton participated in the punitive expedition led by General John J 'Black Jack' Pershing against the Mexican outlaw Pancho Villa in 1916. While in Mexico, Patton led a detachment of 10 soldiers in pursuit of three of Villa's cohorts. He personally shot one of the fugitives and all three were killed. Patton kept a pair of spurs as a memento of this combat and the bodies of the three dead outlaws were strapped to the hoods of the Dodge touring cars the soldiers had used as if they were game trophies.

Patton served in France during World War One and was close to General Pershing, who had once been engaged to Patton's sister Nita. He was promoted captain in the spring of 1917 and at the urging

Patton led the western task force during Operation Torch, the invasion of north Africa, on November 8, 1942. He is shown here with an American light tank in Tunisia in early 1942. (Public Domain)

with landings at Casablanca, Oran and Algiers. General Eisenhower was given overall command in the theatre and Patton led the western task force, including 33,000 troops coming ashore at Casablanca on November 8, 1942. Within three days, the force had captured the city and negotiated terms for a cease-fire with the defending Vichy French troops. Although some resistance had been encountered early in the operation, Torch was successful.

Difficult days

While their baptism of fire had gone well, most American troops in North Africa had not experienced combat against the battle-hardened veterans of the German Afrika Korps and Panzirer Afrika under legendary General Erwin Rommel. The Germans remained full of fight and in February 1943, Rommel hit the Americans hard at Kasserine Pass in Tunisia, driving deep into their lines before his spearheads were halted. The ineptitude of General Lloyd Fredendall had contributed to the embarrassing defeat and Eisenhower relieved him of command before calling upon his old friend George Patton to take charge of the US II corps and restore fighting spirit and discipline.

Patton seized the opportunity and led the Americans in their first successful major engagement with the Germans at El Gutter in March-April 1943. Although the 1st armoured division was still in need of improvement, the 1st infantry division stood fast initially and then gained territory with a spirited eastward advance. Patton led from the front and assumed command of the 1st infantry division personally on at least three occasions. Eventually, the Americans linked up with elements of the British Eighth Army, under General Bernard Montgomery, which had pursued the Axis enemy westward after the great victory at El Alamein in October 1942. German and Italian forces in north Africa surrendered in Tunisia in May 1943.

As the campaign in north Africa reached its conclusion, Patton was given command of the US Seventh Army in preparation for Operation Husky, the Allied invasion of Sicily slated for

GENERAL PATTON SAYS: BUY MORE BONDS!

The Timken Roller Bearing Company, Canton 6, Ohio

Joseph Christian Leyendecker, 1944

General Patton strikes a heroic pose in this War Bond poster from 1944. (Public Domain)

July 9, 1943. Seventh Army was designated to land at the Gulf of Gela, southwest of Montgomery's Eighth Army and provide flank protection for the British as Montgomery drove northward from Syracuse to the port of Messina, just across the narrow straits from the Italian mainland.

True to form, Patton disdained playing a supporting role in Operation Husky and his legendary rivalry with Montgomery erupted during the five-week campaign that followed. When the opportunity appeared, Patton pushed northwest, significantly beyond his original zone of operations and obtained permission from General Sir Harold Alexander, commander of the 15th Army group, to capture the major city of Palermo if possible.

Not only did Seventh Army take Palermo on July 21, but Patton then reoriented his vanguard toward Messina. While executing a series of amphibious operations to outflank German defensive positions, he drove his troops relentlessly, took heavy casualties in stride and

Left: An early advocate for the development of armoured divisions in the US Army, Patton is shown riding in a tank and wearing the patch of the 2nd armoured division. (Public Domain)

Below: In 1914, Pancho Villa (centre) met with General John J 'Black Jack' Pershing (right) at Fort Bliss, Texas. Two years later, Villa was a fugitive from American justice. Patton, an aide to Pershing who also participated in the punitive expedition, is seen over the general's left shoulder. (Public Domain)

Patton (right) confers with naval officers prior to departing the cruiser USS Augusta in the opening moments of Operation Torch, November 1942. (Public Domain)

Generals Dwight Eisenhower (centre) and Omar Bradley (right) meet with General Patton in France in 1944. Patton had begun to lead the Third Army to glory when this photo was taken. (Public Domain)

Following the linkup at Bastogne during the Battle of the Bulge in 1944, General Patton decorates General Anthony McAuliffe, acting commander of the 101st airborne division, for heroism. (Public Domain)

captured Messina on August 16. The effort brought glory to Patton but fuelled the animosity with Montgomery.

Slaps in Sicily

Patton had driven his troops hard during the Sicily campaign and amid the rapid run toward Messina, his patience had been strained on more than one occasion. Although the campaign had resulted in an outstanding feat of arms, Patton had lived up to the nickname of 'Old Blood and Guts'. While historians have scrutinised his conduct of the campaign and pointed to the casualty rolls, the general often reasoned that maintaining the offensive and continually attacking actually saved lives. He once commented: "As long as you attack them [the enemy], they cannot find the time to attack you. You must never halt because some other unit is stuck. If you push on, you will relieve pressure on the adjacent unit and it will accompany you."

While relentlessly pursuing the enemy in Sicily, Patton was intolerant of lacklustre performance and could not abide conduct that he deemed less than heroic. Battlefield cowardice or combat fatigue were simply poor excuses for shirking a soldier's duty. The general's volatile temper got the best of him on two separate occasions during Operation Husky, illustrating the terrible character flaw that caused his detractors to question his true command capability and nearly costing him his lengthy military career.

Patton was visiting an evacuation hospital at the Sicilian town of Nicosia on August 3, 1943 and noticed one soldier who appeared unwounded. Private Charles H Kuhl was suffering from combat fatigue

and Patton flew into a rage when he was informed that the soldier had suffered no physical wound. He slapped the soldier in front of medical personnel. Within a week, the second incident occurred when Patton slapped Private Paul G Bennett at another medical facility. He verbally abused Bennett, unleashing a tirade of profanity on the soldier.

When the incidents were brought to the attention of General Eisenhower, he took action, reprimanding his old friend, who then apologised to the soldiers involved, all personnel who were in the vicinity of the incidents at the time and to units throughout the Seventh Army. Eisenhower recognised the importance of retaining aggressive field commanders for future operations and hoped quietly that the incidents would fade into obscurity. However, a public relations firestorm erupted when journalist Drew Pearson revealed the story on his popular radio programme. Member of Congress and the American public voiced their concerns and called for Patton's removal from command.

Therefore, Eisenhower was compelled to pull the general from active command at a critical time in the war, relegating his old friend to the shadows during the planning for Operation Overlord, the upcoming invasion of Normandy, scheduled for June 6, 1944. In the shuffle, General Omar Bradley, once Patton's subordinate in north Africa, was given command of the US First Army and subsequently 12th Army group during the Normandy invasion and the fighting that continued in western Europe through 1944-1945.

Redemption with Third Army

The Germans had fully expected Patton to lead the Allied forces in the invasion of Normandy, but much to the general's chagrin his rival Montgomery was given command of all Allied ground troops during

Generals Bradley and Patton confer during the spring of 1945. After Bradley had reported to Patton in north Africa, the officers' roles were reversed in France. (Public Domain)

While in Sicily, General Patton visits a group of entertainers and shakes hands with the great Bob Hope. (Public Domain)

General Patton with General Theodore Roosevelt Jr and General Terry Allen of the 1st infantry division at El Guettar in spring 1943. (Public Domain)

General Patton talks to wounded soldiers being prepared for evacuation from Sicily. During the campaign, he got into trouble for slapping two soldiers suffering from battle fatigue. (Public Domain)

the invasion and through much of the later fighting, only relinquishing overall field command to Eisenhower in a pre-planned move on September 1, 1944.

Meanwhile, after sitting idle for months and chafing to get back in the war, Patton had been notified in January that he was to activate and command the newly formed Third Army for future deployment. He set about with zeal, training and equipping the soldiers prior to entering combat. At the same time, Patton had played another key role in the run-up to the Normandy landings. Because the Germans considered him the premiere ground commander among the Allied generals and Patton remained in the dog house for some time, an elaborate deception was conceived with the temporarily disgraced general at the centre – and it succeeded beyond all expectations.

The fictitious First US Army Group (FUSING) was formed around General Patton, complete with dummy troops and equipment, tanks and trucks that were nothing more than inflated rubber decoys, false radio traffic and orders to send phantom units here and there. The ruse was intended to convince the Germans that the D-Day landings would occur some distance north of the Normandy beaches, at the Pas-de-Calais, the shortest distance from England to the European continent. The dummy build-up looked authentic to German spies

Generals Bradley and Patton pore over a map with subordinates during the drive across France in 1944. (Public Domain)

at a distance and it was logical that Patton would lead the mighty force. But FU SAG existed only on paper. The Germans, however, held reinforcements in reserve for a lengthy period even after D-Day, convinced that the real blow would fall at the Pas-de-Calais and with Patton at its head. By the time the German high command realised it had been duped, the Allied foothold in Normandy was secure.

Slow slog and breakout

The weeks following the Normandy landings presented daunting obstacles for Allied expansion of the D-Day lodgement. German defence was vigorous and the timetable for advance was upset, particularly around the city of Caen, which was designated for capture on D-Day. More than a month of fighting was actually required to take the communications and crossroads nexus. The enemy defended every

General Patton confers with Lieutenant Colonel Lyle Bernard, commander of the 2nd battalion, 30th infantry regiment at Brolo, Sicily, in July 1943.

country lane and meadow amid the hedgerow or 'bocage' country of Normandy. The hedgerows were tall mounds of earth that had originally been intended as demarcation lines between farms. However, in the summer of 1944 they became strong impediments to Allied movement as enemy machine gun and mortar positions took a heavy toll on advancing infantry.

During the battle for Caen, Montgomery and his 21st Army group fought heavy Nazi armoured concentrations. With several efforts to dislodge the Germans, they facilitated an opportunity for the Americans, who executed Operation Cobra, a breakout from the hedgerow country, centred on the French town of St. Lo. Carpet bombing of the German positions in the area would be followed by a swift advance through the resulting breach in the German lines. Stunned by the heavy aerial bombardment, the enemy would not be able to respond adequately to a lightning ground thrust. American tanks and infantry would exploit the opportunity, the armoured spearheads breaking into the open country beyond Normandy and dashing across France.

Such an offensive effort was tailor-made for a hell-for-leather general like George S Patton Jr. On July 25, 1944, Operation Cobra was unleashed and the Third Army poured through the gap in the German lines. During the first week of August, it rolled into the town of Avranches and then spilled into Brittany, where its tanks began an epic advance, sometimes even running off the maps that had been distributed to forward elements.

On August 8, Patton's troops captured Le Mans and the time was ripe for another swift movement, on this occasion toward Falaise where thousands of German troops, the remnants of the battered Seventh and Fifth Panzer armies, might be encircled in the vicinity of the town. Bradley understood the magnitude of the opportunity but he hesitated, unwilling to expose the flanks of the Third Army to counter-attack during rapid movement. When the jaws of the trap at Falaise finally closed, thousands of German soldiers had escaped capture, but many others were killed or taken prisoner and their tanks and equipment destroyed.

For several weeks, the Third Army continued its swift advance but the further eastward its columns ventured, the greater the strain on its supply lines became. Trucks were required to bring fuel, ammunition

General Patton is honoured with a great victory parade in Los Angeles on June 9, 1945. (Public Domain)

Generals Bradley, Patton and Eisenhower inspect a cache of precious artwork stolen by the Nazis and recovered during the Allied penetration into Germany. (Public Domain)

After the crisis of the Battle of the Bulge had passed, Generals Bradley, Eisenhower and Patton (left to right) stand amid the ruins of Bastogne. (Public Domain)

and food to the front all the way from the Normandy coastline. At length, the great run ground to a halt and a frustrated Patton was required to allow logistics to dictate the pace of his movement.

When the Third Army resumed its offensive in the autumn, heavy rains plagued the movement. Roads were turned into rivers of mud and debris. Allied forces approached the German frontier at a maddeningly slow pace. By early December, Patton had had enough. He called for the Third Army chaplain, Monsignor James Hugh O'Neill and explained that he wanted the assistance of the Almighty. A 'weather prayer', he said, would be appropriate.

Monsignor O'Neill was a bit sceptical about the request, asking whether it was appropriate to solicit divine intervention in order to kill other human beings. Patton was not dissuaded and the prayer that followed was printed along with a Christmas greeting, 250,000 copies being distributed throughout the ranks of Third Army. It read: "Almighty

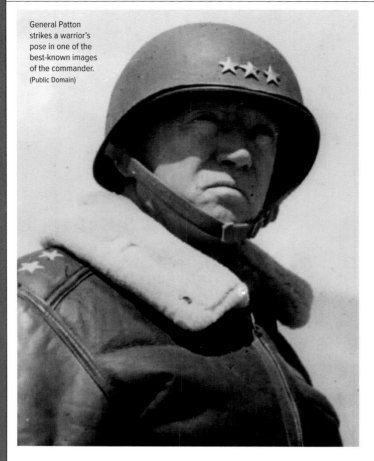

General Patton strikes a warrior's pose in one of the best-known images of the commander. (Public Domain)

taken aback and responded: "Don't be fatuous, George!" Thoroughly in his element, Patton assured the assembled officers that the effort would be successful. As the meeting drew to a close, Eisenhower, newly advanced to five-star general of the army rank, told Patton: "George, every time I get promoted, I get attacked." Smiling broadly, Patton shot back: "Yes and every time you get attacked, I bail you out." He boldly turned to General Bradley and roared: "Brad, this time the Kraut's got his head in the meat grinder and I've got hold of the handle."

True to his word, Patton sent the Third Army northward and the 4th armoured division made contact with the 101st airborne on the day after Christmas. Even the grizzled general was impressed with the elan and fighting spirit of his command. Shortly after the triumphant linkup, he wrote to his wife, Beatrice: "The relief of Bastogne is the most brilliant operation we have thus far performed and is in my opinion the outstanding achievement of this war. Now the enemy must dance to our tune, not we to his. This is my biggest battle."

Patton met a gaggle of newspaper reporters and told them in his straightforward, colourful style, "It's a hell of a lot easier to sit on your rear end and wait than it is to fight into a place like this. Try to remember that when you write your books about this campaign. Remember the men who drove up that bowling alley out there."

Patton's troops and tanks continued to push forward, reaching the Belgian town of Houffalize on January 25, 1945. Elements of the Third Army spent the next month ejecting the Germans from the great salient created during the Battle of the Bulge. By March, the Third Army was again creating havoc in a charge across Germany, catapulting across the River Rhine on the 22nd and then penetrating into Czechoslovakia by the end of the war in May.

During the hectic days of March, however, General Patton committed perhaps the worst command blunder of his long career and in the process, American lives were needlessly lost. The general's son-in-law, Lieutenant Colonel John Waters, had been taken prisoner in north Africa and Patton believed he was being held in Camp OFLAG XIII-B near the German town of Hammelburg. He decided to send Captain Abraham Baum forward with a task force to liberate the camp.

Task Force Baum was ordered on an unnecessary but highly dangerous trek 50 miles behind the German lines. The mission was a fiasco, hurled back by the enemy with 26 men killed and 314 wounded or captured. These casualty figures included every American soldier who took part in the raid. Further, 57 tanks and armoured vehicles were destroyed or captured by the Germans. The Hammelburg raid was indicative of Patton's sometimes erratic behaviour, but the terrible failure was, for the most part, lost in the shuffle of impending victory over the Nazis.

By the end of World War Two in Europe, Patton and the Third Army had amassed a combat record second to none in the European

and most merciful father, we humbly beseech thee, of thy great goodness, to restrain these immoderate rains with which we have had to contend. Grant us fair weather for battle. Graciously harken to us as soldiers who call upon thee that, armed with thy power, we may advance from victory to victory and crush the oppression and wickedness of our enemies and establish thy justice among men and nations. Amen."

Soon, the rains began to slacken and the Third Army picked up the pace of its offensive through the Saar. However, within days the Germans launched their desperate gamble in the west. Hitler conceived the Ardennes offensive, a drive through the heavily wooded area of the Ardennes Forest, penetrating a thinly held section of the American frontline. German tanks would then rush across the River Meuse and on to seize the port of Antwerp. If the panzers could take the Belgian city, Allied supply lines would be severed and the British in the north would be cut off from the Americans in the south. Perhaps there could be a negotiated peace settlement with the western Allies and their tenuous alliance with the Soviet Union might be dissolved.

Grit and glory

The Germans unleashed the Ardennes offensive on December 16, 1944, moving rapidly at first. However, pockets of resistance slowed the advance, particularly at the Belgian crossroads town of Bastogne. As the Battle of the Bulge developed, stemming the enemy tide became a major concern. Patton's vanguard was in the middle of a winter battle at Saarbrucken, far to the south of the breakthrough, but when Eisenhower called a council of war at Verdun on December 19, the Third Army commander attended.

The immediate priority was the relief of the 101st airborne division, combat command B of the 10th armoured division and elements of other units encircled at Bastogne. Plans were formulated to reverse the enemy offensive, but when the problem of Bastogne was on the table, everyone but Patton was rather pessimistic. His staff had already been working on a plan to disengage in the south, pivot northward and relieve the beleaguered garrison at Bastogne.

Patton pledged to attack with three divisions within 48 hours. He would be taxing his men beyond the limit of what many thought was human endurance. But he stood confident. Eisenhower was

A soldier inspects the damaged Cadillac limousine in which General Patton was riding when he was seriously injured in December 1945. (Public Domain)

theatre of operations. During nine straight months of combat, Patton's proud command had killed 145,000 enemy soldiers, captured another 1.3 million and liberated 80,000 square miles of formerly enemy-held territory. It was truly a remarkable performance by men in combat.

The last days

When the war in Europe concluded, Patton sought a battlefield command in the Pacific, but that was destined not to happen – perhaps because the US Army already had its pre-eminent figure in the theatre, General Douglas MacArthur, and the expanse of ocean was not quite large enough for two towering egos.

Instead, Patton was installed as military governor of Bavaria. His pragmatic approach to keeping the necessary public works and services going led to another run-in with the press and his superior officers. He refused to participate in the wholesale 'de-Nazification' of occupied Germany. Taking minor members of the party away from essential services like running telephone switchboards, delivering mail and operating public transportation would be counter-productive as he saw the situation. The outspoken general was also hypercritical of the Soviets, the erstwhile ally of Britain and the United States, in the fight against the Nazi enemy. Suspicious of premier Josef Stalin's intentions, the general denounced Soviet occupation of large areas of eastern Europe during public speaking engagements and press conferences.

Patton once again became a political liability and he was removed from command of Third Army in October 1945. His last command was at Bad Nauheim, Germany, where Fifteenth Army was tasked with writing a history of the conflict that had recently ended.

Patton became depressed in the role with the Fifteenth Army, yearning for more glory in battle and greater adulation. His chief of staff, General Hobart Gay, wanted to cheer up the general and organised a pheasant hunt for December 9 near the town of Speyer, Germany. While travelling to the site that morning, Patton's 1938 Cadillac Model 75 limousine was involved in an accident when the driver of an army truck turned left in front of the general's vehicle.

Although General Gay and the drivers were only slightly injured, Patton had been thrown violently forward into the overhead ceiling light and the steel partition inside the Cadillac. He suffered a broken nose and a large swath of his scalp was peeled back from his forehead. He bled profusely. His worst injury, though, had been the fracture of

Pallbearers carry the casket of General Patton to its final resting place during the funeral on December 24, 1945.

cervical vertebrae three and four, resulting in damage to his spine and paralysis from the neck down.

The general's condition deteriorated and 12 days after the accident, on December 21, 1945, he died of pulmonary oedema and congestive heart failure at the age of 60. He was buried on Christmas Eve in the American Military Cemetery at Hamm, Luxembourg, after previously expressing his wish to be interred among the soldiers he had led to glory in World War Two.

A quarter century after General Patton's death, actor George C. Scott starred in the major film 'Patton' and received the 1970 Academy Award for best actor. The general's spectacular career became known to a generation of Americans who might otherwise never have been familiar with his life and times.

General George S Patton Jr remains one of the most controversial military figures in American history. His battlefield successes are undisputable. However, his brilliant combat record is tinged with errors in judgement and an unquenchable thirst for personal glory, an enigmatic and puzzling combination to say the least.

The grave of General Patton is located in the American Military Cemetery in Hamm, Luxembourg. (Creative Commons Michele Dieleman via Wikipedia)

FIELD MARSHAL WILLIAM SLIM

It seemed highly unlikely that William Joseph Slim would rise to the highest level of command in the British Army. He was the son of a middle-class Birmingham iron wholesaler. He was not of noble birth and the Royal Military Academy, Sandhurst, was out of reach.

Nevertheless, the young man, born August 6, 1891 in Bristol, was bright and academically astute. He gained a scholarship to the local grammar school and his imagination was fuelled by stories of popular military history. Therefore, he embarked on a military career, enrolling in 1912 in the Officer Training Corps at Birmingham University, a unit of the Territorial Army.

Over the next 40 years, Slim would rise to the rank of field marshal and demonstrate extraordinary resilience and command capabilities while fighting the Japanese in Burma during World War Two. Although lesser known than others who led Allied troops in the China-Burma-India theatre (CBI) and elsewhere, he was instrumental in retrieving victory from the proverbial jaws of defeat. He brushed off early losses and guided the British and Commonwealth 14th Army to a hard-won victory against a tenacious enemy and amid some of the world's most difficult weather and thickest jungle.

Tested in the Great War

With the outbreak of World War One, Slim was a 2nd lieutenant in the Royal Warwickshire Regiment. Originally posted to Mesopotamia (modern day Iraq), he experienced combat for the first time in 1915 during the dreadful Dardanelles campaign. The fighting at Gallipoli was particularly bitter and frustrating as Turkish forces pinned down the British, Australian and New Zealander troops at Cape Helles and the neighbouring beaches. Young Slim distinguished himself leading multiple bayonet charges against the entrenched enemy and he was seriously wounded after 18 days of combat in August.

After a lengthy recuperation, Slim returned to action in the Middle East and received the Military Cross for bravery. Wounded a second time, he was determined 'medically unfit for duty' and shunted to India in mid-1917. When the Great War ended, he defied all the odds and remained in the service, transferring to the Indian Army and assuming staff and command positions with the 6th Gurkha Rifles and Indian Army headquarters after attending the staff college in Quetta. By the mid-1930s, he had completed the staff college at Camberley

This portrait of General William Slim was painted while he commanded 14th Army in Burma. Slim was promoted field marshal in 1949. (Public Domain)

and risen to lieutenant colonel. Through the interwar years, he had supplemented his army pay by writing pulp fiction novels.

Early setbacks

On the eve of World War Two, Slim was given command of the 10th Indian Brigade, 5th division, at Jhansi in Upper Pradesh. After 11 months of training, the brigade was detailed to Sudan, where an offensive was planned under the direction of Generals Archibald Wavell and William Platt to eject Italian forces from Eritrea and Ethiopia.

Slim's brigade actually launched the first substantive British offensive of the war in late 1940, but the effort went nowhere. The troops were not adequately supplied, their tanks were obsolete and the advance was poorly co-ordinated. Although Slim blamed himself for the dismal performance, he managed to avoid condemnation and British forces later went on to smash the Italians in East Africa.

In January 1941, Brigadier Slim was wounded for the third time in his career when an Italian aircraft strafed his position. Removed to India to convalesce, he soon joined the planning

General William Slim peers towards Japanese lines during the great offensive of the spring of 1945 that ejected the enemy from Burma. Slim overcame supply shortages, poor morale, deep jungle and a tenacious enemy in winning the victory. (Public Domain)

Soldiers of the 7th Indian division defend their position against a Japanese offensive in the Arakan region in early 1944. (Public Domain)

for a response to Axis inroads in Iraq. Promoted to acting major general, he commanded the 10th Indian division for the next 10 months in both Iraq and Syria. In the spring of 1942, General Wavell suggested Slim as chief of staff of the Indian Army. However, General Claude Auchinleck, commander of British forces in the Middle East, opposed the move, stating that Slim did not possess 'the reputation, personality and experience which would give the Indian Army full confidence'.

At the same time, Gurkha officers who had fought with Slim were aware of his command qualities and fighting spirit. They urged General Harold Alexander, commanding forces in Burma, to appoint Slim commander of the Burma Corps (Burcorps). With some political wrangling, this was accomplished and on March 11, 1942, newly promoted to acting major general, Slim flew to Magwe on the great River Irrawaddy.

It was a turning point in his career and the military situation was nothing short of a disaster in the making.

Uncertainty in the CBI

Slim was optimistic and energetic and his infectious perspective bolstered morale among the troops of Burcorps, who had known only defeat. However, an immediate offensive was thrown back by the Japanese, while the absence of a clear objective and conflicting orders from higher headquarters complicated the effort. In late March, a renewed effort to traverse the valley of the Irrawaddy and assist Chinese troops under American General Joseph Stilwell in their fight against the Japanese at Toungoo in the Sittang Valley was launched. Slim had misgivings from the beginning and this offensive, too, ended in frustrating failure. By the end of April, there was no choice but to withdraw the exhausted British and Indian forces back into India.

The Burma Corps had lost 13,000 casualties and had only 28 artillery pieces left of an original 150. The retreat from Burma covered 900 miles with the Japanese in pursuit and the monsoon season delivering continual torrents of rain. Slim watched the soldiers slog through the mud and muck but retained his pride and remarked: "They might look like scarecrows, but they look like soldiers too."

Field Marshal Archibald Wavell knights General William Slim during ceremonies near Imphal in December 1944. (Public Domain)

Slim's co-ordination of the withdrawal had been remarkable and he assessed: "We, the Allies, had been outmanoeuvred, outfought and out-generaled. To our men, British or Indian, the jungle was a strange, fearsome place. Moving and fighting in it was a nightmare. We were too ready to classify jungle as impenetrable. To the Japanese, it was the welcome means of concealed manoeuvre and surprise. The Japanese reaped the deserved reward for their foresight and thorough preparation – we paid the penalty for our lack of both."

Still, early efforts to reverse the string of defeats met with failure and withdrawal and Slim bore the brunt of criticism in some echelons of higher command – though it was in fact his command ability that had repeatedly saved the British Army from even greater destruction in the CBI. Then, a change of command brought a needed boost, both to the hope for eventual victory and to Slim's flagging career.

Soldiers of the 19th Indian division cheer General Slim as his Jeep passes following the liberation of Mandalay. (Public Domain)

Resurgence at last

In mid-1943, General Sir George Giffard rose to command of 11th Army group, while Lord Louis Mountbatten took the helm of southeast Asia command. Mountbatten stressed a renewal of offensive operations even during monsoon season. Slim's support helped garner command of the 14th Army in October 1943, but even with this new opportunity, Slim admitted: "I must have been the most defeated general in our history."

True to optimistic form though, Slim set to work with the half million soldiers of 14th Army deployed along a 700-mile front from the Bay of Bengal to the Chinese border. Morale had to improve, even though the 14th Army ranked among the lowest priorities in terms of supplies and new equipment. Slim persevered and over the course of several months rebuilt it as a fighting force. He visited his troops regularly, speaking to individual units in their native languages, including Gurkhali and Urdu. The soldiers responded to his spirit.

When his troops were again fit for combat, Slim began with limited actions, deploying overwhelming force against smaller Japanese units to ensure victory and diminish the idea that the enemy were 'supermen' who could not be defeated – even though these engagements were limited. As the soldiers gained confidence, a co-ordinated offensive was taking shape in late 1943 as troops under Stilwell took the city of Myitkyina and reached the Burma Road while the 15th corps advanced to Arakan and the famed Chindits, under Brigadier Orde Wingate, conducted raids deep behind Japanese lines.

When the Japanese saw the offensive building, they took pre-emptive action, launching their own major strike first. Three enemy divisions hit Slim's positions stretched 300 miles along the plain of Imphal. The general called for reinforcements and the ensuing battle for control of the city of Kohima was savage until the last Japanese attacks in the area were beaten back. The enemy retreated in mid-May 1944, after suffering 6,000 casualties.

At Imphal, the Japanese laid siege and battered away at Slim's defenders, who stood their ground and were largely resupplied by air. The advance of the 2nd and 5th Indian divisions broke the siege on June 22, opening the vital Imphal-Kohima Road. The Japanese had lost 53,000 soldiers and pulled back to the River Chindwin. Slim's contribution to the reversal of fortune was recognised and he was made Knight Commander of the Order of the Bath on December 15.

Meanwhile, the intrepid general kept the pressure up on the enemy. He pursued the Japanese across the Chindwin in late 1944 and on January 14, 1945, unleashed the decisive offensive in the theatre. Within three weeks, the communications centre of Meiktila was captured and Japanese links to the Burmese capital of Rangoon were severed. The fabled city of Mandalay fell to the 14th Army on March 21. On May 2, Slim's soldiers liberated Rangoon and by then the enemy had lost a staggering 350,000 men in the recent fighting.

The triumph in Burma is considered by many historians as the most brilliant British land campaign of World War Two.

In the summer of 1945, Slim succeeded General Oliver Leese as commander of Allied land forces in southeast Asia. He was promoted to full general, but still the accolades that were showered on his contemporaries seemed to elude the victor of Burma. Even Winston Churchill had originally snubbed the senior officer who rose to command on merit and steadfastness rather than lofty connection. "I cannot believe that a man with a name like Slim can be much good," Churchill had mused. Then, after victories were won, he softened to add of Slim, "He has a hell of a face."

With the approval of Churchill, Slim became one of the trusted few senior commanders surrounding the great leader. Still, Slim spoke truth to power and frankly informed the prime minister that he did not believe the rank and file of the army would support him in an upcoming bid for re-election in 1945. Churchill did, in fact, lose that election.

In 1946, Slim led the Imperial Defence College. A year later, he served as deputy chairman of the nationalised British Railways. In 1948, he succeeded Field Marshal Bernard Montgomery as chief of the imperial general staff – although Montgomery, for some reason, protested the appointment. At long last, in January 1949, Slim was promoted field marshal.

While serving as Governor General of Australia, he wrote and published his memoirs 'Defeat into Victory', in 1956 and it was well received. Slim became a Knight of the Garter in 1959 and was elevated to the peerage as Viscount Slim of Burma in 1960. In his later years, he served as constable and governor of Windsor Castle. He died in London on December 14, 1970, at the age of 79.

Field Marshal William Slim remains one of the lesser-known Allied commanders who played pivotal roles in World War Two. He has been lauded by historians, but the limelight that has shone on others continues to elude him. Lord Mountbatten, though, was one prominent figure who freely expressed his opinion of Slim's worth, declaring that the Viscount of Burma was 'the finest general the Second World War produced'.

William Slim rose from humble beginnings to the rank of field marshal and the office of chief of the imperial general staff. This photo was taken in 1950. (Public Domain)

GENERAL ORDE WINGATE

O rde Wingate was an enigma – a brilliant tactical planner and leader of men but an eccentric whose reputation for erratic behaviour caused superiors to doubt his fitness for high command.

Wingate led his famous Chindits during long-range penetrations deep behind Japanese lines in the China-Burma-India theatre and wreaked havoc on enemy communications, supply and troop concentrations. His concepts were revolutionary and the exploits of his Chindits in World War Two brought lasting fame to the fighting men and to their leader.

Proving himself resourceful and imaginative, Wingate was nevertheless the object of some scepticism among his peers. He was sometimes seen boiling tea using his socks as strainers. He carried Greek classics by Homer and Plato, perhaps for some light reading while on the campaign trek. And he was known to plot strategy and tactics with subordinate officers in his quarters while not wearing a stitch of clothing.

Born into a military family in India on February 26, 1903, Wingate spent most of his childhood in England. His upbringing was devoutly Christian and Puritan and he attended Charterhouse School in Godalming, Surrey. In 1921, Wingate gained admission to the Royal Military Academy, Woolwich, where future officers of the artillery were moulded. As a young officer, he was known to challenge superior officers and sometimes debate orders.

A committed Zionist, Wingate served in Sudan and then the Middle East in the years between the world wars. He commanded counter-insurgency units in Palestine during an Arab terror campaign that targeted Jewish inhabitants of the region. His 'Special Night Squads' became proficient at clandestine operations, striking oil pipelines and production facilities to choke off the source of the Arabs' financing. The Arabs were forced onto the defensive as Wingate's irregulars tracking them relentlessly.

War in the desert

With the outbreak of World War Two, Wingate was ordered to East Africa and led Gideon Force against the occupying Italians in Ethiopia.

Eccentric but innovative General Orde Wingate was a pioneer of special forces operations. (Public Domain)

Throughout 1940, his command harassed the enemy and Wingate gained a reputation as a superb tactician, deploying well-trained soldiers who were highly motivated and performed well during extended field operations.

Senior officers of the British and Indian armies then fighting the Japanese were impressed and Wingate put forward a suggestion that his tactics might be employed in the China-Burma-India theatre (CBI), where the inhospitable jungle terrain impeded major offensive action. His idea that specially trained and equipped units might be inserted behind enemy lines, patrol for lengthy periods while supplied by air and then be extracted to rest and refit gained support. By then, Wingate had burnished his credibility among senior officers, despite his well-known personality quirks.

To the CBI

General Archibald Wavell, commander of British forces in India, supported the innovative offensive tactic and by late 1942, Wingate was authorised to recruit and train a force of up to 3,000 soldiers. Buoyed by this opportunity, Brigadier Wingate considered options for an appropriate name and dubbed his new force the Chindits, a corruption of the Burmese word chinthe, a descriptive term for the mythical lion prominent in the art and architecture of the Burmese people. Officially, the Chindits were designated the 77th Indian Infantry brigade and their officers prepared them rapidly to assume offensive operations.

The first Chindit foray was launched on February 13, 1943, as Wingate's command intended to cut the rail line that brought supplies to frontline Japanese units. The Chindits crossed the River Chindwin near the town of Imphal and spent two months behind enemy lines. Long marches were oppressive in the stifling jungle heat, while disease took its toll. All the while, the Japanese searched for the raiders and sharp clashes occurred. When they became aware of an expeditionary force 125 miles behind their front, the Japanese were startled. Their respect for the Chindits grew rapidly.

In response to the incursion, the Japanese reoriented substantial forces to their rear to deal with the threat. Moving across the broad plain of the River Irrawaddy, the Chindits had divided their force into five separate columns for the lengthy march. To their disappointment, they found the ground unsuited for sustained operations and the surrounding jungle quite inhospitable. Wingate realised the precarious situation as Japanese pressure mounted and his troops were nearing

Orde Wingate and his Chindit lieutenants confer somewhere in the Burmese jungle in 1944. (Public Domain)

Orde Wingate was killed at age 41 in an aircraft crash in March 1944. (Public Domain)

exhaustion. He chose to break his formations up into small groups that could more easily exfiltrate through the Japanese patrols and main line of resistance to reach the safety of India. Still, it was a fighting retreat and substantial numbers of Chindits were incapacitated by malaria and other tropical maladies. Those who could walk and fire a rifle, though, were tenacious in defensive stands, slowing the enemy pursuit.

When the surviving Chindits, battered but proud of their achievements in the initial action, returned to India, Wingate and his subordinate officers were taken aback by the heavy casualties. While they had undertaken the operation with 3,000 fighting men, more than 800 had been killed, wounded, captured or suffered from disease. The ranks of the Chindits were thinned, but roughly 600 of those wounded or ill did return to active duty. Nevertheless, there were detractors among British senior commanders, some of whom considered the operation an outright failure.

Still, other officers maintained their positive stance on Chindit operations, considering the value of tying down Japanese troops in chasing the irregulars, inflicting damage and casualties and keeping the enemy off balance. Among those who continued to throw their support behind the Chindits was Winston Churchill. The prime minister had long been an advocate of special operations and even briefly considered promoting Wingate to command of all British forces in Burma.

Further, Churchill believed that the Chindits had accomplished something noteworthy, striking back in the wake of a string of unbroken Japanese victories which had taken place in the CBI in prior months. The Chindits had proved that they could exact a price in blood and treasure from the Japanese – and they had proved it in the jungle, where the enemy soldier had become renowned for his fighting prowess. The Chindits had gone toe to toe with the Japanese and come out of the brawl having given as good as they got.

The press could also be useful at a time when the British people were in need of heroes. Orde Wingate was just the sort of combat leader that newspaper reporters and readers could embrace. He was wily, cunning and willing to take a risk to strike a blow at the enemy. And so, following the first Chindit operation, Wingate was promoted major general. At the same time, he was given increased logistical and fire support with American transport aircraft, observation planes, gliders, fighters and bombers.

Flexing Chindit muscles

By early 1944, the ranks of the Chindits had grown to 20,000 and Wingate and his staff envisioned a new offensive in co-operation with the American special operations force known as Merrill's Marauders and Chinese army troops under the command of American General Joseph Stilwell.

Supplies and equipment were to be prepositioned at six sites deep behind Japanese lines and once the irregular troops were on the ground, they would attack enemy communications centres and interdict supply lines as opportunities arose. Resupply would be by air and Stilwell would co-ordinate an offensive that would oust the Japanese from

After the capture of Mogaung during Operation Thursday, Brigadier Mike Calvert gives orders to troops of 77 brigade. (Public Domain)

Chindits board a transport aircraft during the opening phase of Operation Thursday in Burma. (Public Domain)

northern Burma, seize the airfield at the town of Myitkyina and open an Allied overland supply route between India and China.

Codenamed Operation Thursday, the offensive got underway in early March 1944, as the Chindits were inserted by glider and set up supply bases named Piccadilly, Broadway, Aberdeen, White City and others. The beginning was inauspicious as several Dakota transports crashed when their engines were overtaxed by towing two gliders. Piccadilly was not fully prepared to receive gliders since a large number of trees had only just been felled. Those gliders intended for Piccadilly were diverted to Broadway and only 35 of 61 landed without some degree of damage.

The Chindits were aware of the simple fact that hacking suitable bases out of the thick jungle while trying to maintain a timeline was a formidable task, but even so the opening days of Operation Thursday were disappointing. It took 23 agonising days for 16 brigade, under Brigadier Bernard Ferguson, to reach the banks of the Chindwin, the halfway point of its planned trek. Meanwhile, the Japanese were aware of the ruckus and moved adroitly to counter the bold thrust.

Lieutenant General Masakuzu Kawabe led ten battalions of Japanese troops, veteran jungle fighters, against the Chindit lodgements. Two battalions hit Broadway, while White City was assailed by a huge Japanese force of 6,000 soldiers and 77 brigade, under the colourful and capable Brigadier Mike Calvert, fought them hand to hand. Calvert seized the opportunity to take the town of Mogaung but after fighting the Japanese, his effective force had been reduced to just 2,000 men. Of these, half were lost in the effort to take the town.

At the end of August, after six months of fighting, the exhausted Chindits began withdrawing from the jungle with 5,000 of their number killed or wounded.

Meanwhile, on March 24, Wingate had flown to Aberdeen to assess the situation at the base. During the return flight, he was killed when the bomber he was aboard crashed into a mountainside southwest of Imphal. With his death at age 41, one of the most innovative minds in the British Army was lost. The future and what might have been in the CBI during World War Two had Wingate lived provide a basis for robust discourse.

A Chindit column crosses a river in Burma during long-range penetration movements in 1943. (Public Domain)

GENERAL HOLLAND M SMITH

General Holland M Smith of the US Marine Corps is remembered as the father of modern American amphibious warfare doctrine. Smith is credited with developing the tactics and procedures that evolved in the years prior to World War Two and facilitated the landings of both Marine and Army troops during the campaign across the Pacific against Japan.

Smith was a crisp, driven individual who had little patience with incompetent or underachieving personnel. He was opinionated and outspoken, but always maintained a soft approach to young officers and in his later years he worked on behalf of disadvantaged and troubled youth, donating hours of time with charitable organisations.

Smith was born in Seale, Alabama, on April 20, 1882 and graduated ay Alabama Polytechnic University (now Auburn University) in 1901. He showed interest in a military career and joined the Alabama National Guard. After receiving a law degree from the University of Alabama, he practised law in Montgomery, the state capital, briefly before seeking a commission in the US Army. When he was informed that no army commissions were available, he accepted a commission as 2nd lieutenant in the Marine Corps.

Before World War One, Smith served twice in the Philippines and in various posts in the United States. He commanded the Marine detachment aboard the protected cruiser USS *Galveston* and received promotion to captain in 1916 before being ordered to the Dominican Republic. It was there while serving with the 4th Marine Regiment that his volcanic temper earned him the nickname Howlin' Mad from the troops under his command. In 1918, he sailed to France in command of the 8th machine gun company. Attached to the 2nd division, US Army, he was a brigade liaison officer during the fighting at Belleau Wood. After transfer to I Corps, he was an operations officer during offensive actions in 1918, including Aisne-Marne, Oise-Aisne, St. Mihiel and the Meuse-Argonne.

Development and doctrine

After promotion to major in 1920, Smith completed the Naval War College and held several positions at east coast duty stations before reporting to the office of the chief of naval operations in Washington DC, for assignment to the war plans division as the first Marine officer to participate in an Army-Navy planning committee. He subsequently went back to sea as fleet marine officer aboard the battleships *Wyoming* and *Arkansas* and became chief of staff of the Marine brigade stationed in Haiti.

By the mid-1930s, he had steadily assumed positions of greater responsibility and after two years as chief of staff to the Department of the Pacific, Colonel Smith became director of the division of operations and training and then assistant commandant of the Marine Corps. He took command of the 1st marine brigade in August 1939.

Two years later, the need for amphibious capabilities in the American military was recognised and Smith was one of the early organisers of amphibious force, Atlantic fleet, responsible for training the first Marine Regiment and the ninth division of the army in amphibious warfare. In the amphibious role, Smith advanced the concept, first advocated by Major General John Lejeune before World War One, of the Marines as specialists in such operations. While Admiral Ernest J King, commander of the Atlantic fleet, was insistent in retaining navy command of Marine units once they had come ashore, Smith was vigorously opposed. The two men sometimes shouted at one another and King threatened to have the assertive Marine officer relieved. However, Smith refused to back down. The two headstrong officers later repaired their fractured relationship and they co-operated

Above: Marine Corps General Holland M Smith is considered the father of amphibious warfare doctrine in the US military. (Public Domain)

Right: Marines of the 2nd division fight the Japanese at Tarawa atoll in the Gilbert Islands, November 1943. (Creative Commons USMC Archives via Wikipedia)

well during World War Two. In recognition of his proficiency, Smith was promoted major general in October 1941.

Amphibious advance

General Smith was named commander of the fleet Marine force after the Japanese attack on Pearl Harbor, Hawaii, plunged the US into World War Two. Relocating to San Diego, California, in August 1942, he organised the Amphibious Corps, Pacific fleet. In this role, he trained the 2nd and 3rd Marine Divisions and the army's 7th Infantry Division for landings in the Aleutians on the islands of Attu and Kiska. The following year, the command was redesignated V Amphibious Corps and moved forward to Pearl Harbor. It was evident that the long, difficult campaign against the Japanese would require numerous amphibious landing operations and Smith had laid the foundation for the arduous trek across the Pacific.

In February 1943, Smith nearly lost his command and his career. He was arrested for drunk driving and hit-and-run following an incident in which he was observed to crash into another vehicle after apparently

Holland M Smith (right) and secretary of the Navy James Forrestal watch the fighting on the island of Iwo Jima. Mount Suribachi looms in the distance. (Public Domain)

Smith sits at centre with staff officers as they discuss the progress against Japanese defenders on Saipan in the Marianas. (Creative Commons USMC Archives via Wikipedia)

Smith carries an M-1 carbine as he boards a Jeep for a tour on Saipan. While leading troops on the island, Holland Smith relieved Army General Ralph Smith, creating tremendous controversy. (Public Domain)

striking a jaywalking pedestrian who suffered a broken leg. There was no clear evidence that Smith had hit the pedestrian or that he had been drinking to excess. Blackout restrictions were also in place, creating a hazardous situation for drivers. The charges were dropped.

In the spring of 1943, Smith went along to the Aleutians and observed the landings at Attu before reaching Pearl Harbor in September 1943. He assumed command of V Amphibious Corps, at the time engaged in planning for Operation Galvanic, the offensive against the Gilbert Islands which included landings at Tarawa and Makin. At Tarawa, hard lessons were learned in the co-ordination and effectiveness of air support, naval bombardment and transport to hostile beaches aboard landing craft of different types. Smith argued in favour of a larger allotment of the LVTs (landing vehicle, tracked) for the operation and a supplemental number of these proved instrumental in negotiating the coral reef that ringed the lagoon at Tarawa. Still, the number of LTVs was less than optimal and many of the Marines of the 2nd division experienced major difficulties while going in aboard flat-bottomed Higgins boats.

In February 1944, Smith was promoted lieutenant general, and the 4th Marine division and the army's 7th Infantry Division of V Amphibious Corps were landed at Kwajalein in the Marshall Islands. By then, animosity had been building between Smith and senior commanders of the US Army. General Robert Richardson, commander of army forces in the Pacific, was one of several officers who considered Holland Smith a bully and a headstrong individual more concerned with the interests of the Marine Corps than in co-operative operations. Smith had previously clashed with Army General Ralph Smith, commander of the 27th Infantry Division at Makin and Richardson attempted to have V Amphibious Corps dissolved.

Although Richardson's effort failed, the feud simmered at Kwajalein as Smith and General Charles Corlett, commander of the 7th division, were continually at odds regarding the pace of operations. The inter-service rancour boiled over during the operations in the Marianas Islands in the spring and summer of 1944 following landings at Saipan, Guam and Tinian.

Smith versus Smith
For the landings on Saipan, Holland Smith's V Amphibious Corps deployed the 2nd and 4th Marine Divisions and the army's 27th Division. As the fighting progressed, Holland Smith became concerned that the Marines were advancing more rapidly than the army troops, which created problems with

unprotected flanks, upset timetables and subsequently accusations that the army troops were poorly trained and inadequately led.

During the course of the Saipan fight, Holland Smith took the dramatic action of relieving Ralph Smith of command. A firestorm of controversy erupted and in response to the Marine perspective, army observers fired back that the 27th division faced stiffer Japanese opposition than the Marine units. Further, they asserted, Holland Smith had gone beyond the limits of inter-service protocol in relieving an army general.

Richardson was reported to have told Holland Smith: "You had no right to relieve Ralph Smith. The 27th is one of the best-trained divisions in the Pacific. I trained it myself. I want you to know you can't push the army around the way you've been doing. We've had more experience in handling troops than you have and yet you dare remove one of my generals. You Marines are nothing but a bunch of beach runners anyway. What do you know about land warfare?"

An army board of inquiry found, unsurprisingly, that the relief of Ralph Smith was unjustified. However, it also noted that Holland Smith was within his authority to make the change. In the wake of the controversy, Holland Smith was named commanding general, fleet Marine force, Pacific. He commanded task force 56, the Marine expeditionary force that landed at Iwo Jima in February 1945 and took the island after more than a month of bitter combat. That summer, he was reassigned to command of the Marine training and replacement Centre at Camp Pendleton, California.

Pacific postscript
Holland Smith did not actively participate in the April 1945 invasion of Okinawa, the last major amphibious landing and campaign of World War Two and he was disappointed that he did not represent the Marine Corps at the proceedings of Japanese surrender at Tokyo Bay. He retired in August 1946, after 41 years of service and was promoted four-star general shortly afterward. His memoir, Coral and Brass, was published in 1949 and he was sharply critical of the leadership in other branches of the US military.

Nevertheless, he was a devout Christian who was remembered by some as a quiet, calm gentleman, a champion of charitable causes in retirement and quite a contradiction to the persona of Howlin' Mad. He died on January 12, 1967, at age 84.

Smith (second from right) confers with top navy and Marine commanders, including Admiral Richmond Kelly Turner (far right) during the planning for landings at Iwo Jima. (Public Domain)

GENERAL DOUGLAS MacARTHUR

On October 20, 1944, General Douglas MacArthur made good on his promise. American troops had landed on the island of Leyte in the Philippines and the commander of Allied forces in the Southwest Pacific was headed toward the shore.

Moments before MacArthur was to set foot in the Philippines for the first time in more than two years, however, the whaleboat carrying the general and a number of officers and civilians lurched to a hard stop in the pounding surf, grounded fast on a sandbar. The surrounding water was knee deep, but MacArthur was undeterred. In fact, the ensuing moments only heightened the drama as his tall figure left the boat and the general waded ashore, his entourage following closely.

In the dark days of early 1942, World War Two in the Pacific was going badly for the US and its allies. General MacArthur had been evacuated from the Philippines and secretly flown to safety as the invading Japanese tightened their noose around the American and Filipino forces pushed back into defensive positions on the Bataan peninsula and the island fortress of Corregidor in Manila Bay. Just after his plane touched down in Australia, MacArthur declared that he would one day return to the Philippines and defeat the forces of Imperial Japan.

MacArthur holds a riding crop and sits in an ornate chair in France during World War One. (Public Domain)

Now, with the Allies ascendant, MacArthur relished a moment of supreme vindication. As he reached the shore, the general walked a few steps to a portable radio that had been made operational for the occasion. In his deep, authoritative voice, he declared: "People of the Philippines: I have returned. By the grace of Almighty God, our forces stand again on Philippine soil – soil consecrated in the blood of our two peoples. Rally to me!"

General Douglas MacArthur, one of the most famous military commanders in the history of the United States, was also one of its most flamboyant, egocentric and vain. As photographers' flash bulbs popped, the general was truly in his element. A Hollywood script could not have been conceived more perfectly and MacArthur played the role of returning hero to the hilt. The historic return to the Philippines was a sentinel event in the life of General MacArthur, particularly as his military career of more than 40 years had been inextricably bound up with the islands and their people.

Made for the military

Douglas MacArthur was born into a military family on January 26, 1880, the son of Captain Arthur MacArthur Jr, who would later rise to the rank of lieutenant general, and Mary Pinkney Hardy MacArthur.

A corncob pipe clenched between his teeth, General Douglas MacArthur posed for this portrait in August 1945, probably in Manila. (Public Domain)

General Arthur MacArthur Jr received the Medal of Honor during the American Civil War. (Public Domain)

General John J 'Black Jack' Pershing decorates MacArthur with the Distinguished Service Cross. (Public Domain)

He came into the world at Little Rock Barracks, Arkansas, the youngest of three sons and later described his upbringing as that of a military brat.

The family moved often as Captain MacArthur, a recipient of the Congressional Medal of Honor for valour at the Battle of Missionary Ridge during the American Civil War, was assigned to various posts.

Douglas was proud to admit that he had "learned to ride and shoot even before I could read and write – indeed, almost before I could walk and talk". While the family lived in San Antonio, Texas, he was an outstanding student and athlete at the West Texas Military Academy and when the time came, it followed naturally that he would seek admission to the US Military Academy at West Point in New York.

The West Point experience was gruelling. For one thing, Douglas was a bit of a 'mama's boy'. The separation from his mother was too much to bear and she acquired a room in a hotel on the campus to be near her son. The knowledge that MacArthur's mother was living nearby undoubtedly contributed to the relentless hazing he endured from fellow cadets. Nevertheless, Douglas continued to achieve, both athletically and academically. He played left field on the West Point baseball team and served as first captain of his class during senior year, graduating first among 93 cadets in 1903 and receiving a commission as a second lieutenant in the prestigious US Army Corps of Engineers.

Growth and the Great War

Lieutenant MacArthur was posted to the 3rd Engineer Battalion shortly after graduation and made his first visit to the Philippines in October 1903. A month after his arrival, MacArthur was attacked by two assailants. The young officer pulled his pistol and shot them both dead. He contracted malaria and survived. By July 1905, he had returned to the US and served as chief engineer of the division of the Pacific.

In October of that year, he received an appointment as an aide to his father. Travelling in the Far East to Japan and China and then to India, the American officers toured military facilities and major cities across the region. The reputation of the MacArthur men preceded them and one observer during this period wrote: "Arthur MacArthur was the most flamboyantly egotistical man I had ever seen, until I met his son."

After returning to the US in 1906, Douglas remained as his father's aide until summoned to Washington DC to complete the Engineer

Posing with staff officers in France, MacArthur was fond of wearing non-regulation uniforms. (Public Domain)

Violence erupts between Bonus Marchers and police officers in Washington, DC. General MacArthur was ordered to disperse the marchers, generating a public relations disaster. (Public Domain)

School while serving – at the direct request of President Theodore Roosevelt – as an 'aide to assist at White House functions'. In the spring of 1908, Lieutenant MacArthur received his first command, Company K, 3rd Engineer Battalion, at Fort Leavenworth, Kansas. Promoted captain in February 1911, MacArthur was later posted to Texas and Panama before returning to Washington DC and the office of the Army Chief of Staff, a transfer that was arranged to allow him to be close to his ailing mother.

In the spring of 1914, the army was ordered to occupy the port of Veracruz, Mexico and while leading a party to locate railroad locomotives for American use, MacArthur displayed tremendous

personal courage when the group was assaulted several times by renegade Mexicans. MacArthur shot two of the attackers along the rail line and was later recommended for the Medal of Honor.

Promoted to colonel, MacArthur was appointed chief of staff of the 42nd Infantry Division, which arrived in France in 1917 as the US entered World War One. Despite his staff level position, he could not stay away from the front and often found himself in the middle of firefights with the Germans. His heroism was exceptional and he received an astonishing two Distinguished Service Crosses, seven Silver Stars and the French Croix de Guerre in recognition. He was wounded in combat twice, promoted to brigadier general and recommended for the Medal of Honor a second time. At the Battle of St-Mihiel during the decisive Meuse-Argonne offensive, he personally undertook a daring reconnaissance mission which resulted in the recommendation for promotion to major general.

Star in the making

In the peacetime military, MacArthur remained highly visible and garnered a prestigious appointment in 1919, returning to West Point as superintendent and remaining in the post for the next three years. During his tenure, MacArthur revised the curriculum, formalised the previously unwritten cadet honour code and developed training programmes administered by regular army officers. The memories of his merciless hazing led to an effort to bring more army officers into the teaching cadre to minimise the opportunities that upper class men might use to terrorise younger cadets.

In February 1922, MacArthur married wealthy heiress Louise Cromwell Brooks, the mother of two children. He was ordered to the Philippines in the autumn to assume the post of military governor of Manila. The youngest major general in the army, he became friends with prominent Filipino political leaders, including future president Manuel Quezon, and did his best to address pay inequities and persistent prejudices between American soldiers and members of the Philippine military.

Above left: MacArthur in 1919 during his term as superintendent of the US Military Academy at West Point. (Public Domain)

Above right: MacArthur holds a cigarette in this 1925 image. He had already developed a reputation for arrogance and vanity, although his soldierly qualities were acknowledged as well. (Public Domain)

Shacks built by Bonus Marchers go up in flames during the violence of 1932 while MacArthur was chief of staff of the army. (Public Domain)

Left: President Manuel Quezon of the Philippines invited his friend, General MacArthur, to train and improve the Philippine military in the 1930s. (Public Domain)

Returning to the US in 1925, MacArthur held command positions at Fort McPherson, Georgia and Fort McHenry, Maryland and served on the court martial tribunal of the controversial General Billy Mitchell, an early airpower advocate. He was appointed president of the US Olympic Committee and supervised preparations for the country's athletes to participate in the 1928 Summer Olympic Games in Amsterdam.

MacArthur's marriage to Louise foundered. They separated in 1927 and divorced two years later. His military career, however, continued on an upward trajectory despite a growing reputation among his fellow officers as egotistical and arrogant. His previous posting to the Philippines had engendered an affinity for the islands and the people and in 1929 he was detailed there for a year to serve as commander of the Philippine Department.

A year later, MacArthur was back in the United States, commanding the IX Corps area in California and that autumn he was elevated to Chief of Staff of the Army in Washington DC at the relatively tender age of 50. Immediately, he imprinted his style on the high-profile position, padding around his office in a Japanese style kimono, smoking cigarettes in a jewelled holder and hiring his own public relations firm to stoke favour with the press. It seemed that the general's ego grew apace with his increasing responsibility.

In the Great Depression, a large group of World War One veterans and their family members converged on Washington DC to demand early payment of promised financial bonuses. As the crowd grew restive, President Herbert Hoover ordered their large encampment at Anacostia Flats to be levelled and the 'Bonus Army' dispersed. When troops were brought in to carry out the presidential order, the general's aide, then-Major Dwight D Eisenhower, urged him to stay away from the area.

Instead, as the troops used tear gas and the point of the bayonet to remove the protestors and then burned their encampment, General MacArthur was there in full dress uniform. The result was a public relations disaster that smeared his name in the press and though the backlash was temporary, it was a stain on his persona. At the same time, MacArthur was a political pragmatist and although he was a Republican, he maintained a good working relationship with President Franklin D Roosevelt, the New Deal Democrat elected in 1932 to the first of four terms in the White House.

Philippines promotion

In 1935, MacArthur travelled to the Philippines for the fifth time at the request of his old friend President Manuel Quezon. The reason for the invitation was somewhat ominous as Quezon recognised the need to train and modernise the Filipino Army. President Roosevelt agreed to the move in the interest of co-operation and MacArthur was allowed to hold the rank of field marshal of the Philippine Army and maintain his major general rank in the US Army, officially in an advisory role to Quezon.

MacArthur (left) and General Richard K Sutherland sit in MacArthur's headquarters on Corregidor on March 1, 1942. (Public Domain)

Lieutenant Commander John Bulkeley receives the Medal of Honor from President Franklin D Roosevelt. Bulkeley led the PT-boat flotilla that spirited MacArthur to safety in the Philippines. (Public Domain)

Eisenhower was reluctant to accompany his boss to the Pacific and later lost respect for MacArthur when he was blamed for a spending scandal that involved a military parade during times when the Philippine treasury was strapped for cash. Responsibility for the bungled affair rested with MacArthur and was conveniently shifted to Eisenhower, who never forgot the experience along with the Bonus Army fiasco. When asked years later about his time in MacArthur's shadow, Eisenhower wryly responded: "I studied dramatics under him for five years in Washington and four years in the Philippines."

MacArthur married for the second time in 1937. His wife, the former Jean Faircloth, gave birth to a son, Arthur MacArthur IV, in February 1938. The general retired from the army at the age of 57 but remained in the Philippines as an adviser to President Quezon and no doubt because of his love for the people.

By the late 1930s, however, Japanese military incursions on the Asian continent had erupted into full-blown conflict between the aggressors and neighbouring China. With the prospect of an expanded war in the Pacific that would probably involve the United States, Roosevelt federalised the Philippine armed forces in the summer of 1941 and recalled MacArthur to active duty as commander of US forces in the Far East, with the rank of lieutenant general.

Crucible of World War Two

As Far East commander, General MacArthur was responsible for the military preparedness of American forces across the expanse of the region in the event of war. The Philippines would surely be an early

target for Japanese conquest and it would seem logical that MacArthur would take all steps necessary to ensure the defence of the islands. To this day, though, his level of engagement in the effort and the resulting apparent lack of preparedness are topics of historical criticism. And the general's rather inefficient conduct of pre-war training and force fitness has been seen by many as the low point in his career.

When the Japanese attacked Pearl Harbor and other US military installations in Hawaii on the morning of December 7, 1941, the news of the raid was flashed to the Philippines by late afternoon (December 8 as the Philippines are located across the International Date Line) and pre-arranged war plans were activated by order of Army Chief of Staff General George C Marshall in Washington DC. The Far East Air Force (FEAF) sent repeated requests to MacArthur's headquarters to authorise bombing raids against Japanese installations and shipping around the island of Formosa, but these pleas were turned down. At the same time, Japanese air raids targeted facilities, including harbours, airfields and army barracks, across the Philippines. Dozens of American aircraft were caught on the ground and destroyed, crippling the combat effectiveness of FEAF at a critical moment in the burgeoning conflict.

Two weeks after Pearl Harbor, Japanese troops landed at Lingayen Gulf on the Philippine island of Luzon. Although they encountered stubborn resistance at some locations, general progress was rapid. The invaders threatened the capital of Manila and MacArthur's defensive plans began to unravel in the face of the determined enemy. By Christmas Eve, Manila was declared an open city to prevent its destruction. Rumours of relief, vast amounts of materiel and thousands of reinforcing troops that would arrive any day, swept through the ranks of the beleaguered defenders. However, it was a forlorn hope. These brave men in the Philippines could not be reinforced or rescued on a large scale. The best that they could do was sacrifice themselves to buy time for the Allies to marshal forces and strike back elsewhere.

MacArthur confers with Australian Prime Minister John Curtin during operations against the Japanese. (Public Domain)

MacArthur stands second from left during a meeting of senior Allied commanders in the Pacific in October 1942. (Public Domain)

By March 1942, a Japanese victory was a foregone conclusion, only a matter of time. President Roosevelt ordered MacArthur to leave the Philippines while his American and Filipino troops fought doggedly in defence of the Bataan peninsula and the island of Corregidor. Meanwhile, some of the troops realised that their situation was dire. They blamed President Roosevelt and General MacArthur for their predicament and some began to repeat a derisive tune that implied their commander was a coward, not daring to visit the front line. It ran in part: "Dugout Doug MacArthur lies a shaking on the Rock/ Safe from all the bombers and from any sudden shock/Dugout Doug is eating of the best food on Bataan/And his troops go starving on."

Indeed, combat wounded, sick and hungry soldiers held while arrangements were made for the evacuation of MacArthur, his wife and young son and a cluster of close staff officers and advisers. In truth, the general protested Roosevelt's evacuation directive, preferring to share the fate of his command. But orders were orders.

On March 11, 1942, MacArthur and the others boarded a flotilla of fast PT-boats and slipped away from Manila Bay under cover of darkness. The PT-boats were under the command of Lieutenant John

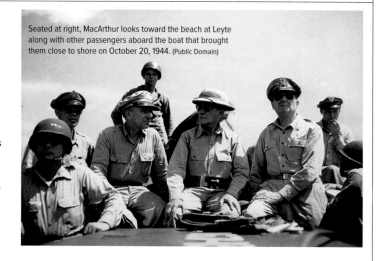

Seated at right, MacArthur looks toward the beach at Leyte along with other passengers aboard the boat that brought them close to shore on October 20, 1944. (Public Domain)

D Bulkeley aboard *PT-41*. The harrowing 35-hour voyage across 560 miles of enemy controlled waters was perilous as the small craft had to avoid contact with Japanese warships in the area. After a couple of close calls, the boats reached the Philippine island of Mindanao. MacArthur turned to Bulkeley and said: "You've taken me out of the jaws of death and I won't forget it."

Five days later, the refugees boarded a Boeing B-17 Flying Fortress bomber that carried them to safety in northern Australia. General Jonathan Wainwright was left in command of the exhausted defenders in the Philippines and the disaster unfolded days later with the surrender of thousands of troops. Many of these were abused, tortured and murdered by their Japanese captors and some were compelled to endure the infamous Death March from Bataan to Camp O'Donnell, a prison many miles away. Wainwright spent the rest of the war in a Japanese prison camp.

When General MacArthur reached Australia, he met a clamouring legion of newspaper reporters, eager to hear his assessment of the situation. With a dramatic flair, he stated: "The President of the United

Left: During the pivotal Hawaii conference of 1944, MacArthur, President Roosevelt and Admiral William Leahy sit while Admiral Chester W Nimitz uses a pointer to mark a position in the Pacific Ocean. (Public Domain)

Below: Wading ashore on the island of Leyte, MacArthur returns to the Philippines, October 20, 1944. (Public Domain)

During ceremonies in Tokyo Bay on September 2, 1945, MacArthur signs documents related to the Japanese surrender aboard the battleship USS *Missouri*. (Public Domain)

States ordered me to break through the Japanese lines and proceed from Corregidor to Australia for the purpose, as I understand it, of organising the American offensive against Japan, a primary objective of which is the relief of the Philippines. I came through and I shall return!"

Even before World War Two, the American people were familiar with the charismatic, flamboyant MacArthur and they were in need of heroes at this nadir in the course of the conflict. MacArthur was a logical choice to be hailed as such. On April 1, 1942, he received the Medal of Honor for 'conspicuous leadership in preparing the Philippine Islands to resist conquest, for gallantry and intrepidity above and beyond the call of duty' as the leader of the defence of the Philippines. Although there were detractors, the controversial gesture did deliver a hero to the American people. Yet, the fact remains that when MacArthur received the nation's highest military recognition for bravery in combat, he had presided over a campaign that was lost and the capitulation of 76,000 American and Filipino soldiers on Bataan was the largest in the history of the US armed forces.

MacArthur's Medal of Honor was received nearly 80 years after his father's exploits during the Civil War and for decades the two remained the only father and son recipients of the Medal of Honor in US history. In 2001, Theodore Roosevelt received the medal posthumously, a century after his bravery during the fighting at San Juan Hill in the Spanish-American War, while his son, General Theodore Roosevelt Jr, received the medal posthumously for bravery in France in 1944.

Pacific resurgence

Following a long rail trip, MacArthur reached Melbourne, Australia, where he set about the task of reversing the Allied fortunes of war in the Pacific. As soon as possible, he ordered Australian and American troops to the island of New Guinea, assuming the offensive there to thwart Japanese attempts to seize the island and threaten Australia itself with invasion. In several pivotal engagements, the Allied soldiers were victorious and the Japanese depleted precious resources of men

MacArthur stands with Japanese Emperor Hirohito at their first meeting in Tokyo in September 1945. (Public Domain)

and equipment that could not be replaced. MacArthur's tactics of amphibious landings along the New Guinea coastline kept the Japanese off balance throughout the campaign and facilitated his planned return to liberate the Philippines.

Still, there were competing priorities in the Pacific War and differing opinions on how to achieve the ultimate victory over the Japanese. In July 1944, President Roosevelt flew to Hawaii to meet with MacArthur and Admiral Chester W Nimitz, US Navy Commander-in-Chief Pacific Ocean Areas, to discuss strategy. The tide of war had turned in favour of the Allies and the issue at hand was the choice of the primary avenue of approach to the home islands of Japan. MacArthur wanted desperately to fight the Japanese in the Philippines and liberate the islands en route to an invasion of Japan itself. In the process, he would fulfil his promise made in defeat more than two years earlier. Nimitz advocated a thrust against Japanese-held Formosa and then against the home islands, bypassing the Philippines.

Roosevelt weighed the merits of each and then came down on the side of MacArthur. The invasion of the Philippines took place at the island of Leyte on that historic October day when the great war commander had returned in sublime triumph. The Japanese, however, put up stiff resistance in the Philippines and fighting continued in the islands until the end of the war.

With the final victory assured, MacArthur was given the honour of presiding over the surrender of the Japanese in Tokyo Bay on September 2, 1945. President Harry Truman had been in a quandary as to how to acknowledge the contributions of all the armed forces to the war effort. In order to give both navy and army their due, it was decided that MacArthur, an army general, would lead the ceremonies on the deck of the battleship USS Missouri, symbolising the might of the US Navy. Amid a throng of onlookers, the general methodically

worked his way through the signing of the documents, giving the Japanese delegates instructions on completing their assigned tasks.

When the ceremony had concluded, MacArthur declared: "These proceedings are closed." But for the great general, a period of new diplomatic and administrative responsibility was just beginning. MacArthur became the military governor and de facto ruler of post-war Japan. He proved adept at running the country in peacetime. Retaining Emperor Hirohito in his ceremonial role, the general rebuilt the Japanese economy, demobilised the country's military and watched over the drafting of a new constitution. In due course, the Japanese economy was revitalised, cities and infrastructure were rebuilt and the nation went on to prosper in the modern world.

At the same time, MacArthur enabled the prosecution of Japanese war criminals during trials in Tokyo and other locations in the Far East. He forcefully rebuffed the efforts of the Soviet Union to participate in the post-war administration of Japan amid the growing Cold War rivalry between east and west. Perhaps the greatest achievement of the general's long career did not occur as a military man, but as a diplomat and administrator from 1945-1951, an American who eventually was revered by the Japanese people.

Still, MacArthur was never far from controversy and during the years in Japan, his public relations team churned out positive stories of the

Japanese defendants stand in the dock during the Tokyo War Crimes Trials in 1946. General MacArthur was the military governor of Japan at the time. (Public Domain)

From the deck of a ship off the Korean coast, MacArthur, holding binoculars, watches the landings at Inchon in September 1950. (Public Domain)

The MacArthur family greets well-wishers during a return visit to the Philippines in 1950.
(Public Domain)

President Harry Truman and MacArthur meet at Wake Island in October 1950. MacArthur was dismissed from command months later.
(Public Domain)

ongoing renaissance in the island nation. Rumours began to circulate that the general might seek the nomination of the Republican Party for President of the United States in 1948, opposing Truman, the incumbent Democrat. MacArthur did not actively campaign for the nomination and Truman worked to undermine any grass roots effort to draft the general. The prospects for future animosity had become real.

Korea and twilight

Although MacArthur may have believed that his days of military command were over by 1950, one more challenge erupted when the army of North Korea plunged across the 38th parallel, invading South Korea on June 25. The general was given command of United Nations forces as the spearheads from the communist north swept down the peninsula and captured the South Korean capital of Seoul. The UN

In April 1951, MacArthur was honoured with a massive parade in Chicago, Illinois.
(Creative Commons Aprad via Wikipedia)

defenders were forced into a narrow pocket around the port of Pusan dubbed the 'Pusan Perimeter'.

The UN forces, primarily American, had operated with limited resources early in the Korean War, as supplies and manpower had faced drastic cuts after World War Two. However, as sufficient strength was gathered to mount offensive operations, MacArthur conceived a bold stroke, one fraught with risk but sure to pay tremendous dividends if successful. While the UN forces hung on grimly at Pusan, he planned a daring amphibious end run that would land thousands of UN soldiers at the port of Inchon, far behind the North Korean lines. Inchon itself presented challenges, with tides that rose and fell precipitously on a daily basis. And no doubt the landings would be contested. Still, MacArthur believed the attempt was worth the risk.

The landings at Inchon, on September 15-19, 1950, were a tremendous success and the enemy was forced to retire hundreds of miles with UN forces at their heels. MacArthur directed his troops to cross the 38th parallel into North Korea, an obvious escalation of the conflict that risked intervention by the communist regime of China. MacArthur impetuously discounted the threat of Chinese involvement and clamoured for bombing of supply lines from that country into North Korea. If necessary, he believed nuclear weapons should be used.

MacArthur's confidence was shattered as his troops approached the Yalu River in the autumn of 1950. A torrent of Chinese troops and tanks attacked, throwing the UN forces into retreat. At the same time, MacArthur and President Harry Truman engaged in a titanic battle of wills over the conduct of the Korean War. Truman wanted to avoid a widening conflict in Asia but MacArthur proved an obstacle, an officer who failed to respect civilian control of the US military and was unafraid to defy the president. Left with little alternative, Truman fired MacArthur on April 1, 1951 and told the American people that limited war was the preferred course of action.

Although his ego had been bruised and his military legacy tarnished, five-star General of the Army Douglas MacArthur remained an authentic American hero. He came home to a welcome fit for a conquering 'caesar' and addressed a joint session of Congress, concluding with the famous words: "Old soldiers never die; they just fade away."

While there was talk of a presidential run in 1952, the Republicans chose Dwight Eisenhower as their nominee. Residing in a luxury suite in the Waldorf-Astoria Hotel in New York, the general became chairman of Remington Rand Corporation, while conferring with presidents, visiting the Philippines one more time and travelling to his beloved West Point in 1962. He died on April 5, 1964, aged 84.

As General MacArthur lay in state in the rotunda of the US capitol in Washington, DC, an estimated 150,000 mourners streamed past his flag-draped coffin. According to his wishes, he was buried near his mother in Norfolk, Virginia. MacArthur remains a towering figure in American military and diplomatic history.

GENERAL JONATHAN M WAINWRIGHT

"I want you to make it known throughout all elements of your command that I'm leaving over my repeated protests," asserted General Douglas MacArthur before his departure from the embattled Philippines in the difficult spring of 1942. "Goodbye Jonathan. If you're still on Bataan when I get back, I'll make you a lieutenant general."

Major General Jonathan M Wainwright had just been handed a no-win situation – and he knew it. Thousands of Japanese troops, flush with victory, had pushed the American and Filipino defenders on the island of Luzon back to the Bataan peninsula and the fortress island of Corregidor in Manila Bay. MacArthur had been ordered to evacuate to Australia to organise the Allied command that would one day turn the tide of World War Two in the Pacific. But Wainwright was left to preside over the largest capitulation of fighting troops in the history of the US military.

Perhaps MacArthur had departed believing that the defenders could hold out against the Japanese onslaught, but in truth food, ammunition and medical supplies were running low. There would be no relief in the form of reinforcements or resupply. The exhausted men were truly the 'Battling Bastards of Bataan'. Wainwright wrote grimly of the situation: "Our perpetual hunger, the steaming heat by day and night, the terrible malaria and the moans of the wounded were hard on the men."

In early April, 70,000 American and Filipino soldiers under the immediate command of Major General Edward King surrendered on Bataan. In early May, the Japanese attacked Corregidor where

General Jonathan M Wainwright surrendered Allied forces in the Philippines in 1942 and endured captivity at the hands of the Japanese. (Public Domain)

Wainwright held on with the last of the defenders in the vicinity of Manila. On the 6th, he gave in to the inevitable and informed Japanese General Masaharu Homma that he would surrender. Although there was some delay in the capitulation of all US troops in the Philippines, Homma was insistent and finally Wainwright ordered Major General William Sharp to surrender the forces on the island of Mindanao.

Corregidor to captivity

Those taken prisoner by the Japanese in the Philippines were to endure immense suffering, some of them subjected to torture, brutality and starvation. The infamous Death March from Bataan to the prison at Camp O'Donnell claimed scores of lives, some of the pitiable men bayoneted for falling behind on the trek or rushing out of line to lap water from a fetid, muddy pool.

Despite his high rank, Wainwright was treated with the same disdain as other American prisoners. He was first moved to northern Luzon, then to Formosa and finally to a prison camp at Liaoyuan in far off Manchuria. He languished there until the end of the war in 1945, spending more than three years in captivity. When liberated by troops of the Soviet Red Army, he was gaunt and frail.

Wainwright wondered what the American people thought of him after allowing 76,000 of their sons and their Filipino allies to surrender to the Japanese in 1942. He had heard no news of the war's progress and thought that if he even survived to make it home, there might be a court martial in his future. Such was the terrible burden he shouldered for seemingly endless months and an unthinkable conclusion it would be for the career of an officer who had devoted his life to the military, having carried on a family tradition of service.

Family vocation

Jonathan Mayhew Wainwright IV was born at Fort Walla Walla, an army post in the state of Washington, on August 23, 1883, the youngest of three children and the only son of Lieutenant Robert Powell Page Wainwright and Josephine Serrell Wainwright. His father was a cavalry officer and he was the grandson of Lieutenant Jonathan Mayhew Wainwright II of the US Navy. The father had fought in the Spanish-American War at the Battle of Santiago de Cuba and succumbed to disease in the Philippines during the Insurrection of 1899-1902. The grandfather had also died for his country, killed during the American Civil War at the Battle of Galveston.

Below left: Wainwright (right) and General Douglas MacArthur greet one another in Yokahama, Japan, August 31, 1945. It was their first meeting since Corregidor in 1942. (Public Domain)

Below right: Colonel Jonathan Wainwright receives the stars of brigadier general rank at Fort Myer, Virginia, in 1938. (Public Domain)

Under the watchful eye of a Japanese censor, General Jonathan Wainwright makes a radio broadcast from captivity. (Public Domain)

Wainwright stands directly behind General Douglas MacArthur during the surrender of Japan in Tokyo Bay, September 2, 1945. (Public Domain)

It followed that the younger Wainwright would seek a commission in the US Army and he graduated as first captain, the top of his class in 1906, from the US Military Academy at West Point. Like his father, Jonathan served in the cavalry, initially with the 1st Regiment at Fort Clark, Texas and then with an expedition to the Philippines to quell the Moro Uprising. He experienced combat there for the first time while on the island of Jolo.

Wainwright married Adele 'Kitty' Holley, the daughter of a fellow officer, in 1911 and the couple had one son, John V, two years later. During World War Two, John V joined the merchant marine and served with distinction, later rising to captain in the US naval reserve.

During World War One, Jonathan Wainwright went to France as assistant chief of staff of the 82nd Infantry Division (later converted to airborne). He participated in the Saint-Mihiel fighting and the Meuse-Argonne offensive. After the armistice, he remained with Third Army at Koblenz in occupied Germany, returning to the US and a series of cavalry postings in 1920. By 1938, he was again posted to Fort Clark to command the 1st Cavalry Brigade with the rank of brigadier general.

To the Far East

In November 1940, Wainwright was once more in the Philippines, commanding a Philippine scout division and then serving as commander of the north Luzon front. In the immediate aftermath of the Japanese attack on Pearl Harbor, December 7, 1941 the Philippines became a prime target for further enemy expansion.

The Japanese landed at Lingayen Gulf on the island of Luzon in late December and though heroic resistance was offered, they pushed the defenders back to Bataan and Corregidor and MacArthur was ordered to depart for Australia, leaving Wainwright with the unenviable task of leading further resistance. While MacArthur understood that the fight against the enemy would continue as long as possible and expected those who might escape a surrender to mount a guerrilla effort against the invaders, Wainwright shared a will to persevere.

After receiving communication from President Franklin D Roosevelt that offered him the latitude to prolong the struggle from Corregidor or surrender as he believed appropriate, Wainwright responded: "I have been one of the battling bastards of Bataan and I'll play the same role on the rock as long as it is humanly possible. I have been with my men from the start and, if captured, I will share their lot. We have been through so much together that my conscience would not let me leave before the final curtain."

When the suffering was too unbearable, even for a veteran soldier like Wainwright, the end came. For 39 months, he languished as a prisoner of war.

Reunion and triumph

After Wainwright's liberation from captivity, he was invited to attend the formal surrender of Japan aboard the battleship USS *Missouri* in Tokyo Bay on September 2, 1945. He stood on the deck alongside General Arthur Percival, who was taken prisoner with the fall of Singapore in early 1942. General MacArthur presided over the ceremonies and gave each officer a pen he had used to sign the instrument of surrender on behalf of the Allied nations.

Three days later, Wainwright was promoted to four-star general. The advance in rank came as a surprise, as did the response to the lingering question that had gnawed at his psyche for so long. With his return to the United States, he learned that he was considered a hero. In fact, he had been recommended for the Medal of Honor while in captivity in 1942. MacArthur, however, opposed the recommendation in the belief that the defenders of the Philippines could have held out longer and it was dropped.

Nevertheless, the recommendation for the highest US honour for courage in combat was revived in 1945. This time, MacArthur offered no opposition, perhaps in recognition of the outstanding service Wainwright had rendered and the privations he had suffered. President Harry Truman presented the medal at the White House on September 10, 1945 and the citation read in part: "Distinguished himself by intrepid and determined leadership against greatly superior enemy forces. At the repeated risk of life above and beyond the call of duty in his position, he frequented the firing line of his troops, where his presence provided the example and incentive that helped make the gallant efforts of these men possible."

Wainwright bore no bitterness toward MacArthur, either for the Philippines affair or the slight regarding the Medal of Honor. In fact, when MacArthur was considered for the Republican Party's nomination for President of the United States in 1948, Wainwright was prepared to make the nominating speech at the party convention.

In January 1946, Wainwright took command of the Fourth Army at Fort Sam Houston, Texas. He retired in August 1947 after reaching the mandatory age of 64 and solemnly noted: "For an old soldier to say that it is a pleasure to take his last review, to address his troops for the last time and to make his last public appearance as a commander, is in my mind at least a stretch of the imagination and a far cry from the truth."

General Wainwright, a faithful and dutiful officer, suffered a stroke and died at the age of 70 on September 2, 1953. He is buried in Arlington national cemetery.

This photo of Jonathan Wainwright as a West Point cadet appeared in the Academy yearbook. (Public Domain)

GENERAL FREDERICK 'BOY' BROWNING

His words were prophetic – and they proved haunting. When General Bernard Montgomery delivered a briefing to General Frederick 'Boy' Browning on the upcoming Operation Market Garden, Browning asked how long the Red Devils of the 1st Airborne Division were supposed to hold the bridge across the Neder Rhine at the Dutch town of Arnhem.

Montgomery replied that the lightly armed airborne troops would be relieved by the ground advance of XXX Corps within two days. Confident in the fighting ability of the 1t airborne, Browning shot back that the troopers could hold for four days, but then he warned: "Sir, I think we may be going a bridge too far."

Operation Market Garden was a spectacular and costly failure. Intended to position Allied spearheads to plunge like daggers into the Ruhr, the industrial heart of Germany and perhaps end World War Two in Europe by Christmas 1944, Market Garden ended with the 1st Airborne Division shattered as General Roy Urquhart had led 10,000 troops into the September 1944 operation and emerged with only about 2,000 remaining fit for service.

During the Market Garden effort, Lieutenant General Browning was deputy commander of the Allied First Airborne Army and though he had expressed reservations, he threw his considerable support behind the operation, later bearing significant criticism for its failure. The tragedy of Market Garden was a lingering blemish on an otherwise admirable 30-year career for Browning.

Becoming Boy Browning

Frederick Arthur Montague Browning was born the son of wine merchant Frederick Henry Browning and Ann Alt, daughter of noted scientist and author George Earl Alt, in Kensington, London, on December 20, 1896. His family called him Tommy, and the boy showed great promise, excelling in athletics and academics at West Downs School in Winchester and then Eton College, where he was poised and succinct as a member of the debating team.

After Eton, Tommy aspired to the Royal Military Academy, Sandhurst, sitting for the entrance examination in November 1914. World War One was already underway. 'Tommy' passed the English and French sections but failed history/geography and mathematics. However, Edward Lyttleton, headmaster at Eton, came to the rescue. Authorised to recommend individuals for admission to the Army Council, he boosted Browning, who entered Sandhurst in December.

The exigencies of war required that young officers should be graduated on an accelerated schedule and after six months of whirlwind study, Browning was commissioned as a lieutenant in the prestigious Grenadier Guards. By October 1915, he was in command of a reinforced battalion in the trenches of the western front.

The origin of the long-lasting nickname 'Boy' can probably be traced to the time in the trenches, as officers of the Grenadier Guards often addressed one another informally. Logically, because of his youth, he may have become Boy at the time. Otherwise, he may have shared a name with an older soldier of the unit and the nickname might have been bestowed to differentiate the two.

When future prime minister Winston Churchill visited the western front in November 1915, he arrived without his greatcoat. Browning offered his own to ward off the autumn chill and it was a

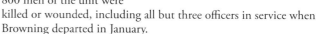

King George VI (left) and General Browning inspect an airborne Jeep fitted with a Vickers machine gun in spring 1942. (Public Domain)

gesture that Churchill never forgot. In January, Browning fell seriously ill. He spent two weeks in hospital and did not return to the 2nd Battalion until September, missing the great summer bloodletting on the Somme in which 800 men of the unit were killed or wounded, including all but three officers in service when Browning departed in January.

Despite the stark realisation that war was a bloody, destructive business, Browning yearned to fight. He found the opportunity. Once while under heavy German fire, he seized a rifle and emptied the weapon at the enemy. In the summer of 1917, the 2nd Battalion fought at the Battle of Passchendaele and in December at Cambrai, where Browning led No 2 company in an attack on Gauche Wood, defended by at least 10 German machine-gun nests.

Browning watched the attacking companies falter. When most of the officers were killed or wounded, he took command of the remaining troops, organising defensive positions as two enemy counter-attacks were repelled and 2nd Battalion suffered 26 killed, 115 wounded and 11 missing. Browning received the Distinguished Service Order for his heroism, a rare occurrence for officers of junior rank and just short of the Victoria Cross.

The 2nd Battalion helped repulse the last German offensive of the Great War in March 1918, blunting the drive near Amiens. In September, Browning became aide to General Sir Henry Rawlinson of 4th Army and as the war ended, he returned to the Grenadier Guards as adjutant of 1st Battalion. The experience of combat had been harrowing and Browning was plagued by periodic nightmares for the rest of his life.

Between the wars

Browning was promoted to captain in 1920 and became adjutant at Sandhurst, establishing a tradition in 1926 as the first adjutant to ride his horse up the steps of the old college and dismounting at the grand entrance. In 1928, he left Sandhurst exhausted and spent eight months on sick leave, completed a refresher course at the small arms school, received promotion to major and was posted again to the 2nd Battalion, Grenadier Guards.

Throughout the 1920s, Browning trained regularly as an athlete. He competed in the 1928 Winter Olympics in St. Moritz, Switzerland, as a brakeman with the bobsleigh team, which finished 10th. He also cultivated a lifelong passion for sailing.

In 1932, Browning married acclaimed novelist Daphne du Maurier. Although the two often led separate lives, the marriage endured for 33 years. They had three children. By 1936, Browning was a lieutenant colonel commanding the 2nd Battalion, Grenadier Guards during 18 months in Egypt.

Lieutenant General Frederick 'Boy' Browning was a leader in British Army airborne development. (Public Domain)

Browning observes airborne training at RAF Netheravon in October 1942. (Public Domain)

Right: After returning to Britain from a visit to the front lines in Normandy, Browning stands in front of a Douglas Dakota transport aircraft. (Public Domain)

To the airborne

Promoted to brigadier and posted first as assistant commandant and then commandant of the small arms school, Browning missed the debacle of the Battle of France. In mid-1940, he was given command of the 128th Infantry Brigade and in February 1941, the 24th Guards Brigade group.

As World War Two progressed, the concept of airborne warfare emerged and in October 1941, Churchill appointed Browning commander of the newly formed 1st Airborne Division with the rank of major general. Some foundational work had already been done with the fledgling airborne, but Browning may rightly be considered the father of the British airborne forces. He worked tirelessly to procure men and materiel, applying superb organisational skills.

Browning designed his own uniform complete with swagger stick, introduced the distinctive maroon beret and commissioned the famous airborne shoulder flash depicting the Greek hero Bellerophon riding the winged horse Pegasus. He designed the army air corps wings badge after qualifying as a glider pilot at age 46 and made two parachute jumps, sustaining slight injuries in both.

Although he was an efficient administrator, Browning sometimes presented himself as aloof and condescending. Perhaps such was unintentional and the by-product of his clipped and matter-of-fact conversational style. Nevertheless, his demeanour did not play well with Britain's American allies when Browning travelled to the US in the summer of 1942. Although he had far less practical airborne experience than his hosts, he seemed at times more lecturer than ally. To his credit, Browning acknowledged that he may have been perceived as overbearing, but relations with senior American commanders remained prickly for the duration of the war.

In the spring of 1943, Browning was elevated to adviser on airborne training and operations at the headquarters of General Dwight Eisenhower, supreme command of Allied forces in Europe. While his direct influence on airborne operations was limited, he rightly criticised the prospects for success in the glider-borne assault during the campaign in Sicily. In August, he returned to England to assist in training the new 6th Airborne Division. After travelling to India to inspect the 50th Indian Parachute Brigade, he was promoted lieutenant general and given command of the 1st Airborne Corps, including the 1st and 6th Airborne Divisions, Special Air Service Brigade and later the 1st Polish Independent Parachute Brigade and 52nd Lowland Division.

Market Garden and memory

By the autumn of 1944, the 6th airborne had performed admirably in the D-Day operations. When the First Allied Airborne Army was formed, Browning hoped to lead it. However, command was given to American General Lewis Brereton. Browning resented the fact that he was passed over. His cold relationships with the Americans may have impacted Eisenhower's decision. During Browning's tenure as deputy commander, his dealings with them deteriorated such that he offered to tender his resignation. However, when he realised that Brereton was willing to accept it, he backed off.

Operation Market Garden started in mid-September and Browning rode into Holland aboard a glider, which bumped to a stop in a cabbage patch at the edge of the Reichswald Forest and on the German frontier. As soon as he was able, he bounded into the trees. Moments later, he returned with a grin, explaining that had wanted to be the first Allied officer to relieve himself in Germany.

As for the outcome of the airborne-ground offensive, Browning had discounted the photographic evidence that two German SS panzer divisions were near Arnhem and though he had no personal authority to scrub the effort, he might have been vocal with an alarm. Additionally, he rankled Brereton when news was received that he had communicated with Montgomery and committed his command to Market Garden without higher approval. To make matters worse, Browning later admitted that his headquarters was wholly unprepared for deployment to the field. He remarked, "My staff is almost more inefficient than I could possibly imagine."

When Market Garden was over, there was plenty of blame to go around. Although Browning received no censure for the failure, he received no further promotion. He was posted to southeast Asia as chief of staff to Admiral Lord Louis Mountbatten and rewarded as Knight Commander of the Order of the British Empire.

Post-war pride and twilight

Browning was named military secretary in 1946. He left active service a year later and became comptroller and treasurer to the household of Princess Elizabeth. Officially retiring from the military in 1948, he became treasurer to the Duke of Edinburgh.

Browning's health began to decline in later years. As a result of heavy smoking, he developed chronic bronchitis. He was subject to bouts of depression, drank heavily and suffered a nervous breakdown in 1957. He died on March 14, 1965, aged 68.

Actor Dirk Bogarde portrayed Boy Browning in the 1977 film A Bridge Too Far, based on the book by author Cornelius Ryan. Although Ryan's treatment of Browning is generally considered reasonable and balanced, the film cast him as something of a fall guy.

In the final analysis, based on his contributions to victory and lifetime of service, Frederick Browning probably deserved better.

Above left: General Browning addresses a crowd during ceremonies in Ceylon in 1945. (Public Domain)

Above right: Browning (left) confers with General James Gavin of the US 82nd Airborne Division. Browning's support for the failed Operation Market Garden left a blemish on his career. (Creative Commons Regionaal Archief Nijmegen via Wikipedia)

FIELD MARSHAL ARCHIBALD WAVELL

One of the most senior officers in the British Army with the outbreak of World War Two, Archibald Wavell was perhaps given the most difficult tasks of any Allied commander of the period. His successes and failures marked the course of the early years of the conflict, but he remains somewhat obscure among the war's major strategists.

By the end of 1940, the war had gone badly. The British expeditionary force had been ejected from the European continent at Dunkirk, France had surrendered to the Nazis and Italian fascist troops threatened the British Empire in north and east Africa, where the loss of Egypt and the Suez Canal might prove catastrophic. For a year – June 1940 to June 1941 – it was Wavell's command alone that fought the Axis enemy on land.

While Britain braced itself for a possible Nazi invasion, the Commonwealth forces under Wavell were active across a land area of 1,700 miles by 2,000 miles. As commander-in-chief Middle East, General Wavell was confronted early with the daunting tasks of repulsing the Italian forces that greatly outnumbered his own troop strength and then with securing the wider Middle East against Vichy French and German control.

Although his soldiers won victories, they also sustained numerous setbacks as the war in the North African desert ebbed and flowed and Wavell was compelled to fight with diminished resources against long odds on several occasions. He was removed from command twice by Winston Churchill and was on each occasion brought back with greater responsibilities. At the end of his career, he was the only man to achieve the rank

While serving as Viceroy of India, Wavell sits with Field Marshal Bernard Montgomery (left) and Field Marshal Claude Auchinleck (right) in New Delhi, India. (Public Domain)

Left: Field Marshal Archibald Wavell is shown with the rank of major general in this portrait from 1936. (Public Domain)

Below: Wearing civilian clothes, Wavell works at his desk in Delhi, India. The field marshal commanded the Indian Army during World War Two. (Public Domain)

of field marshal in the British Army and to serve as Viceroy of India. While Wavell's combat record is marked by defeats in both the Middle East and China-Burma-India theatres, his achievements are often overlooked. By the end of his career, he had been criticised and lauded, perhaps in unequal measure.

Son of the army

The son of Major General Archibald Graham Wavell and Lillie Percival Wavell, Archibald Wavell was born May 5, 1883, in Colchester, Essex. He was educated at Winchester and graduated from the Royal Military Academy, Sandhurst, receiving a commission in the famed Black Watch in the spring of 1901. He fought in the Second Boer War and later as a lieutenant in the Bazar Valley campaign to quell a frontier uprising in India. He turned in an excellent academic performance at the staff college and was detailed to Russia in 1911 as a military observer and to become proficient in the language.

Promoted captain on his return, Wavell served as a staff officer and was assigned to the Directorate of Military Training. He was again sent to Russia in 1913 and as he tried to leave the country, he was temporarily detained on charges of spying. However, he managed to hide incriminating evidence before his hotel room in Moscow was searched by the authorities.

On staff, in action

On the eve of World War One, Wavell returned to his staff officer posting and by November 1914, he had been ordered to France, where he was posted to the headquarters of the British expeditionary force. Within weeks, he was transferred as brigade major of the 9th infantry brigade. Seriously wounded by a shell splinter at the second battle of Ypres in the spring of 1915, the young officer lost an eye. He received the Military Cross for heroism. While convalescing, he married Eugenie Marie Quirk, daughter of an army officer and the couple had three children.

Returning to a staff position in France in December 1915, he progressed in staff officer grades and received temporary promotion to lieutenant colonel. He travelled to Russia for a third time, as a liaison officer in the Caucasus, and then to Egypt and expeditionary force headquarters. When the Great War ended, he was a brigadier general and staff officer with XX Corps.

Between the world wars, Wavell rose to assistant adjutant general in the War Office, served on the staff of the 3rd Infantry Division and commanded the 6th Infantry Brigade. He became aide-de-camp to King George V in 1932, serving until the following October and rising to the rank of major general. After his second period of unemployment and half pay in the 1930s, he took command of the 2nd Division. Transfer to Palestine followed and during a period of growing unrest he was named to command British forces in the region and received promotion to lieutenant general in January 1938. Weeks before World War Two broke out, he was given charge of Middle East command and by early 1940 widening responsibilities included much of the eastern Mediterranean, Greece, and East Africa.

Desert drama

In the spring of 1940, Italian forces invaded Egypt, probably expecting to overwhelm the British whom they greatly outnumbered. Wavell faced more than 400,000 enemy troops and gave ground initially. At the end of the year, he authorised General Richard O'Connor to launch Operation Compass. Intended as a brief counter-thrust, Compass was so successful that it became a full-blown offensive. British forces repeatedly defeated the Italians, inflicting huge casualties and capturing large numbers of prisoners, 130,000 alone at the Battle of Beda Fomm in February 1941. Further victories were won in Ethiopia and Eritrea.

Wavell had delivered the first major Allied victories on land during World War Two, but his seizure of the initiative in East Africa and Libya was soon halted due to orders from Churchill. Against his protests, much of Wavell's experienced troop strength was transferred to Greece to defend against a German invasion. He believed that the Commonwealth positions there and on the island of Crete could not be held long term – and he was correct.

Perhaps Wavell's relationship with Churchill, which was always somewhat dysfunctional, played a role in the prime minister's decision. After their first meeting, Churchill had declared that Wavell came across like the chairman of a suburban golf club.

During that fateful February of 1941, the German Army entered the desert war as the Afrika Korps, under General Erwin Rommel, arriving at the Libyan port of Tripoli. Soon after organising, Rommel struck the depleted British forces in Libya and drove them back into Egypt.

Meanwhile, as the situation in Greece deteriorated, an effort by Nazi-sponsored forces to seize power in Iraq was defeated, although troops from India were required and Churchill was disappointed with Wavell's lack of involvement with the campaign there. By June, Wavell did act decisively against the Vichy French governments in Syria and Lebanon, which had supported the enemy in Iraq.

Wavell was wounded in World War One and became the first British ground commander to deliver a significant victory against the Axis in World War Two. (Public Domain)

At the same time, the rapid German advance in Libya had led to a siege of the port of Tobruk and Wavell attempted to break through to the garrison. However, the counter-offensive of Operation Battleaxe, launched on June 15, 1941, ended in failure and contributed to Churchill's decision to relieve Wavell of command in favour of General Claude Auchinleck.

To the CBI

In effect, Wavell and Auchinleck traded roles as Auchinleck assumed Middle East command and Wavell became commander of the Indian Army. Again, Wavell was thrust into a difficult situation, lacking manpower and equipment to effectively fight the Japanese, who declared war on Britain in December 1941.

When the Japanese mounted a strong offensive into Malaya and Burma, Wavell was hardly able to mount a meaningful response. The enemy captured Singapore in February 1942 and pushed the British and Commonwealth forces out of Burma. The retirement to India was costly and embarrassing. Meanwhile, as the Dutch East Indies fell to the Japanese, Wavell's ABDACOM, American-British-Dutch-Australian Command, was dissolved. From India, he observed the retreat from Burma, unable to do much in response.

The withdrawal from Burma was completed in May 1942, just after the capable Generals Harold Alexander and William Slim took command of forces in the country and the ground troops of Burcorps respectively. Eventually, the fortunes of war would reverse in Burma, but Wavell would not take part. In January 1943, he was promoted to field marshal and returned to London. At mid-year, he was appointed Viceroy of India.

Viceroy and veneration

With his role as a combat commander over, Wavell worked to relieve the suffering of the Bengal famine. He struggled to maintain good relations with Indian leaders during the discussions of a framework for the country's independence and was replaced by Lord Louis Mountbatten in 1947.

Wavell had received titles reflective of earlier service, including Viscount of Cyrenaica and of Winchester and Viscount Keren of Eritrea and Winchester and was created 1st Earl Wavell of Eritrea and Winchester in 1947 as he assumed the office of High Steward of Colchester. In his last years, Wavell compiled a collection of well-known poetry along with commentary and titled his work Other Men's Flowers. He also contributed poetry of his own to the volume.

Wavell died from complications following surgery on May 24, 1950. His legacy is one of both victory and defeat, hard-fought campaigns often conducted on a shoestring, but with a willingness to continue the struggle. The verdict of history, for better or worse, has been to relegate his brightest military achievements to the shadows of prominent setbacks.

Wavell confers with Winston Churchill (left) and Admiral James Somerville (right) aboard the SS Queen Mary in May 1943. (Public Domain)

Right: Wavell greets a soldier of the British Army in Singapore, Malaya, in 1941. Within months the Japanese had captured the great city. (Public Domain)

GENERAL OMAR N BRADLEY

"Omaha Beach was a nightmare," wrote General Omar N Bradley, commander of US ground forces going ashore in French Normandy on D-Day, June 6, 1944. From the deck of the cruiser USS *Augusta* offshore, Bradley watched the assault waves of the US 1st and 29th Divisions wade into battle while strong German defences steadily pounded the troops.

Men struggled in the surf, landing craft were blasted and smoking from direct hits and some soldiers had sought shelter behind the beach obstacles the Germans had placed to impede the progress of the American assault. Omaha was one of two beaches designated for American D-Day landings. At Utah, further west, elements of the 4th Infantry Division had landed in the wrong place but were making progress. To the east, where General Miles Dempsey was in command, British forces at Sword and Gold and Canadian troops at Juno were also moving off the beaches against stiff German resistance.

But at Omaha, Bradley faced a tremendous command decision as the minutes ticked by. The troops on the beach were in danger of being pushed into the sea and it was Bradley's decision whether to evacuate them and divert further reinforcements to other beaches or continue at Omaha, slugging it out with the Germans who held the high ground.

"Even now it brings pain to recall what happened there on June 6, 1944," Bradley continued years later. "Omaha Beach remained a bloodbath for too long. Six hours after the landings, we held only ten yards of beach. The whole of D-Day was for me a time of grave personal anxiety and frustration. I gained the impression that our forces had suffered an irreversible catastrophe, that there was little hope we could force the beach., I agonised over the withdrawal decision, praying that our men could hang on."

Bradley elected to stay the course and continued to peer through binoculars toward the embattled swath of sand. Just as the situation appeared bleakest, individual men, junior officers and clutches of soldiers, on their own initiative, began to move toward the enemy machine gun nests and bunkers, slowly but surely turning the tide. Finally, the Americans at Omaha secured a toehold on the French coastline. Although they had paid a terrible price, Bradley had made the right call.

While in command of the 82nd Infantry Division, Bradley confers with General Lesley McNair, commander of Army Ground Forces, during field exercises. (Public Domain)

By 1944, Omar Bradley had served in the US Army for nearly 30 years and those anxious hours at Omaha Beach were perhaps the defining moment of his career. His journey to that time and place were marked by extraordinary personal dedication, an affinity for the common soldier and a resolve that had been honed and nurtured from his earliest days as a member of the famed West Point class of 1915. However, it had been a long, tough road to reach the highest echelons of military command.

From America's heartland

Omar Bradley's early years were difficult. He was born in Clark, Missouri, on February 12, 1893, to schoolteacher and administrator John Smith Bradley and Sarah Hubbard Bradley. He was their only surviving child. The boy enjoyed the outdoors and his father taught him how to handle a rifle and hunt at a tender age. When Omar was 15, tragedy struck with the untimely death of his father. Predictably, financial hardship followed and his mother lost a house to foreclosure, unable to make monthly payments.

Despite the early challenges, Omar graduated from high school in nearby Moberly, Missouri, in 1910, with outstanding academic performance. He was also an excellent athlete, a star of the baseball team. After graduation, he took a job with the Wabash Railroad to help ease his mother's financial burden and hoping to save enough money to finance attendance at the University of Missouri.

While finances were a substantial obstacle to higher education, Bradley's prospects improved when he learned from his Sunday School teacher that young men appointed to the US Military Academy had their expenses paid by the US government. The teacher encouraged him to take the competitive entrance examination at Jefferson Barracks in St Louis, Missouri, and he secured an appointment from a local congressman when the favourite for the slot failed the rigorous battery of tests. The examination had not been easy for Bradley. In fact, it was a sentinel event in his young life. He was completely stymied during the mathematics section and at one point

Above left: Photographed while serving as chairman of the Joint Chiefs of Staff, General of the Army Omar Bradley wears the five-star rank insignia on his shoulder. (Public Domain)

Above right: Shown in cadet uniform while at West Point, Bradley was a top performer on the baseball and football teams at the academy. (Public Domain)

GENERAL CHARLES DE GAULLE

Charles de Gaulle was the foremost Frenchman of the 20th century. De facto leader of the Free French movement that opposed the Nazis and their Vichy minions in the wake of the horrendous defeat in the spring of 1940, he carried the soul of France with him through desperate days and emerged in triumph to lead the nation in the post-World War Two era.

De Gaulle was the man of the hour as former national hero Field Marshal Philippe Pétain sold out to the Nazis and concluded a peace agreement that made his government a puppet of Hitler's regime. Following lengthy discussions with the British government intended to keep France fighting, de Gaulle knew the cause was lost and hopped on a plane bound for London to carry on the fight. At the time, he held no post of consequence in the French government and only the rank of a brigadier general in a broken army.

Nevertheless, his will to fight gained attention and shortly after he landed in Britain, he took to the BBC airwaves with a call to his people to resist. Known to history as the Appeal of June 18, he exhorted them: "I, General de Gaulle, now in London, call on all French officers and soldiers now present on British territory or who may be so in the future, with or without their arms to get in touch with me. Whatever happens, the flame of French resistance must not and will not be extinguished."

Days later, Winston Churchill, impressed with de Gaulle's courage and aware that the Pétain government had, or would soon, impose a death sentence on the officer as a traitor, summoned de Gaulle to 10 Downing Street and said bluntly: "You are all alone. Well then, I recognise you alone."

Charles de Gaulle, pictured in 1942, preserved the honour and the place of France among nations during World War Two. (Public Domain)

Forever France

Charles de Gaulle, born November 22, 1890 in the industrial city of Lille, was 39 years old when he stepped from relative obscurity. He had completed a requisite year in the French Army, joining the 33rd Regiment at Arras in the autumn of 1909, before applying to the military academy at Saint Cyr and was one of only 221 accepted from a pool of 800 applicants. He completed the course of study in 1912, ranking 13th in a class of 211.

De Gaulle was the son of a lifelong educator Henri de Gaulle and the third of five children. His heritage and upbringing were filled with stories of earlier generations, their contributions to the welfare of the nation and the illustrious history of France. De Gaulle was devoted to his country, his passion greater than that of most. However, his early career was marked by indifferent comments from superior officers, some of whom considered him unfit for more than non-commissioned officer rank. Nevertheless, he maintained a self-confidence that seemed to rankle others at times, and before he left Saint Cyr had earned nicknames such as 'Grand Constable' and 'Le Coq'.

After Saint Cyr, de Gaulle returned to his old 33rd Regiment, then commanded by Pétain. The two were destined to form a relationship that influenced the course of world events, first as mentor and student, then as adversaries. Although Pétain gained lasting fame as the Hero of Verdun during World War One, his capitulation to the Nazis forever tarnished his legacy. Still, it was Pétain's prestige and goodwill that bailed de Gaulle out of hot water on more than one occasion during the younger officer's career.

In the winter of 1916, the 33rd Regiment was transferred to the killing fields, stark fortifications and fetid trenches of Verdun. Already wounded once and with the coveted Croix de Guerre pinned to his chest, Captain de Gaulle was seriously wounded a second time and captured, spending nearly three years as a prisoner of the Germans. Afterwards, he was one of 2,000 officers sent to advise the army of a reconstituted Poland during its fight against Bolshevik Russia. He proceeded to complete the prestigious army Ecole Superieure, although his reputation as Pétain's protégé and his behaviour at Saint Cyr made him something of a marked man. He graduated with a punitive rating of 'good' rather than the desired and deserved 'very good'.

Pétain and de Gaulle were enraged by the slight and the senior marshal rescued his pupil from a dead-end assignment to help write a history of the army in the Great War. Pétain then arranged sweet revenge, appointing de Gaulle to deliver a series of lectures to the cadre of officers at the Ecole Superieure who had insulted their pride.

The officers were a captive audience, forced to listen to this junior upstart and swallow their collective rage at the same time. Sadly, the relationship between de Gaulle and Pétain foundered over the rights to the published Great

Above left: Charles de Gaulle in the uniform of a cadet at Saint Cyr in 1910. (Public Domain)

Above right: Charles de Gaulle posed for this photo along with a fellow prisoner of the Germans in the autumn of 1916. (Public Domain)

Charles de Gaulle reviews Free French naval personnel aboard a warship in June 1942.
(Public Domain)

War history, ghost written by de Gaulle under the prestigious name of Pétain but claimed by Pétain exclusively later. The coup de grace occurred with the terrible Vichy affair, but after World War Two, de Gaulle did commute Pétain's death sentence as a collaborationist to life in exile.

Armour and the will

Throughout his life, de Gaulle was a prolific author, writing dozens of books and articles on a variety of military topics. One of these was the introduction of the tank on the modern battlefield. He had not witnessed the armoured behemoth's combat debut during the Great War but heard stories of it while a prisoner.

Soon enough, de Gaulle became a tireless champion of the new weapon of war, so much so that he again gained the ire of fellow army officers and earned the derisive nickname of 'Colonel Motor'. His promotion to full colonel was blocked in 1936, but he persevered and continued to advocate for the development of the tank and its tactical deployment while war clouds gathered again in Europe.

By the outbreak of World War Two, de Gaulle could rightly be considered the foremost expert on armoured warfare in the French Army. Still, his advice was not thoroughly heeded and the armoured authorisation was increased to four divisions only in mid-May 1940, just weeks before the collapse of the French military before the Nazi juggernaut that ended with German infantry goose-stepping down the Champs-Elysées.

Brigadier General de Gaulle led the 4th Armoured Division in heroic resistance to the enemy onslaught, getting the better of the Germans at times. However, the outcome of the Battle of France was inevitable. The role of Colonel Motor soon escalated to one of minor office holder in the teetering French government and then to one of national hero, carrying the honour of his country in an attaché case as he fled to Britain.

Through sheer force of personality and an unshakable will to maintain the place of France among nations, de Gaulle gained support from French military men and from the far-flung colonies that were out of the immediate fight, at least temporarily. Although the relationship with Churchill was rocky at times, de Gaulle maintained the independence of France as well as he possibly could. He was aghast when the Royal Navy fired upon elements of the French fleet at Mers el-Kébir in July 1940 and endured the embarrassment of the failure of the British-Free French co-operative effort to take control of the Vichy port of Dakar, Senegal.

Then, if the relationship with the British government was somewhat contentious, relations with the US government, which still recognised Vichy as the true representative of France for some time, were frosty at best. One of the darkest periods was before and during Operation Torch, the Allied landings in North Africa in November 1942. President Franklin D Roosevelt had declared that the Free French were not to be involved in the landings and de Gaulle was not made

aware of Torch until it was well under way. He was furious and further animosity surfaced when the Americans tried to install General Henri Giraud as either a successor or at least an alternative to the intransigent de Gaulle in early 1943.

Roosevelt remained insistent that de Gaulle was to be kept out of the planning for the D-Day landings in Normandy on June 6, 1944 and de Gaulle was briefed on Operation Overlord only two days before it started. Still, he refused to allow the Americans or the British to direct the future of post-war France. He was determined that a liberated France would be ruled by the French people and that he would be the head of state.

When the British and Americans had both finally acknowledged that de Gaulle and the Free French were in fact the leaders of France, he wryly noted: "The government of France is pleased to be called by its name."

To liberation

On June 14, 1944, Charles de Gaulle boarded the French destroyer *Combattante* and sailed to the vicinity of Courseulles, setting foot on French soil for the first time in four years. On August 15, Allied forces made a second landing in the south of France during Operation Dragoon. Ten days later, the French 2nd Armoured Division rumbled into the streets of Paris, liberating the city of light.

Before the triumph, de Gaulle had become aware that General Eisenhower, Supreme Allied Commander, intended to bypass the French capital. He implored Eisenhower to take the city, prevent wanton destruction and assist the guerrillas then fighting the Germans in the streets. He also told American commanders that French formations would further be taking orders from the French government rather than American officers. Although the declaration was a bit boastful, since the French depended on US arms and supplies, it was nevertheless a bold gesture. And surely, the appearance of de

Charles de Gaulle addresses a gathering at Brazzaville, French Equatorial Africa, in 1944. (Public Domain)

During a tense meeting at Casablanca in 1943, General de Gaulle sits third from left with General Henri Giraud (far left), President Franklin D Roosevelt and prime minister Winston Churchill. (Public Domain)

of the gunfire, de Gaulle stood fully erect, ignored the danger and strode 200 feet down the aisle to his seat.

Some spectators and a BBC radio commentator would offer that in that moment Charles de Gaulle solidified his hold on the people of France and their post-war future.

Tough talking

In the years to come, de Gaulle maintained a tough stance toward allies and former foes alike. His demands for a French occupation zone in Germany were granted after a tense statement released to the press that said France would not abide by the terms of any agreement reached if the country were not directly represented at the negotiating table.

De Gaulle served intermittently not only as leader of the provisional government of the French Republic but also as prime minister and president of the Fifth Republic, leaving office in 1969 after a decade. During his post-war service, he facilitated a formula for the independence of Algeria, survived another assassination attempt and opposed British entry into the European Common Market. He always kept the US at arm's length as well. France under de Gaulle was stubbornly independent.

On the evening of November 9, 1970, the soul of France sat down to a game of solitaire and suffered an aortic aneurysm, never to regain consciousness. He was 13 days short of his 80th birthday and in keeping with his wishes, there was no elaborate state funeral, no grand eulogy and his epitaph was to simply read: "Charles de Gaulle, 1890-...."

Gaulle in the coming Parisian victory parade would send a clear message of control to doubters, including the communists and other factions that sought to increase their influence during a turbulent time.

And so, on the glorious day of the liberation of Paris, de Gaulle followed French tanks into the city, heading to the war ministry and then to the main police station to secure the co-operation of the gendarmerie. He met briefly with the various resistance leaders whose forces were roaming the capital and as he spoke, his Gaullist lieutenants were quietly asserting control throughout the liberated areas of the country. At 8pm he stepped onto the small balcony of the Hotel de Ville and greeted an enthusiastic throng that had waited to catch a glimpse of the saviour of France.

On August 26, 1944, de Gaulle led the tumultuous victory parade. He walked to the Place de la Concorde and then took a short ride to the cathedral of Notre Dame, where a service of thanksgiving was to be held. As he stepped from the car, rifle shots rang out and it appeared the leader was the target of a would-be assassin. Apparently disdainful

De Gaulle and Churchill confer during a meeting at Marrakesh, Morocco in January 1944. (Public Domain)

General de Gaulle strides down the Champs-Elysées in Paris following the 1944 liberation of the City of Light. (Public Domain)

FIELD MARSHAL ERWIN ROMMEL

Adolf Hitler was dismayed. The forces of his Italian cohort Benito Mussolini had been roughly handled by their British and Commonwealth adversaries in the desert war. Despite outnumbering the British significantly, the Italians had suffered embarrassing defeats and at times they appeared on the brink of collapse.

The Führer, therefore, was determined to intervene and turn the tide of World War Two in North Africa in favour of the Axis. The Deutsches Afrika Korps was dispatched to the region in mid-February 1941 and as the first German tanks and troops were put ashore from transport ships at the Libyan port of Tripoli, their commander, General Erwin Rommel, arrived.

A rising star in the German Army, Rommel was a combat veteran and he knew the desert command would be the greatest challenge of his career. In the event, he proved himself a superb tactician, taking advantage of every opening allowed by the British and utilising intelligence gleaned from reliable sources, to push

Field Marshal Erwin Rommel was the most respected German field commander to emerge during World War Two. (Creative Commons Bundesarchiv Bild via Wikipedia)

the Afrika Korps and the Axis Panzerarmee Afrika across the Egyptian frontier, at times wreaking havoc and threatening the great port of Alexandria, the capital city of Cairo, the Suez Canal and even the vital oil fields of the Middle East.

While accomplishing tremendous feats of arms via shrewd flanking attacks, rapid exploitation of breakthroughs, and the outstanding 88mm flak cannon in an innovative anti-tank role, Rommel became the stuff of legend. He fought the British to their absolute limit despite frequent shortages of reinforcing troops, new tanks, fuel and other supplies. Rommel earned the grudging respect of his enemy and the nickname of the 'Desert Fox'.

Prime minister Winston Churchill was so preoccupied with Rommel that he once groused: "Rommel! Rommel! Rommel! What else matters but beating that man." But even Churchill admitted that the Desert Fox was 'across the havoc of war, a very great general'.

Left: Lieutenant Erwin Rommel posed for this photo while serving with the German Army in Italy in 1917. (Public Domain)

Below: Rommel met Adolf Hitler for the first time in 1934. He is shown here with the Führer in the city of Goslar. (Creative Commons Bundesarchiv Bild via Wikipedia)

Von Rundstedt meets with Italian dictator Benito Mussolini and Adolf Hitler in Russia in summer 1941. (Creative Commons Bundesarchiv Bild via Wikipedia)

During a meeting in December 1943, von Rundstedt (left) and Erwin Rommel discuss plans for the defence of German occupied territory in western Europe. (Creative Commons Budesarchiv Bild via Wikipedia)

allow German aircraft to complete the defeat of Allied forces around the port of Dunkirk. Rundstedt, his tanks and infantry in need of rest, agreed to halt ground operations for a critical period. The pause was a grave tactical error, which allowed the British to evacuate thousands of soldiers at Dunkirk.

Nevertheless, plans for Operation Sea Lion, the invasion of England, proceeded in the summer of 1940 and Rundstedt was promoted field marshal in July. The Luftwaffe failure to achieve air superiority over the Channel during the Battle of Britain forced the cancellation of Sea Lion and Rundstedt was given command of occupation forces in the west.

Operation Barbarossa
One of Hitler's great blunders of World War Two was the decision to invade the Soviet Union on June 22, 1941. The reach of the German Army exceeded its grasp, but for a time it appeared that the Nazi juggernaut would sweep to victory. As planning for Operation Barbarossa was underway, Rundstedt was called to the eastern front. He led 52 infantry divisions and five panzer divisions in army group south in a drive through Ukraine. With the encirclement of Kiev, the Germans captured more than 650,000 Red Army soldiers. The cities of Kharkov and Rostov were taken by November and Rundstedt argued against continuing the offensive into the teeth of the bitter Russian winter. His advice was not heeded and though the 65-year-old field marshal suffered a heart attack at the end of the month, he refused to leave his command, directing the response to a Soviet counter-offensive.

Hitler flatly refused Rundstedt's requests to halt for the winter and the result led to privations for the troops who had not been issued cold weather clothing. They shivered in summer uniforms while engines and weapons locked up, unable to operate in sub-zero temperatures. The Red Army drive in late November compelled the Germans to fall back from Rostov, at least temporarily.

Hitler was livid, countermanding Rundstedt's order for the retreat. Rundstedt refused to comply and was relieved of command in favour of General Walther von Reichenau. As the subsequent misfortunes of the German Army unfolded on the eastern front, Rundstedt was occupied elsewhere.

Command in the west
Rundstedt was sidelined only temporarily. He was recalled to duty in March 1942 and given command of OB west with responsibility for more than 1,700 miles of coastline that the German Army was required to defend as the possibility of an Allied invasion of western Europe became more likely. Under Rundstedt, the building of the Atlantic wall defences was begun in earnest as thousands of workers of the Todt Organisation and forced labourers erected steel and concrete bunkers and casemates to house large-calibre shore batteries and machine-gun emplacements were dug.

Subsequently, Field Marshal Erwin Rommel was ordered to France as commander of army group B. Rommel and Rundstedt disagreed on the proper disposition of panzer forces at the Pas-de-Calais and Normandy to be ready to repel an invasion. Neither received their preferred arrangement after Hitler intervened and took personal control of the bulk of the armoured forces from Berlin.

After the D-Day landings, Rundstedt commanded German forces who fought with tenacity in Normandy. However, overwhelming Allied air support and the growing presence of British and American ground forces on the European continent facilitated offensive operations that pushed the Germans back along a broad front. At the same time, tremendous pressure was exerted by the Red Army, advancing towards the German frontier from the east.

Rundstedt was pragmatic and saw the situation for what it was – inevitable defeat. He did advocate for peace but his opinion fell on deaf ears. His reward for speaking truth to power was being relieved of duty yet again, replaced by General Gunther von Kluge. After the unsuccessful July 20, 1944 attempt on Hitler's life, Rundstedt was a member of the army court of honour that dismissed dozens of officers from the military and allowed them to be prosecuted in sham trials. Apparently, as far as Rundstedt was concerned, the court of honour was part of a soldier's duty. He had not actively participated in the plot against Hitler and again saw the role of the soldier as simply to follow orders.

In the autumn of 1944, Rundstedt was restored to command of OB west. Although his forces were able to contain and then reduce the Allied airborne-ground offensive of Operation Market Garden in September, Rundstedt opposed Hitler's Ardennes offensive, launched on December 16,1944. In the resulting Battle of the Bulge, the Germans lost troops and tanks that had first been transferred from the eastern front, weakening the resistance to the advancing Red Army and then sacrificed in a high-risk enterprise that was doomed to fail.

The end in Europe
By the spring of 1945, Hitler had once again tired of Rundstedt's objection regarding strategy and tactics in the last days of the Third Reich. The Führer sacked Rundstedt one final time as the field marshal argued for a negotiated peace as soon as possible. Rundstedt was captured by troops of the US 36th infantry division a week before the end of World War Two in Europe.

Transported to Britain and held in various prison camps, Rundstedt was charged with war crimes related to the invasion of the Soviet Union. Because of failing health and advanced age, he was never brought to trial. He died in Hanover, Lower Saxony, aged 77 on February 24, 1953, an example of a soldier having done his duty as he could comprehend that duty, to the last.

Von Rundstedt delivers the eulogy at the funeral of Field Marshal Erwin Rommel in October 1944. (Creative Commons Bundesarchiv Bild via Wikipedia)

FIELD MARSHAL FRIEDRICH PAULUS

The surrender of the German Sixth Army at Stalingrad was a turning point of World War Two. More than 90,000 soldiers had been captured by the victorious Red Army and among them was the first Prussian or German field marshal ever to be taken prisoner by an enemy force.

Friedrich Paulus, commander of the ill-fated Sixth Army, had been promoted to the highest rank in the German Army only hours earlier and the implications of it were clear. Adolf Hitler expected Paulus to commit suicide. However, Paulus is said to have remarked that he would not 'shoot myself for that Bohemian corporal'. Paulus went into Soviet captivity and later made propaganda speeches against the Nazi regime.

He was held in the Soviet Union until 1953, when he was allowed to return to his native country, although the nation had been divided. He lived in the city of Dresden in communist East Germany working briefly as a police inspector and died there at the age of 66.

The road to Stalingrad was long and Paulus may well have been ill-served when he was given command of the Sixth Army. His experience with formations larger than a battalion was limited but nevertheless, in the summer of 1942 he was handed a task that proved to be virtually impossible.

Case Blue and capitulation

Germany invaded the Soviet Union on June 22, 1941, its spearheads striking deep into Soviet territory but stalling just shy of the capital city of Moscow. After enduring a harsh winter, the Wehrmacht was to resume offensive operations again when the weather improved. The Soviets were sure that a renewed drive on Moscow was to come. However, Hitler redirected the focus of the latest offensive, codenamed Case Blue, to the oil fields of the Caucasus to the south.

Case Blue was unleashed on June 28, 1942 and at first good progress was made. However, lengthening supply lines and stiffening Red Army resistance led the Führer to modify the strategic aims of the offensive. Issuing Führer Directive No 45 on July 23, he divided army group south into separate army groups A and B. While the oil fields remained an objective, Paulus's Sixth Army, a component of army group B in the north, was given the task of advancing along the River Don and capturing the city of Stalingrad, an industrial and communications centre on the banks of the great River Volga. Although Stalingrad was not a target of substantial consequence, it bore the name of Soviet premier Josef Stalin. Its capture would provide a propaganda coup for the Nazis and Hitler became obsessed with its seizure.

On August 23, one month after beginning its drive eastward, army group B crossed the River Don, advancing that afternoon into the suburbs of Stalingrad. Sixth Army had come to Stalingrad from the

Hitler and Paulus with other senior German officers during a meeting at the headquarters of army group south on June 1, 1942. (Creative Commons Bundesarchiv Bild via Wikipedia)

Paulus arrives at an airfield in southern Russia in January 1942. He led sixth army to its fate at Stalingrad months later. (Creative Commons Bundesarchiv Bild via Wikipedia)

Field Marshal Friedrich Paulus was destined to lead the German sixth army to ruin at Stalingrad. (Creative Commons Bundesarchiv Bild via Wikipedia)

north, establishing control over about five miles of the west bank of the Volga on the 23rd and gaining control of about 90 percent of the city by November. However, the Soviets unleashed a massive counter-offensive, Operation Uranus on November 19 and succeeded in trapping the Sixth Army inside the city.

Weeks of bitter combat continued and a relief attempt mounted by General Erich von Manstein and elements of army group D failed to break the red army ring, partially because Paulus did not initiate a drive to break out and meet his would-be rescuers. Apparently, he was intent on carrying out Hitler's orders to hold the city regardless of circumstances.

Efforts to supply the Sixth Army by air were futile as the Luftwaffe could not transport enough materiel to sustain the embattled troops. As the fighting continued and the Soviet noose tightened, Paulus sought permission to surrender. Hitler denied the request and ordered the Sixth Army to fight to the last man. But by January 31, 1943, the situation was hopeless. Paulus and his staff surrendered and the last German soldier laid down his arms on February 2.

Paulus spent his last years working for the East German Military History Research Institute and sometimes made public speeches critical of Western nations, particularly the United States. During one encounter with the media, he addressed the German families of the thousands of prisoners captured at Stalingrad and on the eastern front

From inside the embattled city of Stalingrad, Paulus peers toward positions of the soviet red army. (Creative Commons Bundesarchiv Bild via Wikipedia)

during World War Two. He reassured them that their family members in the Soviet Union were being treated well. In truth, only a fraction of the German soldiers who were captured lived to return to Germany.

Rising through the ranks

For Paulus, a military career that ended in spectacular defeat began rather unremarkably. He was born on September 23, 1890 in Breitenau, the son of a financial executive. After determining to pursue a military career, his application to become an officer cadet in the navy was rejected, probably due to the family's lack of social standing. He studied law for a few months and then joined the German Army in 1910, receiving promotion to lieutenant a year later.

During World War One, Paulus served as a staff officer and saw combat in France and on the eastern front. He remained in the interwar army, the Reichswehr, occupying various staff positions and serving as an infantry instructor. He was promoted to the rank of lieutenant colonel in 1934. He was appointed commander of motor transport section three and became an acknowledged authority on the development of tanks and armoured warfare tactics as the German Army became more mechanised.

Paulus succeeded the famed General Heinz Guderian as chief of staff of the army's mechanised forces in 1935 and received promotion to major general as director of training for its light divisions in 1939, including motorised infantry, artillery and reconnaissance regiments. During his rise to higher command, Paulus was supported by his mentor, General Walther von Reichenau, and on the eve of World War Two he became chief of staff of the Tenth Army. In the early days of the conflict, he participated in the invasion of Poland and in the campaign against France and the low countries in the spring of 1940.

Operation Barbarossa

Paulus was promoted lieutenant general in June 1940 and participated in the planning for Operation Barbarossa. At the urging of General Reichenau, Hitler appointed Paulus to command the sixth army in December 1941, six months after the invasion of the Soviet Union had begun. After a Soviet counter-attack brought the advance of sixth army to a halt and Paulus was required to issue orders to give ground in early 1942, he rallied.

Sixth army launched a counter-attack on May 20, regaining the initiative as the Germans killed or captured nearly 250,000 Soviet soldiers. Paulus received the Knight's Cross for the achievement and may well have reached the zenith of his military career in the process. Within weeks, he was leading 250,000 troops toward disaster at Stalingrad. The fighting inside the city of Stalin was street to street and house to house. Casualties were horrendous on both sides, but the Soviets were tenacious during three months of combat.

When the end came, Colonel Wilhelm Adam, an aide to Paulus, recorded his impression of the surrender drama in his diary. "My God, what a contrast between the two sides! The German soldiers, ragged and in light coats, looked like ghosts with hollow, unshaven cheeks. The red army fighters looked fresh and wore warm winter uniforms.

Involuntarily, I remembered the chain of unfortunate events which had prevented me from sleeping for so many nights. The appearance of the red army soldiers seemed symbolic. At 9am sharp the HQ commander of the sixth army arrived to take the commander of the vanquished German sixth army and its staff toward the rear. The march toward the Volga had ended."

Postscript for Paulus

Hitler was furious when he received the news that Paulus had surrendered and had not taken his own life. Just before he agreed to surrender, Field Marshal Paulus sent his wedding ring to his wife aboard one of the last aircraft to depart the encircled city of Stalingrad. He had not seen her since his departure for command in 1942 and she died in 1949 while he was still a prisoner of the Soviets.

Immediately after he was captured, the Soviets pressured Paulus to make propaganda radio broadcasts encouraging German troops to surrender. He refused to co-operate until news of the July 20, 1944, assassination attempt against Hitler was received. Afterwards, he made several broadcasts and in later years he served as a mouthpiece for the communists, commenting on political affairs in West Germany and elsewhere. He appeared as a witness for the prosecution during the post-war Nuremberg war crimes trials, acknowledging his role in the planning and execution of Operation Barbarossa but refusing to incriminate other high-ranking Nazi officers.

Paulus was diagnosed with amyotrophic lateral sclerosis (ALS), a fatal neuromuscular disease, in 1956 and died within months. According to his wishes, he was buried in Baden-Baden, West Germany, beside his wife.

Right: Paulus speaks during a press conference in East Berlin in 1954. (Creative Commons Bundesarchiv Bild via Wikipedia)

Below: Paulus walks away from the meeting with soviet officers moments after his surrender at Stalingrad. (Creative Commons Bundesarchiv Bild via Wikipedia)

GENERAL HEINZ GUDERIAN

The German panzers of XIX Corps rolled into the French cities of Calais and Boulogne on May 23, 1940. Their swift advance had covered an astonishing 220 miles in 11 days and their commander, 51-year-old General Heinz Guderian, was at the zenith of his career. Guderian is acknowledged today as one of the foremost advocates of armoured warfare of his age. His theories of rapid exploitation of a breakthrough with the mailed fist of the tank were proven and he is remembered by many as the father of the blitzkrieg, or lightning war, tactic that took Poland and much of Western Europe by storm in the early months of World War Two.

On the heels of the stunning panzer advance, Guderian believed that his armoured forces could deliver the final blow in the west, compelling the surrender of the British expeditionary force and remaining French Army units with the capture of the French port cities along the English Channel. He thoroughly disagreed with the stop order issued by Adolf Hitler to allow the Luftwaffe of Reichsmarschall Hermann Göring to deliver the knockout blow against the Allies in France. It was not the first time Guderian would clash with the Führer and the Luftwaffe effort failed, allowing the Allied evacuation at Dunkirk at the end of May.

Guderian had already demonstrated the veracity of the blitzkrieg in Poland and he would go on to warn Hitler not to invade the Soviet Union in 1941. He spoke out against the Ardennes offensive of late 1944 while raising the alarm that a Soviet Red Army offensive would be unleashed in early 1945. Although his advice went unheeded, he remained steadfast in his commitment to the German Army and its panzer arm. He was sacked by Hitler in 1941 and recalled to duty months later by the Führer, whom he did not fear and openly defied when he felt it necessary. Guderian was innovative, flexible and driven in command.

A soldier for life

Born in Kulm, East Prussia, on June 17, 1888, Guderian was the son of an aristocratic army officer. He attended the Karlsruhe cadet school in Baden and the principal cadet school in Berlin before assignment to the 10th Hannoverian Jaeger battalion at Bitche, under his father's command. He received a lieutenant's commission in February 1907. He met and married Margaret 'Gretel' Goerne while serving in the Harz mountains.

The young officer took posts in communications units and started a three-year course of study at the Berlin war academy in October 1913.

General Heinz Guderian, photographed in 1941, was an early proponent of armoured warfare in the German army. (Public Domain)

The outbreak of the Great War interrupted the studies and Guderian was given command of a wireless station at the age of 26. He transferred to the headquarters of the 4th infantry division and was promoted to captain. He held various staff positions through the remainder of the war and although disenchanted by its outcome and the onerous provisions of the Versailles Treaty, he chose to remain in the post-war Reichswehr, an army of just 100,000 men.

In January 1922, Guderian was ordered to the office of the inspectorate of transport troops, the early organisation that dealt with armoured vehicle development and deployment in the German military. At first, he considered it a dead-end assignment. However, he pitched into the job with determination and learned all he could about the tactical use of tanks on the battlefield. He was heavily influenced by the writings of foreign military men, including Captain Basil Liddell Hart and Colonel J F C Fuller of Britain and Colonel Charles de Gaulle of France.

In later years, Guderian wrote: "These far-sighted soldiers were even then trying to make of the tank something more than just an infantry support weapon." The officer read voraciously and attended the manoeuvres of the British experimental mechanised force in 1923. His dedication to the development of an effective armoured force for the German Army was rewarded with promotion to major and command

Considered the father of the blitzkrieg, Guderian rides aboard a transport plane during a 1943 visit to the eastern front. (Creative Commons Bundesarchiv Bild via Wikipedia)

of a motor transport battalion in February 1930 and then as chief of staff to his friend, General Oswald Lutz, chief of transport command. Guderian demonstrated tank performance to Hitler, who responded enthusiastically: "That's what I need! That's what I want to have!"

The German Army's panzerwaffe grew to three divisions by 1935 and the following year Guderian was given command of the 2nd panzer division, along with promotion to brigadier general. He wrote the book Achtung! Panzer! that year and described the tactical use of the armoured fighting vehicle in swift operations that slashed into enemy rear areas. He predicted in 1937: "Where tanks are, is the front. Wherever in future wars the battle is fought, tank troops will play the decisive role."

Guderian visits the forward headquarters of a panzer regiment during Operation Barbarossa in 1941. (Creative Commons Bundesarchiv Bild via Wikipedia)

In November 1938, Guderian was made Lieutenant General of panzer troops and by early 1939 five panzer divisions were operational, while a sixth was being formed. As commander-in-chief of panzer troops, he supervised the preparations of the panzerwaffe for war.

The lightning war

On August 22, 1939, just nine days before the invasion of Poland, General Guderian was given command of the XIX panzer corps. When the offensive started, Guderian's tanks and motorised infantry swept across the southern end of the Polish corridor and made the furthest eastward penetration into Poland of any German command. They captured Brest-Litovsk, just 100 miles from the Polish capital of Warsaw, in 16 days. The dazzling advance earned praise from Hitler and a Knight's Cross.

After the Polish success, Guderian devoted the next nine months to increasing tank production and refining the training and tactics of his hard-hitting, fast-moving tank formations. When case yellow, the conquest of France and the low countries, began on May 10, 1940, the panzers were at their best during the dash towards the Channel and the movement that doomed the British and French to defeat.

Slashing through the Ardennes forest in eastern Belgium, Guderian's XIX corps breached French lines, blasted its way through defences at Sedan and established a bridgehead across the River Meuse in three days. German tanks burst into open country, defeated a French armoured counter-attack led by Colonel de Gaulle and used the existing road network to reach the Channel coast. The world watched in awe and came to know the meaning of the word blitzkrieg. Guderian earned the nickname 'Hurrying Heinz' for his rapidity of movement.

Guderian then advocated additional panzer divisions and the number reached 20 within a year. However, he was concerned that the number of available tanks was inadequate for long-term, sustained operations.

When Hitler revealed his plan for Operation Barbarossa, the invasion of the Soviet Union set for June 22, 1941, Guderian was aghast. He discounted assessments that the Soviet military would collapse within days and warned not to engage in a prolonged war against an opponent with seemingly endless resources. Nevertheless, he led Second Panzer Army into Russia, covering 200 miles in five days and co-ordinating a pincer movement with other forces to destroy or damage an astonishing 3,300 Soviet tanks and take 324,000 prisoners around the city of Minsk.

Towards the end of 1941, Soviet resistance stiffened, German supply lines lengthened and the invading troops began to suffer from the freezing temperatures of the harsh Russian winter. Their uniforms were light summer issue and no provision had been made for winter clothing. Engines and weapons froze and were rendered inoperable by sub-zero temperatures.

An autumn push against Moscow had ground to a halt amid torrential rain that turned roads into quagmires and another thrust was stopped with the spires of the city in sight. Then, the Red Army unleashed a counter-offensive that pushed the Germans back nearly 150 miles in some areas. Guderian wrote: "Our attack on Moscow had broken down. All the sacrifices and endurance of our brave troops had been in vain. We had suffered a grievous defeat." His pleas to Hitler for a withdrawal to consolidate defensive positions fell on deaf ears.

Guderian's argument with Hitler and disagreements with superior officers led to his relief from duty on Christmas Day 1941. He was sidelined until early 1943, when Hitler recalled him to the post of inspector

During the course of World War Two, Guderian was sacked and reinstated by Hitler. (Creative Commons Bundesarchiv Bild via Wikipedia)

general of panzer troops. He worked for months to improve German tank performance, including the installation of more powerful guns in the Panther medium and Tiger heavy tanks. Still, Guderian clashed regularly with Hitler over strategy and tactics. He never achieved the tank production figures he believed necessary to win the war.

Despite his disagreements with the Führer, Guderian declined to actively participate in the July 20, 1944 plot to assassinate Hitler. He did serve on the military court of honour that cashiered many officers and led to their swift prosecution in the sham 'People's Court'. Many were sentenced to death.

War and remembrance

During the final months of the war, Guderian opposed the winter offensive in the Ardennes that led to the Battle of the Bulge and his prediction of a Soviet offensive came true in early 1945. In the spring, the western allies were across the great River Rhine and the red army was on the banks of the River Oder, just 40 miles from Berlin.

Guderian was sure that Hitler had lost his mind and the two nearly came to blows during a heated exchange at the Reich Chancellery in Berlin on March 28. Hitler forced Guderian to take six weeks of sick leave, but the general was actually glad to leave his staff post. He did rejoin the headquarters of the panzer inspectorate in May and surrendered to American troops on the 10th.

Charges of war crimes were dropped, but Guderian remained in Allied custody until June 1948. After his release, he lived in Bavaria and wrote his memoirs, Memories of a Soldier, released in 1951. The next year another book, Panzer Leader, became a bestseller. Guderian died in 1954 at the age of 65. He remains a towering figure in the history of armoured warfare.

Right: This photo of General Heinz Guderian was probably taken in Russia sometime in 1944. (Creative Commons Cassowary Colorizations via Wikipedia)

Below: Guderian and Adolf Hitler stand at centre during a review of panzer troops in Poland. (Public Domain)

MARSHAL GEORGI ZHUKOV

Above left: Marshal Georgi Zhukov was the foremost military commander of the Soviet Union in World War Two. (Public Domain)

Above right: A youthful Georgi Zhukov as a regimental commander during the 1920s. (Creative Commons Savitskiy Vadim via Wikipedia)

The most prominent and militarily successful senior officer of the Soviet Red Army during World War Two, Marshal Georgi Zhukov played a leading role in the Soviet response to the Nazi invasion of June 22, 1941.

At the time of the invasion, Zhukov was serving as chief of the general staff with responsibilities for the establishment of plans in the event of war with Nazi Germany. Historians have surmised that a plan for a pre-emptive attack against Germany had been devised by the spring of 1941, but whether it was formally approved by Soviet premier Josef Stalin or whether it existed at all remain open questions.

The Soviet Union and Nazi Germany had signed a non-aggression pact in 1939 Stalin refused to believe that Adolf Hitler would initiate such a betrayal. His refusal to heed warnings of impending disaster and desire that Soviet forces maintain a defensive posture to avoid provoking the Nazis undoubtedly contributed to the Soviet unpreparedness in the spring of 1941 and the initial German penetrations deep into the country.

Zhukov responded to the shocking news of the invasion with orders to surround and destroy the Germans as they plunged eastward. However, there were problems with communications and the swiftness of the enemy advance crippled a cohesive defence.

Left: Zhukov in 1940 with Marshal Semyon Timoshenko. (Public Domain)

Right: Zhukov delivers a speech during a 1941 meeting. In that year, the Nazis invaded the Soviet Union. (Public Domain)

When Zhukov recommended that Red Army forces fall back from Kiev, the capital of Ukraine, just over a month after the invasion was launched, Stalin relieved him of his post.

Reassigned to command of the Reserve Front in the autumn of 1941, Zhukov was responsible for the defence of Leningrad, which was surrounded by the Germans and withstood a siege of 900 days. He also delivered the first substantial victory over the Germans during World War Two in the east. Executing the Yelnya offensive from August 30 to September 8, 1941, he commanded Red Army troops that drove the enemy from a salient southeast of Smolensk that might have been used as a staging area for a German thrust toward the Soviet capital of Moscow.

Despite the early defeats and the loss of hundreds of thousands of Red Army soldiers, Zhukov's determination, along with strategic and tactical skill, had propelled him again to the forefront of the Soviet military leadership.

From conscript to command

Georgi Zhukov was born the son of a peasant cobbler in the village of Strelkova, Kaluga Province, south of Moscow, December 1, 1896. He grew up in abject poverty and as a boy was apprenticed to an uncle in Moscow to learn the furrier trade, working long hours in difficult conditions.

In 1915, Zhukov was conscripted into the Tsarist Russian Army. A cavalryman during World War One, he showed aptitude for higher command and within a year was selected for training as a non-commissioned officer. While serving with the 10th Dragoon Novgorod Regiment, he was wounded in action and decorated twice for bravery. In the wake of the Bolshevik revolution of 1917, he joined the Communist Party and fought in the Russian Civil War after surviving a near-fatal bout of typhus. By 1921, he had received a cavalry officer's commission and the Order of the Red Banner for outstanding service.

During the interwar period, Zhukov remained in the Red Army and rose steadily in rank. In 1923, he was given command of the 39th Cavalry Regiment and this was followed by completion of the cavalry school and the prestigious Frunze Military Academy by the end of the decade. In 1933, he received command of the 7th Cavalry Divisio, and in 1938 he became deputy commander of the Belorussian

Military District. During this period, he is said to have kept a packed suitcase near the door of his home in the event that he became subject to arrest during Stalin's brutal, paranoid purge of the senior ranks of the Red Army that occurred in the 1930s.

Foreign exchanges

By 1938, Japanese expansion on the continent of Asia threatened the security of Soviet territory in the East. Incursions from Japanese-occupied Manchuria into Mongolia were occurring with alarming regularity. Zhukov was given command of the First Soviet Mongolian Army Group and tasked with putting the Japanese in their place.

Zhukov's forces won a victory at the Battle of Lake Khasan in the summer of 1938, ejecting a Japanese incursion. When the fighting resumed in the spring of 1939, the Battle of Khalkhin Gol was a decisive Soviet victory. Zhukov utilised tank brigades to execute a swift manoeuvre outflanking the Japanese, taking prisoners, slashing into rear areas and creating confusion. The defeat of the Japanese Sixth Army quelled the threat of further military action. Zhukov was hailed a Hero of the Soviet Union, one of four of these prestigious awards he would receive in his lifetime.

Meanwhile, Soviet concerns related to the possibility of invasion by Nazi Germany prompted demands that neighbouring Finland cede territory along with other concessions that would improve Soviet security. When the Finns refused to co-operate, the Soviets invaded the country, leading to the costly and sometimes embarrassing losses of the Winter War of 1939-1940. Zhukov served as chief of staff of the Red Army during the period and the Soviets sustained heavy casualties at the hands of the resourceful Finns. However, the outcome was inevitable as the Soviets forced Finnish leaders to the negotiating table through sheer weight of numbers and firepower.

Subsequently, Zhukov was given command of the Kiev Military District and returned to the post of chief of the general staff in January 1941.

Turning the eastern tide

After the early setbacks against the invading Nazis, Zhukov was elevated to deputy commissar of defence and first deputy commander-in-chief of the Soviet armed forces, a close advisory role to Stalin. He organised the defence of Stalingrad as the 62nd Army, under General Vasily Chuikov, fought doggedly against the Germans around the industrial centre on the River Volga that bore the name of the Soviet premier.

While the fighting raged at Stalingrad, Zhukov led the planning of Operation Uranus, the offensive that succeeded in surrounding the German Sixth Army in the city and led to the great victory in early 1943 that changed the course of World War Two in the east. Concurrently, he executed Operation Spark in the north, opening a supply route to the besieged city of Leningrad. He was promoted Marshal of the Soviet Union and participated in the planning to blunt Operation Citadel, the German offensive against the Kursk salient, in the summer of 1943. Focusing again in the north, Zhukov led Red Army forces in finally lifting the 900-day siege of Leningrad in January 1944.

Mounted on horseback, Zhukov takes part in a post-war victory parade in 1945. (Creative Commons Mil.ru via Wikipedia)

Soviet histories of the Great Patriotic War refer to 1944 as the year of Stalin's 10 Blows or the Year of 10 Victories, alluding to the successes of Soviet offensive operations that pushed the Germans back across hundreds of miles to their own frontier. Zhukov launched Operation Bagration, intended to clear the enemy from Belarus and eastern Poland, on June 22, 1944, exactly three years after the Germans had launched Operation Barbarossa.

The Red Army pitched into the Germans at multiple locations and won victory after victory. Soviet spearheads were slowed only as their supply lines became overextended and armoured formations were outdistancing their infantry support. Zhukov capably led the 1st and 2nd Belorussian Fronts and then the 1st Ukrainian Front.

The final offensive against the Nazis began in earnest in early 1945. Zhukov's 1st Belorussian Front and Marshal Ivan Konev's 1st Ukrainian Front crossed the River Oder and were pitted against one another in a race to subdue the Nazi capital of Berlin. Stalin challenged each commander to conquer the city.

Soviet forces executed a giant pincer movement to defeat the Germans and the fighting was bitter at Seelow Heights, the gateway to Berlin. Zhukov sent waves of Red Army soldiers and tanks against the entrenched enemy and it took four days to clear the road to the Nazi capital. Zhukov entered the city from the north, while Konev's forces attacked from the south and Berlin fell to the Red Army on May 2, 1945.

Zhukov was given credit for the final capture of Berlin while Konev was diverted southwest to link up with American forces at Torgau on the River Elbe. The Soviets lost 80,000 killed and wounded in the epic battle. In retribution for German cruelty earlier in the war, the Red Army advance to Berlin was marked with brutality, looting and destruction of property.

Zhukov postscript

Zhukov's status as a national hero was burnished with the victory in Berlin and he was chosen to represent the Soviet Union during surrender ceremonies in the city. Zhukov was praised for his leadership and became military governor of the Soviet occupation zone in Germany, but he was also a marked man. Stalin began to perceive the great war hero as a threat to his own pre-eminence. Within months of the triumph, Zhukov was shunted to a series of inconsequential posts.

After Stalin's death in 1953, Zhukov re-emerged on the Soviet political and military scene. He was appointed defence minister under Premier Nikita Krushchev, but further disagreements over policy led to his retirement. He died in 1974 at the age of 77.

Without question, Zhukov was one of the great military leaders of World War Two. His command skills served the Red Army well and his contribution to the defeat of Nazi Germany was substantial.

Zhukov (centre) and Ivan Konev (right) confer during the Battle of Kursk in the summer of 1943. (Public Domain)

MARSHAL KONSTANTIN ROKOSSOVSKY

"The German Army is a machine and machines can be broken!" so noted Konstantin Rokossovsky, a high-ranking officer of the Soviet Red Army during the life and death struggle against the Nazis on the Eastern Front during World War Two.

In fact, Rokossovsky was a man who had refused to be broken, even surviving arrest and brutal torture at the hands of the NKVD, the Soviet secret police, during Premier Josef Stalin's paranoid purge of the Red Army officer corps in the 1930s. Born in the city of Velikiye Luki, in Russian-ruled Poland, on December 21, 1896, he had enlisted in the Tsarist Russian Army and served as a non-commissioned officer during World War One. Wounded twice, he received the Cross of St George.

With the outbreak of the October revolution, he joined the Bolshevik Party and subsequently the Red Army. His troubles began in the summer of 1937, after more than 20 years of military service. He was accused of being a spy for both Poland and Japan but refused to confess to any false charges. Subjected to harsh beatings, he suffered broken ribs and fingers and perhaps worst of all, he was subjected to at least two mock firing squads, only to be returned to his cell.

The road to redemption for Rokossovsky began in early 1940, as the Red Army had been embarrassed by the efficiency and tenacity of the neighbouring Finns. The Soviets had invaded Finland after failing to coerce territorial concessions and other favours that would improve the country's defensive posture in the event of an invasion by the German Army. When the Finns refused to co-operate, the ensuing Winter War went badly for the Red Army, which suffered extremely high casualties. A reversal and final victory in the war of 1939-1940 was achieved when the Soviets deployed overwhelming military might – and restored men such as Rokossovsky, deemed to be rehabilitated, to senior command.

Service and severance

Although the Rokossovsky (Russified from the original Polish spelling of Rokossowski) family was of the Polish nobility, Konstantin's father worked as a railroad official and his mother was a teacher. The family further had a long tradition of supplying officers to the cavalry regiments of the old Polish Army.

The boy was apprenticed as a stone mason in 1911, but the coming of the Great War had brought a new focus to his future. His courage and leadership were exemplary and during the Russian Civil War, he commanded a squadron of the Kargopolsky Red Guards Cavalry, fighting White Russian forces in the Ural Mountains. In one harrowing incident, Rokossovsky was wounded in the shoulder but later killed the officer who shot him.

Rokossovsky then served during unrest in Mongolia, where the Red Army defeated separatist forces and was wounded yet again. In 1929-1930, he led a cavalry brigade during a dispute with a China warlord related to control of the Chinese Eastern Railway. Eventually, the Soviet soldiers defeated the renegade army and restored joint control of the railroad to the Soviet and Chinese governments.

Rokossovsky confers with another officer during the fighting around Moscow. (Creative Commons Mil.ru via Wikipedia)

One of the first officers of the Red Army to realise the potential of the tank in modern warfare, Rokossovsky was associated with Marshal Mikhail Tukhachevsky, also an armour advocate and proponent of a tactical field strategy he referred to as 'Deep Battle'. Tukhachevsky was executed during the purge.

Rokossovsky also ascribed to the Deep Battle concept and the relationship with Tukhachevsky may have created enough friction with old line cavalry officers to also make Stalin wary of the Polish-born

Polish-born Marshal Konstantin Rokossovsky was hero of the Red Army during World War Two. (Public Domain)

Rokossovsky watches action in the Stalingrad area during his command of the Don Front in 1942. (Public Domain)

officer. Following his arrest, Rokossovsky skilfully defended himself at a trial and pointed out that one of the Soviet officers who supposedly had implicated him was dead before the accusations of spying and negligence of duty were even made.

By this time, Rokossovsky was acquainted with both Georgi Zhukov and Semyon Timoshenko, also future Marshals of the Soviet Union. At various times during World War Two, he would serve under them both. After Rokossovsky was released from prison in 1940, Timoshenko provided command of the 5th Cavalry Corps with the rank of colonel. Within months, promotion to major general and command of the 9th Mechanised Corps followed. When the Nazis invaded the Soviet Union on June 22, 1941, the corps became heavily engaged, losing 252 of its original complement of 316 tanks.

During the Battle of Smolensk in the summer of 1941, Rokossovsky commanded the 4th Army with the rank of lieutenant general. His command kept a corridor of retirement open during the see-saw battle and fought to halt the German advance against an ever-shrinking pocket of Soviet resistance, finally stabilising the front in its sector. In September Rokossovsky was personally appointed by Stalin to take command of the 16th Army and supervise the defence of Moscow. The ensuing German offensive spent itself after making some gains and Rokossovsky challenged Zhukov's authority during a dispute over potential withdrawal of the 16th Army to more favourable defensive positions. When Zhukov rescinded an order from higher command and the withdrawal did not take place, heavy losses were experienced.

In March 1942, Rokossovsky was seriously wounded by shrapnel. He spent two months in hospital recovering and then returned to command 16th Army until July 1942, when Stalin personally placed him briefly in command of the Bryansk Front. On Zhukov's recommendation, Rokossovsky was transferred to the south that autumn and given command of the Don Front. After playing a supporting role in Operation Uranus, the encirclement of the German Sixth Army at Stalingrad, Rokossovsky was ordered to eliminate German resistance in the city.

When the German surrender was complete and the great victory sealed, Rokossovsky, promoted colonel general, wrote: "The troops of the Don Front at 4pm on February 2nd, 1943 completed the rout and destruction of the encircled group of enemy forces in Stalingrad. Twenty-two divisions have been destroyed or taken prisoner."

In July 1943, the Germans launched Operation Citadel, intending to reduce the Kursk Salient. In response, Rokossovsky had deployed his Central Front forces in supporting defensive rings, which engaged elements of German Army Group Centre and held their positions. The Battle of Kursk was the largest tank engagement of World War Two and during the thrust and counterthrust fighting, both sides suffered horrific losses in troops and armoured vehicles.

Fight to the finish

In the summer of 1944, the Red Army unleashed Operation Bagration, but not before Rokossovsky openly disagreed with Stalin's proposed strategy and prevailed in a heated exchange witnessed by other senior officers. The scene was remarkable and indicative of the esteem that Stalin held for Rokossovsky after nearly having him executed during the earlier purge.

Rokossovsky argued for two points of penetration of the German defensive lines during the early stages of Bagration, rather than a single breakthrough as Stalin had proposed. The veteran officer held his ground while the others waited for Stalin's volcanic temper to erupt. Quietly, Rokossovsky repeated: "Two breakthroughs, Comrade Stalin, two breakthroughs." In response Stalin placed his hand on Rokossovsky's shoulder. The others waited for Stalin to tear away Rokossovsky's colonel general's rank insignia. Instead, to everyone's

Rokossovsky poses for this post-war photo in the uniform of the Polish Army. (Creative Commons Mil.ru via Wikipedia)

amazement, Stalin replied: "Your confidence speaks for your sound judgment."

The central front was renamed the 1st Belorussian Front and Rokossovsky commanded the army group during its advance through Belorussia and into Poland. During its advance, the 1st Belorussian Front shattered Army Group Centre, destroying 28 of its 34 divisions. Controversy followed as Rokossovsky halted his drive at the River Vistula and declined to send any aid to the Polish fighters during the Warsaw Uprising. Observers have debated his motivation. Whether it was too great a logistical challenge in the face of continuing German resistance outside the city or an opportunity to allow SS troops to annihilate the Polish fighters that might oppose Stalin in the aftermath of the war remains the subject of debate today.

In mid-1944, Rokossovsky was promoted Marshal of the Soviet Union. By autumn he was transferred to command of the 2nd Belorussian Front, which fought its way through East Prussia and northern Poland to make contact with British Field Marshal Bernard Montgomery's 21st Army Group surging from the west. During the 1945 Red Square victory parade in Moscow, Marshal Rokossovsky rode a brown stallion, accompanying Marshal Zhukov, mounted on a white charger.

After the war, Rokossovsky commanded Red Army forces in Poland and later served as Polish Minister of National Defence with the approval of Stalin. He was named Marshal of Poland and later became deputy chairman of the Council of Ministers of Poland's communist regime. He worked to suppress a Polish independence movement that would have taken the country out of the Soviet orbit and remained loyal to Stalin. He sent troops and tanks to suppress protesters in the city of Poznan who sought better working conditions.

In the mid-1950s, Rokossovsky was forced by political rivals to leave Poland. He returned to the Soviet Union and served as Deputy Minister of Defence while commanding the Transcaucasian Military District. In 1958, he was elevated to chief inspector of the Ministry of Defence. He retired in 1962 and died of cancer five years later.

Konstantin Rokossovsky proved his loyalty to the Soviet Union but once muttered: "The Russians think I'm a Pole and the Poles think I'm a Russian." Regardless, his impact on the course of World War Two was substantial.

Right: Marshal Rokossovsky was honoured with this Russian postage stamp in 2021. (Public Domain)

Below: Rokossovsky discusses troop dispositions with General Filipp Golikov. (Creative Commons Mil.ru via Wikipedia)

GENERAL TOMOYUKI YAMASHITA

General Tomoyuki Yamashita, commander of Japanese forces in Malaya in the opening days of World War Two in the Pacific and later defender of the Philippines, executed one of the most dazzling military campaigns in the history of modern warfare, culminating with the capitulation of Singapore on February 15, 1942.

Yamashita used speed and bluff to achieve the capture of the great British bastion at Singapore and during the rapid movement of his 25th Army earned the nickname 'Tiger of Malaya'. His troops, however, committed atrocities against civilians and prisoners of war both in Malaya and in the Philippines. Yamashita was put on trial after the war and paid for these crimes with his life.

Towards the military

Tomoyuki Yamashita was born on the island of Shikoku on November 8, 1885. He was the second son of a local physician and attended schools that prepared him for a military career. He graduated from the Imperial Army Academy at Ichigaya, Tokyo, in 1905, ranking 16th among 920 aspiring officers. He was commissioned as a lieutenant in the Japanese Army and fought for control of German-owned railroads in the Chinese province of Shandong during World War One.

Promoted to captain in 1916, Yamashita attended the Army War College and graduated sixth in his class. He developed into an acknowledged expert on Germany and became an officer of the general staff. From 1919 to 1922, he was assigned as military attaché in Bern, Switzerland and then Berlin. He was promoted to major in early 1922 and assigned to the Military Affairs Bureau of the War Ministry to begin working on a project to restructure the Japanese Army. Stiff opposition from several factions was encountered and Yamashita incurred the wrath of some senior officers.

Promoted to lieutenant colonel in 1925, Yamashita became involved in political wrangling within the officer corps of the army and sponsored a controversial reduction programme, again incurring the enmity of other officers, particularly the powerful General Hideki Tojo, future wartime prime minister. Tojo opposed some of the controversial measures that Yamashita favoured, such as a reorganised army and air command structure, mechanisation of the ground forces and the establishment of a defence ministry and cadre of officers to foster inter-service co-operation. From 1927 to 1930, Yamashita was shunted far from the epicentre of authority as a military liaison officer in Vienna.

Palace intrigue

Despite having fallen into disfavour, Yamashita was given command of the 3rd Imperial Infantry Regiment, Imperial Guards Division, promoted full colonel in 1930 and then elevated to major general in 1934. Soon afterwards, however, controversy found the officer once again. In 1936, an attempted coup by young, zealous military officers intent on ridding the government and the army of existing leadership and liquidating political rivals, culminated in 'The February 26 Incident'. When the coup was put down, 19 ringleaders were executed and another 40 imprisoned.

Yamashita appealed for leniency to Emperor Hirohito but was rebuffed and his own career suffered a setback as the monarch's trust waned. Although Yamashita decided to resign his army commission, a group of senior

General Tomoyuki Yamashita and staff officers pore over a map during the drive to Singapore. (Public Domain)

officers talked him out of the career-ending act. He then accepted an inconsequential post as commander of an infantry brigade in Korea. Historians have seen this period as one of reflection and re-instilling discipline for General Yamashita, as he spent time in meditation and the practice of Zen Buddhism.

By the late 1930s, the Japanese Army had been encroaching on Chinese territory for nearly a decade and in 1937, open hostilities erupted with the Second Sino-Japanese War. The Japanese Kwantung Army seized the Chinese province of Manchuria and proclaimed it the puppet state of Manchukuo. Although Yamashita had advocated for an end to the fighting in China and co-operative relations with the United States and Great Britain, the diplomatic rift only widened. Promoted lieutenant general in November 1937, Yamashita was given command of the 4th Infantry Division, already embroiled in the war in China. He served in that role for the next three years.

Diplomatic mission

On September 27, 1940, Japan signed the tripartite pact with Nazi Germany and Fascist Italy. In December, Yamashita was sent on a diplomatic mission to Germany, leading a delegation. Hitler apparently intended to press the Japanese into declaring war on Great Britain and the United States. However, Yamashita's agenda was quite different. Japan was still engaged in the war with China amid a growing number of troops committed to the Asian continent. At the same time, border incidents had sparked a shooting war with the Soviet Union.

The Japanese were immediately concerned with preventing a widening war with the Soviets, solidifying their gains in China and determining

General Tomoyuki Yamashita led the Japanese 25th Army in the swift conquest of Malaya. (Public Domain)

Above: General Tomoyuki Yamashita presses General Arthur Percival for the unconditional surrender of Singapore. (Public Domain)

Left: In September 1945, General Tomoyuki Yamashita and his staff surrender to the Allies. (Public Domain)

their future course in promotion of the Greater East Asia Co-Prosperity Sphere, a euphemism for Japanese hegemony in Asia and the Pacific. Yamashita and his delegation were interested in procuring German technology and learning more of the successful tactics the Nazis had employed during their lightning conquest of Poland and Western Europe.

The Germans were reluctant to share information. They deflected the primary questions and instead showed the Japanese some of the sites related to their recent feats of arms. The situation left Yamashita unenthusiastic. A meeting with Hitler left him unimpressed and he commented: "He may be a great orator on a platform, but standing behind his desk listening, he seems much more like a clerk." Prior to his departure for Japan, Yamashita softened his comments for the press and noted that the objectives of the Japanese and German governments were in concert with one another, which he saw 'almost as a surprising coincidence'.

Maelstrom of war

On December 8, 1941, Yamashita launched the Japanese attack on British Malaya from bases in occupied Indochina. The mission was predicated on speed and the growing Japanese prowess in jungle warfare. Yamashita had only 30,000 troops under his command and the opposing forces on the Malay peninsula outnumbered the 25th Army significantly.

Progress was swift and some Japanese soldiers rode bicycles during the advance. When the tires went flat, they rode on the rims. British preparations for defence proved inadequate and many of the heavy guns that were meant to defend Fortress Singapore were pointed seaward in anticipation of an attack along the coast rather than a concerted drive overland. They were useless against Yamashita's ground onslaught.

While the swift campaign had taken its toll on the Japanese attackers, they rolled from victory to victory and when Yamashita approached Singapore, he presented the illusion that his force was much stronger than it actually was. After a week of fighting, the Japanese had bombed and seriously damaged the mainland reservoirs

that supplied water to the city. Threatening an all-out attack that would bring further destruction on the civilian population as well as the defenders, Yamashita convinced General Arthur Percival to surrender and 80,000 Commonwealth soldiers marched into terrible captivity. It was the largest surrender of an armed force in British military history.

Winston Churchill called the fall of Singapore the 'greatest disaster' and commented: "I do not see how anyone could expect Malaya to be defended, once the Japanese obtained command of the sea and while we are fighting for our lives against Germany and Italy."

Seated at centre during his trial, Yamashita was convicted of war crimes and sentenced to death. (Public Domain)

In July 1942, Yamashita was reassigned again to northern China, where he commanded the First Area Army. Tojo had become prime minister and the appointment to a backwater area may well have been in retribution for their earlier differences. Yamashita was promoted to full general and after Tojo resigned as prime minister in the summer of 1944, he was ordered to the Philippines, where the US would soon land forces intent on liberating the islands.

Yamashita took command of the 14th Area Army in the Philippines on October 10, just 10 days before the American landings on the island of Leyte. The initial US offensive was followed in early 1945 with further amphibious landings at Lingayen Gulf on the island of Luzon. The fighting for the Philippine capital of Manila was bitter and casualties, both military and civilian, were high. The Japanese were forced into the rugged mountains and exerted determined resistance until the surrender of the Empire's armed forces.

Yamashita was taken into custody after the forces in the Philippines laid down their arms and he was soon tried as a war criminal. The proceedings in Manila lasted from October 29 to December 7, 1945 and the charges were related to atrocities committed in Malaya, the battle for Manila and the execution of prisoners of war in the Philippines. Although evidence was presented that he did not actively participate in the killings of innocent people, he did little or nothing to stop the bloodshed. Still, he denied awareness that his troops were committing atrocities and asserted that he would have issued orders to immediately cease such actions if he had known.

The tribunal found Yamashita guilty and sentenced him to death by hanging. General Douglas MacArthur, commander of Allied forces in the Pacific, reviewed the proceedings and found no mitigating circumstances. He wrote: "This officer, of proven field merit, entrusted with high command involving authority adequate to responsibility, has failed this irrevocable standard; has failed his duty to his troops, to his country, to his enemy, to mankind; he has failed utterly his soldier faith. The results are beyond challenge."

Further appeals were denied, and US president Harry Truman declined to intervene. The convicted war criminal was hanged at the Philippine Detention and Rehabilitation Centre near Manila on February 23, 1946.

Moments after the verdict of death by hanging is rendered, Yamashita is led from the courtroom. (Public Domain)

GENERAL MASAHARU HOMMA

General Masaharu Homma was a man with perspective. However, he chose to keep that perspective to himself.

"War against the USA would be a disaster, I knew, but I could not show any feeling in it as I would have been called a traitor," he wrote after the defeat of Japan in World War Two. "[Prime Minister] Tojo did not understand Anglo-Saxon temperament and its potential strength. Japan was already exhausted from its prolonged war in China and was not in a position to wage another against the US and Great Britain. It was sheer madness."

And so it was that the commander of the Japanese 14th Army and conqueror of the Philippines during the heady early days of the war in the Pacific would ironically doom himself years later. Homma was arrested after hostilities ceased, tried for war crimes and shot by firing squad on April 3, 1946. He was 58 years old.

Further irony exists in Homma's fate. True enough, he had commanded the Japanese soldiers who overran the Philippines and accepted the surrender of the American and Filipino troops cornered in the Bataan peninsula and the fortress island of Corregidor in the spring of 1942. It was also true that the soldiers under his command committed heinous atrocities against many of the near 80,000 prisoners they took. Despite orders he personally issued that the POWs should be treated humanely, the Japanese soldiers were violent, vindictive and heartless – and Homma was held to account in the sense that an officer is responsible for what his troops do or fail to do.

An estimated 5,500 American and Filipino prisoners died at the hands of their captors during the infamous Death March, a horrific trek of 85 miles from Mariveles to Camp O'Donnell on the western edge of the central plain on the Philippine island of Luzon.

East meets West

Homma was a cultured man, known to many in the Japanese Army as the 'Poet General'. He had written extensively, published magazine articles and music lyrics and travelled widely during his military career. Early aspirations to become an author had given way to a life in the

Above left: Photographed in 1943, General Masaharu Homma was familiar with the West at the outbreak of World War Two. (Public Domain)

Above right: While in custody of American authorities after World War Two, Homma was tried for war crimes. (Public Domain)

Imperial Japanese Army and Homma developed an affinity for western thought and culture well before the outbreak of World War Two.

Born on Sado Island in the Sea of Japan on November 27, 1887, Homma joined the Imperial Japanese Army at the age of 17 in 1905 amid a wave of patriotic fervour as the Russo-Japanese War was underway. He was a 1907 honour graduate of the Imperial Japanese Army Academy at Ichigaya, Tokyo, ranking 14th in his class. Among his fellow students was future prime minister and nemesis Hideki Tojo. In 1915, Homma graduated from the Army Staff College and while serving with the Imperial General Staff he became a military liaison officer in Great Britain.

In the middle of World War One, Homma was sent to learn the English language and he experienced combat on the Western Front while attached to the East Lancashire Regiment of the British Army. He exhibited courage under fire and received the Military Cross in 1918. Such adventure was exceptional for a Japanese soldier.

Through his experience, Homma gained a deep interest in European culture and society and from 1930 to 1932, he was again posted to Britain as a liaison officer. He went on to serve as a Japanese delegate to the 1932 Geneva Disarmament Conference and as an officer in the press department of the Army Ministry, putting his English language skills to good use. Through the end of the 1930s, he held command of the army's 1st Infantry Regiment and 32nd Infantry Brigade prior to appointment as an aide to Prince Chichibu, brother of Emperor Hirohito.

The Second Sino-Japanese War erupted in 1937 and within months, Homma was promoted to lieutenant general and given command of the 27th Division. For the next two years, his troops were engaged in Tientsin, where foreign concessions, trade areas ceded to Western countries by China, were blockaded. He carried on negotiations with the British during the tense period. Homma became critical of Japanese policy in China and had stated publicly that Japan would suffer defeat in a prolonged war.

After the December 1937 capture of the Chinese city of Nanking and the subsequent atrocities perpetrated by Japanese soldiers against the civilian population, Homma remarked: "Unless peace is

Homma comes ashore in the Philippines in December 1941. (Public Domain)

achieved immediately it will be disastrous." He had also maintained that early low opinion of Tojo, commenting: "His dogmatic character was deeply repugnant to me and his pro-German idea was widely in variance with my liberal views."

In combination, these sentiments led some senior government officials and military leaders to believe Homma was too westernised. He was removed from frontline command in China and appointed commander of the Taiwan Army District in 1940.

Above: American prisoners pause during the horrific Death March from Bataan in the spring of 1942. Homma was executed by firing squad for the atrocities committed under his command. (Public Domain)

Left: Homma meets with Filipino officials in Manila in 1943. (Public Domain)

Fortune and the Philippines

Despite his prior difficulties with Tojo and others, Homma was given command of the 14th Army just before the outbreak of World War Two in the Pacific. The Philippines was an obvious target for Japanese expansion and within hours of the December 7, 1941, attack on Pearl Harbor, elements of the 14th Army landed at Lingayen Gulf on Luzon. The ensuing campaign lasted until May 1942, when conquest of the islands was concluded.

Although the occupation of the Philippines was successfully completed, Homma had been the subject of criticism for several reasons. Some detractors believed that he was too close to his soldiers, caring too much for their individual safety to commit them to desperate fighting against stout American and Filipino defences that would certainly have meant a higher toll in dead and wounded. As a result, repeated cables reached Homma's headquarters from Army Chief of Staff General Hajime Sugiyama in Tokyo urging a faster pace for 14th Army. Further, Homma had also ordered his troops to treat the Filipino people as friends rather than a subjugated population.

Such conduct attracted attention and Homma gained the enmity of his superior officer, Count Hisaichi Terauchi, the general commanding the Southern Army based in Indochina. Terauchi sent derogatory reports to Tokyo and these sullied Homma's reputation further. At the same time, subordinates within the 14th Army were undermining their commanding officer. Colonel Masanobu Tsuji issued an order in Homma's name that nearly led to the assassination of a Philippine Supreme Court justice and of the former speaker of the Philippine House of Representatives. Homma was informed of the unauthorised order just in time to prevent the tragic deaths of the officials.

When the defenders of Bataan and Corregidor surrendered in the spring of 1942, the Japanese expected to deal with roughly 25,000 prisoners. However, the number taken was substantially higher. There

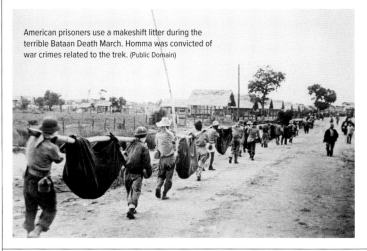

American prisoners use a makeshift litter during the terrible Bataan Death March. Homma was convicted of war crimes related to the trek. (Public Domain)

had been no planning or provision made to deal with such large numbers of POWs. To make matters worse, many of the captured men were ill with malaria and other tropical diseases. They were hungry, thirsty and exhausted. Their captors, for that matter, had suffered from the long jungle campaign and were not inclined to extend relief on a large scale.

During the course of the Death March, Japanese soldiers brutally beat and often executed prisoners on the spot. Those who broke ranks to drink water from a fetid ditch or mudhole were bayoneted or clubbed to death with rifle butts. Officers beheaded stragglers with their swords. One survivor of the infamous trek admitted that he would commit suicide rather than repeat the ordeal.

Shortly after the conclusion of the Philippine campaign, criticism of Homma's performance re-emerged. His desire for the lenient treatment of prisoners and civilians was the proximate cause of the demise of his military career and such action stands in stark contrast to the horror of the Death March that was apparently in progress around him. He was forced into retirement and lived in relative obscurity in Japan until the end of the war.

Homma was arrested by American authorities in December 1945 and charged with 48 counts of violating the international rules of war. Returned to the Philippines, he was tried in Manila from January 3 to February 11, 1946. He was supposedly shocked to hear reports of the inhumane treatment meted out by his soldiers in the Philippines and declared: "I am horrified to learn these things happened under my command. I am ashamed of our troops." He further explained that he had heard nothing of the mistreatment of prisoners until he appeared in court more than three years after the fact. Additionally, Homma stated that in the immediate aftermath of the surrender on Bataan, he was consumed with planning an assault on Corregidor and unaware of the poor treatment of the prisoners. He had assumed that staff officers were carrying out his directive to treat them well.

Although testimony was offered in support of Homma's position, witnesses also offered damning first-hand accounts of the harrowing Death March. One witness indicated that it was impossible for Homma not to be aware of the misery occurring on the route of the march just 500 feet from his headquarters.

The outcome of the trial was a foregone conclusion and some critics of the proceedings have asserted that Homma was convicted unjustly. The controversy persists to this day and relates directly to the degree of accountability Homma should have borne for the actions of subordinates far below his position in the chain of command.

The fact that Homma was allowed to be executed by firing squad, in the military sense a death more honourable than hanging, offered only cold comfort.

MARSHAL OF THE ROYAL AIR FORCE ARTHUR TEDDER

Air Chief Marshal Arthur Tedder in Italy while in command in the Mediterranean in 1943. (Public Domain)

Tedder stands to the right of General Dwight Eisenhower with Allied commanders, including Montgomery, Bradley and General William Simpson. (Creative Commons via Wikipedia)

One of the foremost Allied air commanders of World War Two, Marshal of the Royal Air Force Arthur Tedder began his military career as an infantryman. A fortuitous knee injury prompted a request for transfer to the Royal Flying Corps in the middle of the Great War and Tedder went on to high command during a military career of 38 years.

Tedder occupied the key role of Deputy Supreme Commander of the Allied Expeditionary Force, second only to General Dwight D Eisenhower in the chain of command during the preparation and execution of Operation Overlord, the Allied invasion of Normandy on June 6, 1944. He was known for his ability to co-operate with Britain's American allies and he forged a strong working relationship with Eisenhower, who wrote of Tedder: "Certainly in all matters of energetic operation, fitting into an allied team and knowledge of his job, he is tops. Moreover, he is a leader type."

A Scotsman, Tedder became well known for his advocacy of tactical air power and he capably commanded Allied air forces during the extensive campaigns in the Mediterranean theatre. His experience in planning major air operations, honed in North Africa, Sicily and Italy, prepared him for the task in Normandy. He proved capable of determining priorities, such as the German transportation system in France, crippling the enemy's ability to move troops and supplies in response to the D-Day landings.

From foot to flight

Arthur Tedder was born on July 11, 1890, at Glenguin, north of Glasgow. His father was a customs official and as a boy he grew up in various locations throughout Great Britain. He was a graduate of Cambridge and spent the summer of 1912 in Germany, becoming familiar with the language. In the autumn of 1913, he joined the Dorsetshire Regiment, commissioned in the reserve as a second lieutenant. In February 1914, he enlisted as a cadet with the colonial service and travelled to Fiji, returning after a brief stay when World War One broke out.

Early service with the Dorsetshire Regiment ended with the knee injury

and Tedder actively sought transfer to the Royal Flying Corps. This was accomplished only after several months and in January 1916, he entered No. 1 School of Aeronautics and then later Central Flying School. Promoted to captain, he earned his pilot's wings in June 1916 and was posted to No 25 Squadron on the Western Front. Flying the Bristol Scout C, the squadron performed reconnaissance flights and Tedder was a flight commander by August. He was elevated to major and given command of No 70 Squadron on January 1, 1917, followed by command of No 67 Squadron at mid-year.

By early 1918, Tedder was transferred to Egypt in command of the School of Navigation and Bomb Dropping. In June he was given command of the 38th Wing and elevation to lieutenant colonel followed.

During the interwar years, Tedder commanded No 274 Squadron, flying Handley Page V1500 bombers at RAF Bircham Newton. He attended the Royal Navy Staff College in 1923-1924 and was promoted to wing commander and head of No 2 Flying Training School. By the spring of 1934, he had served with the Directorate of Training at the Air Ministry, completed the Imperial Defence College, commanded the Air Armament School at RAF Eastchurch and achieved the rank of air commodore.

In the autumn of 1936, as rumours of war began to criss-cross the globe, Tedder was named Air Officer Commanding RAF Far Eastern Forces, with bases in the Indies, Hong Kong and Burma. In July 1937, he was promoted air vice marshal and a year later made Director General for Research with the Air Ministry. After the outbreak of World War Two, the Ministry of Aircraft Production absorbed Tedder's research and development command and strained relations with senior political figures facilitated a

Tedder at his desk in Cairo while commanding air forces in the Middle East. (Public Domain)

GENERAL HENRY 'HAP' ARNOLD

He was only a junior officer, but he was willing to display tremendous courage. It was not a combat situation, but Major Henry Harley Arnold would no doubt come under fire for his support of a 'heretic' among US Army Air Corps commanders.

The courtroom was tense with excitement during the court martial of General William 'Billy' Mitchell, on trial for insubordination. Assistant Chief of the US Air Service, Mitchell was an outspoken advocate of air power and a proponent of establishing an air service separate and autonomous from the US Army. He was vocal, direct and loud – a recipe for repercussions. As he lobbied for the recognition of the aircraft as a decisive weapon of war, Mitchell had gained the enmity of many, but he had also cultivated a following.

Among those who supported Mitchell, 'Hap' Arnold had been asked to testify on behalf of the accused during the proceedings. He had been warned that doing so would be detrimental to his career, but Arnold stood by his own convictions and followed through. Mitchell was found guilty in 1925 and, as expected, Arnold felt the repercussions of his support. Although their concepts of the aircraft in wartime were proven in the years to come, such was in the future.

Now, Arnold was in the crosshairs. He was offered the option to resign his commission or face his own court martial. He chose the latter, forcing the hand of the senior officers involved. Instead of another high-profile courtroom drama, they chose to banish Arnold to Fort Riley, Kansas and command of the 16th Observation Squadron, a backwater post far away from the epicentre of Air Corps activity and the controversy he had chosen to participate in. A derogatory entry was also placed in Arnold's personnel file. It read: "In an emergency, he is liable to lose his head."

Rather than wallowing in self-pity, Arnold served his time in exile and compiled an admirable record from that point forward. He was destined to emerge from the trauma as one of the most respected and visionary air leaders in American military history. In the twilight of his life, he was promoted to five-star General of the Army rank and subsequently held the same in the US Air Force, the only officer ever to achieve the rank in two service branches.

Good man rising

Hap Arnold was already something of a local celebrity before he embarked on a military career. Born in Gladwyne, Pennsylvania, on June 25, 1886, he took the entrance examination to the US Military Academy at West Point after his brother refused to do so and had disappointed their father, a prominent local physician. Although Hap's academic record was unremarkable, he did graduate in 1907 and receive a commission as a 2nd lieutenant.

His famous nickname 'Hap' was said to be short for 'Happy'. Some historians have asserted that his wife, Bee, was the originator, while others believe it came into common usage as he was working in silent films in the 1920s. Earlier in his life, Arnold was known by several other nicknames, including 'Sunny', according to family members. During his term at West Point, he was called 'Benny' and 'Pewt'. When he rose to the pinnacle of US air command, he was called simply, 'The Chief'.

Swiftly, Hap found that he did not like the infantry and petitioned for a transfer to the fledgling aviation section of the Signal Corps. He

General Henry 'Hap' Arnold was responsible for all US Army Air Forces activities during World War Two. (Public Domain)

then completed pilot training under Orville and Wilbur Wright, famed for their flight at Kitty Hawk, North Carolina, in 1903. A certified aviation pioneer, he received pilot certificate No 29 and military aviator certificate No 2.

Ironically, early in his career, Arnold actually developed a fear of flying. A fellow aviator, Al Welsh, was killed in a plane crash in June 1911 and Arnold began to have doubts about his own flying skills. Later, he crashed a plane in high winds in Massachusetts Bay, learned of another classmate's death in a crash and survived a second accident during an artillery spotting exercise. He grounded himself, took a leave of absence and then found the intestinal fortitude to conquer his fears, making his first solo flight in five years in November 1916.

Detailed to train new pilots, Arnold also set aerial records, first to carry US mail by air, first to fly over the US capitol building and established a new altitude mark at 3,260 feet. He did perform in two silent films as a young aviator. During World War One, he held staff positions in Washington DC and served in the Panama Canal Zone before boarding a ship for France. En route to Europe, he contracted influenza, recovering in time to reach the Western Front on November 11, 1918, the day the war ended.

While the hubbub surrounding the controversial Billy Mitchell had nearly cost him his career, Hap Arnold was headstrong and unwilling to bow out of the service. He worked to rehabilitate his reputation and found support, particularly from Chief of the Army Air Corps Major General James E Fechet. He was an excellent author and wrote numerous articles related to air power. His fitness reports reflected an intelligent, driven officer with potential and by 1928 he had gained a recommendation to the Command and General Staff School at Fort Leavenworth, Kansas, graduating in 1929.

Arnold was given command of March Field, California, in 1931 and his authority was expanded to include three

Right: Arnold as a young army officer while serving in the War Department in the spring of 1918. (Public Domain)

Below: General Billy Mitchell stands during his 1925 court martial. Arnold risked his career in support of the officer. (Public Domain)

zones of mail delivery operations. By
early 1935, he had reached the rank
of brigadier general, an astonishing
accomplishment for someone so highly
scrutinised, and assumed command of
the 1st Wing of General Headquarters
Air Force at March Field. Meanwhile,
he continued to advocate for a well-
equipped and well-trained bomber
force, believing that the aircraft
would be a decisive weapon in wars of
the future.

During the interwar years, one of
Arnold's greatest accomplishments was
the development of the Boeing B-17
Flying Fortress heavy bomber. Arnold
championed the B-17 and it became
a primary weapon of World War Two,
iconic in its performance. Along with
the Consolidated B-24 Liberator, the
B-17 served as the backbone of the
Eighth Air Force bombing campaign
and with other Allied air forces
during the war, delivering tremendous
bombloads on Axis targets.

By 1936, Arnold was a familiar
presence in the halls of power in
Washington DC. He rose to become
assistant chief of the Air Corps and was promoted to its command in
the autumn of 1938 with the rank of major general. Following US
entry into World War Two, General Arnold's title was revised to chief
of the Army Air Forces and he was promoted lieutenant general.

Leadership in war

Arnold was responsible for all Army Air Forces operations during
World War Two and from 1941-1945, the forces under his
command increased from 22,000 and just 3,900 aircraft to 2.5
million personnel in service and 75,000 combat, transport, and
auxiliary planes. Arnold was responsible for key appointments that
advanced the role of US air power during the war years. Among
them were General Carl 'Tooey' Spaatz, initial commander of the
Eighth Air Force in England, and General Ira C Eaker, commanding
Eighth Bomber Command and later Eighth Air Force and the
officer responsible for laying the foundation for US air operations
in Europe. Arnold also placed General Jimmy Doolittle, hero of
the bombing raid on Tokyo in 1942, in key command roles in the
Mediterranean and in England.

Through the course of World
War Two, Arnold was known for a
willingness to take risks, to remove
incompetent or ineffective commanders
and to stay the course through the
difficult days and the heavy losses in
planes and aircrew during the strategic
bombing offensive against Nazi
Germany. One of his most controversial
appointments was that of General Curtis
LeMay to lead the Twentieth Air Force
in the Pacific. LeMay unleashed waves
of Boeing B-29 Superfortress bombers,
based in the Marianas Islands, against
Japanese cities. The heavy firebomb
raids gutted Tokyo and other population
centres and the devastation raised
questions of the necessity of such raids.
Still, it may rationally be concluded that
the firebombing was responsible in part
for bringing about the surrender of the
Japanese Empire to end the war in 1945.

Above: A formation of US Army
Air Forces B-17 Flying Fortress
bombers heads for a target in
Nazi-occupied Europe in 1944.
(Public Domain)

Right: Shortly after World War Two,
Arnold poses wearing the rank of
General of the Army. (Public Domain)

Although he was plagued
by health issues during the
war years, including gastric ulcers that were the result of overwork
and stress and four heart attacks suffered between 1943 and 1945,
Arnold was also abroad, taking a lengthy tour of air installations
in North Africa, the Middle East, India and China. The trek was
35,000 miles long and the general attended high-level command
conferences as Allied grand strategy was shaped. He was promoted
to four-star general in March 1943. In early 1946, a bout of heart
arrhythmia forced the suspension of a trip to
South America and brought about retirement
after nearly four decades of military service.
Promoted to five-star General of the Army in
March of that year, the rank was changed to
General of the Air Force to reflect his role more
accurately. In 1947, to Arnold's delight, the US
Air Force became a separate and distinct arm of
the American military.

Arnold spent his last years at his ranch in
Sonoma, California and continued to write. As
his memoir, Global Mission, went to press in
1948, he suffered his fifth heart attack and spent
three months in hospital. In retrospect, it appears
that General Arnold had willingly sacrificed his
own health in the pursuit of Allied victory in
World War Two. He died at his home on January
15, 1950, at age 63 and was buried at Arlington
National Cemetery with full military honours.

Arnold sits at the controls of a training aircraft at the Wright Flying
School in Dayton, Ohio, 1911. (Public Domain)

GENERAL JIMMY DOOLITTLE

The twin engines of the North American B-25 Mitchell medium bomber sputtered and roared to life. Moments later, the US Army Air Forces plane was speeding down – of all things – the flight deck of the aircraft carrier USS *Hornet*.

The pilot, Lieutenant Colonel Jimmy Doolittle, throttled up and the bomber, never intended to operate from such a platform, dipped toward the wavetops, struggled against the winds and clawed its way skyward. Doolittle was the leader of 16 B-25 crews that were about to make a bold statement during the darkest days of World War Two for the United States.

On April 18, 1942, the American airmen executed the famous Doolittle Raid on the Japanese capital of Tokyo. Just four months after the devastating Japanese air raid on Pearl Harbor and other US military installations on the island of Oahu in Hawaii had brought the two nations to armed conflict, the American people received a badly needed morale boost. And Doolittle and company responded.

The raid did little physical damage, but the blow to the collective psyche of the Japanese high command reverberated across the remainder of the Pacific War. The Japanese had been convinced that no American bomber would threaten their home islands and the raid caused an abrupt reprioritisation of the empire's war aims. The defensive perimeter necessary to guard hard-won gains in the Pacific would have to be extended. The resulting operations to do so led to the setback at the Battle of Coral Sea in May 1942 and catastrophic defeat at the Battle of Midway, the turning point of the war, a month later.

Jimmy Doolittle and his intrepid raiders, therefore, own a large portion of credit for the turning of the tide of the war. But then, Doolittle had always been a risk taker.

General Jimmy Doolittle led the spectacular air raid on Tokyo on April 18, 1942. (Public Domain)

A rising star

Although he was just a lieutenant colonel, a relatively common offer rank in the US Army Air Forces, Jimmy Doolittle was an uncommon man. He was widely known as an officer with great potential, nerves of steel and a tremendous command presence. He was the obvious choice to lead the daring raid on Tokyo, most likely because senior officers knew that he was virtually fearless. He had already proven so.

Doolittle was born on December 14, 1896, in Alameda, California, and spent five early years in Alaska. The family returned to California when he was eight and he was educated in the public schools of Los Angeles. At a tender age, he took up boxing and he eventually gained a reputation as a formidable bantamweight along the West Coast. He considered a career as a mining engineer, but attending an air show in 1910 altered the course of his life. He became enamoured with flight and when the US entered World War One in April 1917, he set aside his pursuit of a degree in mine engineering and joined the Army Signal Corps Reserve as a flying cadet. He received a 2nd lieutenant's commission in the Signal Corps Aviation Section in March 1918 and earned his pilot's wings. Disappointed that he did not see combat during World War One, he served as a flight and gunnery instructor at Camp Dick, Texas, Wright Field, Ohio and other bases.

Two weeks after the Great War ended, Doolittle made his debut as a stunt pilot during an air show in San Diego. The pioneer aviator remained in the air service and received a degree from the University of California in 1922. In the same year, he embarked on the first of numerous hazardous cross-country flights. By the mid-1920s, he had received a doctorate of science degree from the prestigious Massachusetts Institute of Technology with emphasis on engineering.

Through the remainder of the decade, he performed as a stunt pilot and took up air racing. In 1925, he competed in the Schneider Cup races, piloting a borrowed US Navy Curtiss R3C2 floatplane, and won the international competition. On leave of absence from the army in 1926, he broke both ankles in a crash but continued to fly with them in casts. He continued making cross-country flights and became the first pilot to complete a dangerous outside loop aerial manoeuvre.

In 1930, Doolittle resigned his army commission and went to work for Shell Oil Company to manage its aviation department. Retaining his major's commission in the Reserve Officer Corps, he continued racing and won the Bendix Trophy in 1931, flying an average speed of 225mph. He also took the Harmon Trophy and piloted the

Doolittle stands with the Curtiss floatplane he flew to win the Schneider Trophy in 1925. (Public Domain)

Doolittle smiles before entering the cockpit of an aircraft pre-World War Two. (Public Domain)

Doolittle attaches his Japanese medal to a bomb prior to the April 18, 1942, raid on Tokyo. (Public Domain)

800-horsepower, stubby-winged GeeBee Super Sportster to claim the Thompson Trophy with an average speed topping 250mph. He retired from racing in 1933 and was elected president of the Institute of Aeronautical Sciences in 1940. A year later, as war loomed, he was recalled to active duty in the Army Air Corps with the rank of major.

Wings at war

Quickly promoted to lieutenant colonel, Doolittle was assigned to the headquarters of the Army Air Forces. At age 45, he was soon recommended for the most hazardous mission of an already risk-filled lifetime.

As senior army and US Navy officers put together the ambitious plan to strike back at the Japanese, they cut orders for the procurement of the necessary land-based B-25 bombers, believed to have the best opportunity for success if launched from the deck of an aircraft carrier, and passed the word that 24 five-man aircrews were sought from a pool of volunteers to train and possibly participate in a clandestine mission. The selected airmen were ordered to Eglin Air Base, Florida, for intense training in carrier take-offs. Doolittle took command and went through the training alongside the men.

To the casual observer, the mission looked like a suicide run. The bombers were to take off from the carrier, drop their modest bombloads on industrial and military targets in Tokyo and nearby cities, then fly on to airfields in China. There was no possibility for recovery aboard the carrier and fuel supplies would be nearly exhausted even if the pilots reached the Chinese airfields and they had not been overrun by Japanese ground troops in the intervening period.

And so, *Hornet* put to sea on April 2, 1942, passing from San Francisco Bay beneath the Golden Gate Bridge. Fifteen days later, all had been quiet. That is, until a Japanese patrol boat was spotted and in turn had surely spotted the US aircraft carrier and its escorts. Gunfire from the light cruiser USS *Nashville* quickly dispatched No 23 Nitto Maru, but it was likely that a radio report of *Hornet's* sighting had been sent to Tokyo.

On the horns of a dilemma, Doolittle met with Admiral William F 'Bull' Halsey, the task force commander, and Admiral Marc Mitscher, skipper of the *Hornet,* and the trio weighed its options. Aborting the mission was anathema. They could sail on to the anticipated launch position, risking attack by overwhelming Japanese forces, or commence launching right where they were, 200 miles further away from Japan and 10 hours earlier than anticipated. They unanimously decided to launch as quickly as possible.

Doolittle assembled his airmen, informed them of the change in plans and attached a medal given to him by the Japanese

government in peacetime to one of the bombs, returning it to sender. At 8.20am, he roared off the flight deck of *Hornet* into overcast skies and circled while the rest of the bombers joined up. The B-25s flew low, hugging the coastline of Honshu and surprise was complete. Schoolchildren waved to the planes from their playgrounds while citizens shuffled through the streets of Tokyo, ignoring the now familiar drone of engines from above.

The American bombers swept in, dropped their bombs and then headed off to an uncertain fate. The Japanese response was negligible, a few puffs of anti-aircraft fire and the arrival of defensive fighter planes was too late.

Meanwhile, the raiders made for China. As the saga unfolded, one plane landed at Vladivostok in the Soviet Union, its crew interned for the duration of the war. Unable to raise the friendly airfield at Chuchow, Doolittle parachuted into a rice paddy. Other B-25s, their fuel tanks also drained, ditched in the sea or crash landed. Miraculously, only one man of the 80 participants was killed. The Japanese captured eight fliers, paraded them before a kangaroo court and then flew them to Tokyo, where three were beheaded and one died in prison.

Doolittle and the remaining raiders managed to get out of China with the help of friendly villagers along the way. Sadly, the Japanese terrorised the civilian population and committed many atrocities

In 1985, President Ronald Reagan and Senator Barry Goldwater pin the four-star rank of full general on the uniform of Jimmy Doolittle (Public Domain)

during their search for the Americans. Doolittle believed that he would face harsh criticism when he returned to the US, thinking that the raid was a failure because of the losses in aircraft and personnel. He was wrong.

Doolittle was a national hero and received the Medal of Honour for heroism. The other 79 raiders received the Distinguished Service Cross, the nation's second-highest award for valour. Doolittle rose to the rank of general during the war and went on to command Twelfth Air Force in North Africa, Fifteenth Air Force in the Mediterranean and Eighth Air Force in Britain. After the war, he returned to reserve status and rejoined Shell Oil.

The Doolittle Raid altered the course of World War Two in the Pacific and when a reporter asked President Franklin D Roosevelt where the planes had come from, he grinned broadly and replied: "Shangri-La." Of course, he knew the truth and he revered the stout-hearted leader of a courageous group of airmen.

Jimmy Doolittle attended many social functions and spoke publicly on numerous occasions during his later years. An aviation pioneer whose career spanned the earliest of flights to the Space Age, he died on September 27, 1993. He was 96.

Doolittle went on to command air forces in North Africa, the Mediterranean and Britain during World War Two. (Public Domain)

AIR CHIEF MARSHAL HUGH DOWDING

Few historians, if any, would argue against the assertion that the individual most responsible for the resounding Royal Air Force victory in the Battle of Britain was Air Chief Marshal Hugh Dowding.

Head of RAF Fighter Command since its inception in 1936, the outbreak of World War Two had postponed the retirement of the 58-year-old Dowding in June 1939. At the request of Winston Churchill, he agreed to stay on until March 1940. When the Battle of Britain started, his term was extended until July and then until November. During the previous four years with Fighter Command, Dowding had prepared the island nation's air defences meticulously, possibly becoming the most important military man in Britain during the darkest days of the conflict.

When Britain stood alone against the German armed forces, Dowding directed much of the RAF response to the Nazi air offensive intended to establish control of the skies above the English Channel in preparation for Operation Sea Lion, the anticipated seaborne invasion of the British Isles.

During the run-up to the decisive air battle, fought July 10 to October 31, 1940, Dowding had organised Fighter Command into four sectors under group commanders. Air Vice Marshal Quintin Brand led 10 Group in Wales and southwest England, while 11 Group under Air Vice Marshal Keith Park was responsible for London and southeast England, 12 Group under Air Vice Marshal Trafford Leigh-Mallory covered northern England, East Anglia and the industrial Midlands and 13 Group under Air Vice Marshal Richard Saul took Northern Ireland, parts of northern England and southern Scotland. Each group was divided into sectors with main airfields identified as sector stations with huts constructed as operations centres to direct fighters on courses to intercept enemy air attacks.

Dowding had previously advocated the modernisation of the RAF with state-of-the art metal monoplane fighters during the 1930s. The result was the development and manufacture of the Supermarine Spitfire and Hawker Hurricane models, icons of the Battle of Britain that fought Nazi Messerschmitt Me-109 fighters and Heinkel, Dornier and Junkers bombers for air supremacy. Perhaps most importantly, he established an early warning radar network, referred to as Chain Home, that provided critical notice to Fighter Command bases and allowed pilots to scramble to meet German air raids at the most advantageous time and place and in sufficient strength to put up a stout fight.

Because of his rather brusque demeanour, Air Chief Marshal Dowding was known as 'Stuffy'. He was the senior

Air Chief Marshal Hugh Dowding appears all business in this wartime portrait. Dowding's preparation of air defences and adroit deployment of Fighter Command contributed substantially to RAF victory in the Battle of Britain. (Public Domain)

officer serving with the RAF at the time of the Battle of Britain. When the air battle was won and the threat of German invasion began to wane, Dowding was removed from command in the midst of an internal power struggle. It was an end not befitting a true hero, visionary and focused military man who had rendered such great service to his country.

Early years
Hugh Dowding was born in Moffat, Scotland, on April 24, 1882, the son of a teacher. He was educated at St. Ninian's School and Winchester College before entering the Royal Military Academy Woolwich. He received a 2nd lieutenant's commission in the Royal Garrison Artillery in August 1900. He served overseas with the artillery in Ceylon, Hong Kong and Gibraltar and then with No 7 Mountain Artillery Battery in India before returning to England to attend the Army Staff College in 1912.

A year later, the young officer was promoted captain and soon he became fascinated with flight. Obtaining his aviator's certificate at the Vickers School of Flying in late 1913, he subsequently attended Central Flying School and received his pilot's wings. He was briefly added to the Royal Flying Corps reserve list, returning to his artillery post, and then called to duty with RFC No 7 Squadron at the outbreak of World War One.

During the Great War, Dowding commanded several squadrons, as well as the Wireless Experimental Establishment at Brooklands. Promoted to major in December 1915, he held various commands in Britain for the remainder of the war as a series of promotions reaching brigadier general followed.

Wearing civilian clothes and a bowler hat, Dowding stands with a group of RAF pilots, just a few of the valiant airmen who won the Battle of Britain. (Public Domain)

Between the world wars, Dowding received a permanent commission in the RAF, assuming the rank of group captain. He was appointed chief of staff for RAF Iraq in the summer of 1924 and two years later director of training with the Air Ministry. At the end of the decade, he was an air vice marshal with administrative responsibilities in air fighter defence and then supply and research. In 1933 he was promoted to air vice marshal and three years later appointed head of Fighter Command. In this highly visible post, he began to develop the Dowding System, which integrated the use of radar (then known as RDF or Radio Direction Finding), observers watching the skies, central plotting and tracking of incoming air raids and radio communication and vectoring of aircraft.

Dowding strolls with King George VI and Queen Elizabeth on September 1, 1940. (Public Domain)

Proving the system

With the Battle of Britain looming, the Dowding System was put to the test. Its most innovative feature was the Chain Home radar system, which consisted of as many as 56 towers standing 240 feet high and ringing the eastern and southern coasts of Britain. As their radio waves stretched 150 miles across the Channel and into occupied France, the radar apparatus could detect approaching aircraft at altitudes from 1,000ft to 30,000ft.

Dowding addresses the crowd at RAF Biggin Hill during the laying of the cornerstone for the Royal Air Force chapel, now St. George's Chapel of Remembrance, in 1951. (Public Domain)

In sequence, telephone operators at RDF stations transmitted information on incoming aircraft, including speed, course, estimated number and range, to the filter room at Fighter Command headquarters, Bentley Priory, Stanmore, Middlesex. Operations personnel called tellers then passed information from the filter room to the underground operations room and then to the affected groups and sectors. The raids were tracked on large maps with blocks and arrows indicated the incoming enemy. Squadrons of fighters were then alerted and scrambled to meet the threat.

In the event, RAF Spitfires and Hurricanes shot down so many black-crossed Luftwaffe planes that the threat of Nazi invasion was thwarted. In his landmark History of the Second World War, Churchill praised Dowding's creation. "All the ascendancy of the Hurricanes and Spitfires would have been fruitless but for this system which had been devised and built before the war. It had been shaped and refined in constant action and all was now fused together into the most elaborate instrument of war, the like of which existed nowhere in the world."

Big wing brouhaha

At the moment of supreme victory for the RAF in the Battle of Britain, internal strife came to a head. A continuing argument over effective tactics had festered for some time even as the enemy wolf was at the proverbial British door. The essence of the internal discord lay in the conduct of the Battle of Britain and in the future of the RAF. Dowding and Park, whose 11 Group had faced the brunt of the Luftwaffe onslaught, opposed Leigh-Mallory and Air Vice Marshal William Sholto Douglas, Deputy Chief of the Air Staff.

This statue of Air Chief Marshal Hugh Dowding stands at St Clement Danes, the Strand, London. (Creative Commons Elliott Brown via Wikipedia)

The main issue surrounded the concept of the Big Wing, advocated by Leigh-Mallory and Douglas along with fighter ace and national hero Douglas Bader, and the tactic endorsed by Dowding and Park, who appreciated the fact that RAF fighters were the first line of defence against the Luftwaffe and understood that the supply of planes and trained pilots was limited. Dowding and Park favoured the deployment of individual squadrons subjecting the enemy to continual attack while their formations were broken up and stragglers shot down.

The other faction favoured large formations of fighters, three to five squadrons, massed to meet the oncoming Germans over the Channel, hopefully inflicting substantial damage on the raiders before they dropped their cargoes of destruction on airfields, radar installations, industrial targets or British cities.

Dowding believed it was crucial to maintain a fighter reserve and that the Big Wing theory would put too many fighters at risk at the same time, resulting in losses that Fighter Command might find unsustainable. To make matters worse, Park and Leigh-Mallory did not get along, perhaps a result of Leigh-Mallory's jealousy over Dowding's appointment of Park to No 11 Group.

While the Big Wing debate rages even today, Dowding was also criticised for failing to develop effective night fighter defences as the horror of the Blitz developed in late 1940. Using Big Wing and night fighters as levers, Dowding's critics clamoured for his relief even as the Battle of Britain was underway. Dowding, however, stuck to the business at hand and seemed either unconcerned or oblivious to the internal hubbub.

On October 17, 1940, Douglas, who some say kept stirring the pot as he jockeyed for Dowding's job, presided over a meeting at the Air Ministry. It devolved into a scathing indictment of Dowding's tactical command methods – and Park was guilty by association. Secretary of State for Air Archibald Sinclair and Air Chief Marshal Charles Portal, newly appointed Chief of the Air Staff, supported the Big Wing faction and though Churchill defended Dowding early in the dust-up, he acquiesced when the time to make a command change occurred.

On November 25, 1940, Dowding was relieved of his duties without fanfare or further discussion. Douglas rapidly took over as head of Fighter Command and Dowding, it was said, greeted his successor on the day of the transition with only an abrupt: "Good morning." Leigh-Mallory took command of No 11 Group as Park was shunted away from meaningful command. Park's transfer was the epitome of collateral damage in a drama that had all the makings of a Shakespearean tragedy.

Dowding, considered a member of the RAF 'Old Guard', was dispatched to the US on behalf of the Ministry of Aircraft Production. He retired from active service in 1942, following a 42-year career in which he had been showered with honours. A peerage as 1st Baron Dowding followed in 1943. In his later years, one of the truest heroes of the Battle of Britain became interested in spiritualism and an advocate of animal rights. He died at age 87, on February 15, 1970.

During observances of the third anniversary of the Battle of Britain in 1943, Dowding salutes while standing next to his rival Air Marshal Trafford Leigh-Mallory at Bentley Priory. (Public Domain)

MARSHAL OF THE ROYAL AIR FORCE ARTHUR HARRIS

At the inception of the Royal Air Force bombing campaign that laid waste to German cities during World War Two, Air Chief Marshal Arthur 'Bomber' Harris quoted the Bible, specifically Hosea 8:7.

Aircraft of the Nazi Luftwaffe had ravaged cities across Europe and subjected Britain to the horror of the Blitz. Harris declared in early 1942: "The Nazis entered this war under the rather childish delusion that they were going to bomb everyone else and nobody was going to bomb them. At Rotterdam, London, Warsaw and half a hundred other places they put their rather naïve theory into operation. They sowed the wind and now they are going to reap the whirlwind."

From his appointment to lead RAF Bomber Command in February 1942 through to the end of the war, Harris did his utmost to deliver on that promise. Early raids were limited due to the dearth of available aircraft – the RAF had only 349 bombers at the outbreak of war in 1939. Harris, however, continually pressed for more and better planes, capable of delivering heavier bombloads, and pressed for raids that would include 1,000 or more aircraft. This impressive number was achieved in May 1942 with a large-scale raid on the German city of Cologne. As the war progressed, the US Eighth Air Force joined the campaign against targets in Nazi-occupied Europe and into the Third Reich.

Losses were heavy at times, but Harris persevered. In doing so, he became one of the most controversial figures to emerge amid the Allied command structure during the war. He remained a believer in the war-winning capacity of strategic bombing and asserted that the round-the-clock offensive against German industry, military targets and population centres alone could win the war. While such belief was proved misguided, there is no doubt that the bombing offensive hastened the end of the war.

In the event, however, there was criticism not only regarding RAF losses in planes and personnel, but also in the continued bombing of German cities, which caused civilian casualties to steadily mount. For example, in the summer of 1943, Bomber Command and the Eighth Air Force executed Operation Gomorrah. Beginning July 24, they bombed Hamburg, the second-largest city in Germany, for eight days and seven horrific nights. The heart of the city was devastated by a resulting firestorm and estimates of civilian casualties reached 40,000 to 60,000 men, women, and children.

In October 1943, Harris felt compelled to explain to the British people the rationale for the bombing effort and proposed such an outreach to government officials. He commented: "The aim of the Combined Bomber Offensive should be unambiguously stated. The destruction of German cities, the killing of German workers and the destruction of civilised life throughout Germany, the destruction of houses,

A stern and resolute Air Chief Marshal Arthur 'Bomber' Harris sits at his desk at Bomber Command headquarters. (Public Domain)

public utilities, transport and lives, the creation of a refugee problem on an unprecedented scale and the breakdown of morale both at home and at the battle fronts by fear of extended and intensified bombing, are accepted and intended aims of our bombing policy. They are not by-products of attempts to hit factories." There it was. Frank and brutal.

Making an air officer
Arthur Harris was an adventurer from the start. Born in Cheltenham on April 13, 1892, he was the son of an engineer and architect in the Indian Civil Service. He was educated in Britain while his parents were in India and at the age of 17, defied his father's wishes by travelling to Rhodesia and working as a gold miner, farmer and coach driver.

His father had hoped Arthur would enlist in the army and with the outbreak of World War One, he joined the 1st Rhodesian Regiment, fighting the Germans in Africa. By 1915, he had returned to England and joined the Royal Flying Corps. He trained at Brooklands, received promotion to flying officer in 1916 and served in posts in Britain before deployment to France in 1917 as a flight commander and then commanding officer of No 45 Squadron. Flying the famed Sopwith Camel and Strutter aircraft, he destroyed five German planes before returning to Britain to command No 44 Squadron.

During the inter-war years, Harris became station commander at RAF Digby and then served in India, Iraq and Iran. He once became disenchanted with his choice to remain with the RAF and in 1922 decided to tender his resignation. However, colleagues persuaded him to remain in the service rather than return to Rhodesia. The decision proved fortuitous and by the summer of 1927, he had been promoted wing commander.

Harris attended the Army Staff College, Camberley, from 1927 to 1929. He commanded a flying boat squadron and developed night

Left: This portrait of Arthur 'Bomber' Harris dates to 1943 and the height of Bomber Command activity. (Public Domain)

Right: The devastation wrought on the German city of Dresden by RAF and US Army Air Forces bombers in February 1945, is readily apparent. (Creative Commons Deutsche Fotothek via Wikipedia)

flying procedures and was promoted group captain in June 1933. He served as Deputy Director of Plans with the Air Ministry and in Egypt as senior air staff officer with Middle East Command. In 1938 he was placed in command of the bombers of No 4 Group and the following year he was promoted air vice marshal while serving as Officer Commanding RAF in Palestine.

The storm breaks

Just as Harris returned to Britain in September 1939 to take command of No 5 Group, World War Two broke out. Within months he was named deputy chief of the air staff and promotion to air marshal followed in the spring of 1941.

Concerns were raised regarding the accuracy of the RAF bombing effort early in the war and in August 1941, the Butt Report brought rather dismal news – just slightly more than 30 percent of the bombers sent on hazardous missions were getting within five miles of their assigned targets. In response, Harris was handed responsibility for the future of Bomber Command.

Through the course of the war, RAF bombers meted out destruction on a grand scale but paid a heavy price during continual nocturnal raids, as did the US Eighth Air Force, its commanders opting to bomb in daylight with the hope of improving their own accuracy. Harris ordered a prolonged air assault against the German capital of Berlin, lasting from November 1943 to March 1944. Also in March, the bombers hit Nuremberg but absorbed brutal losses with 94 bombers shot down and 71 damaged from a complement of 795 planes.

During the preparations for the D-Day landings of June 6, 1944, Harris protested an order to switch target prioritisation to the rail and road transport network in France. Although the idea was to interdict German movement of troops and supplies to Normandy to defend against the Allied landings, he believed the refocus from cities and industrial targets would only allow a resurgence of German manufacturing output.

Once the Allies were firmly established on the European continent, Harris was redirected to resume the earlier tactic of area saturation

Harris listens to the debriefing of Wing Commander Guy Gibson's aircrew following the famous Dam Buster Raid by No 617 Squadron RAF. (Public Domain)

Harris receives the Soviet Order of Suvorov at the embassy in London, 1944. (Public Domain)

Harris and other RAF officers examine a map of Germany during World War Two. (Public Domain)

bombing. He was promoted air chief marshal in August 1944 and six months later the combined Allied bombing offensive conducted the most controversial series of air raids of World War Two in Europe.

Despite the rain of bombs that had fallen on other German cities, Dresden had been virtually unscathed. That changed dramatically on the night of February 13, 1945. Waves of RAF bombers touched off a firestorm that inflicted thousands of civilian casualties and US Army Air Force planes added to the conflagration by day. Questions as to the military necessity of bombing Dresden emerged, but the response indicated that there were valid reasons for the devastating raids.

Harris was resolute, responding to critics who questioned the rationale behind the Dresden affair: "No doubt in the past we were justified in attacking German cities. But to do so was always repugnant and now that the Germans are beaten anyway we can properly abstain from proceeding with these attacks. This is a doctrine to which I could never subscribe. Attacks on cities like any other act of war are intolerable unless they are strategically justified. But they are strategically justified insofar as they tend to shorten the war and preserve the lives of Allied soldiers. I do not personally regard the whole of the remaining cities of Germany as worth the bones of one British Grenadier."

But Churchill felt the growing pressure to end the heavy bombing of German cities during the final weeks of the war. He told Harris bluntly: "It seems to me that the moment has come when the question of bombing German cities simply for the sake of increasing the terror should be reviewed. Otherwise we shall come into control of an utterly ruined land."

When the war ended in May 1945, Harris and RAF Bomber Command had left their mark on Germany and on modern history. Harris retired from active service in September 1945 and was promoted Marshal of the Royal Air Force the following year. He wrote the book Bomber Offensive in 1947, detailing the saga of Bomber Command in wartime. He was dismayed that the moral and ethical debate over area saturation bombing and the bombing of enemy population centres remained robust in peacetime. He lived in South Africa from 1946 to 1953 and in that year was made a baronet after declining a peerage.

Harris died at his home on Oxfordshire eight days before his 92nd birthday on April 5, 1984. However, his legacy remains one of controversy. When the Bomber Harris Trust, a veterans' organisation, decided to erect a statue of the air leader outside the RAF Church of St Clement Danes, in London in 1992, a wave of protest occurred. Queen Elizabeth II dedicated the statue, but protesters shouted accusations that Harris had been a war criminal.

Such is the terrible tale of woe that follows the great human tragedy of modern war.

AIR CHIEF MARSHAL TRAFFORD LEIGH-MALLORY

With the Allied victory in the Normandy campaign in hand, Trafford Leigh-Mallory was impatient. He had received promotion to air chief marshal and a new post as Air Commander-in-Chief South East Asia Command (SEAC). His work as the Commander-in-Chief Allied Expeditionary Air Forces in preparation for and support of the D-Day landings of June 6, 1944, had gone well.

Now, on November 14, he was ready to board the Avro York aircraft, along with his wife Doris, for the first leg of the long flight from England to SEAC headquarters in Burma, but the pilot and aircrew were hesitant. The weather was rough over the French Alps and they warned Leigh-Mallory to wait for conditions to improve. The plane took off and a short while later crashed into a French mountainside, killing everyone aboard.

Air Chief Marshal Trafford Leigh-Mallory posed for this portrait shortly before his death in an aircraft crash in 1944. (Public Domain)

A formal inquiry found that the weather had indeed been the proximate cause of the tragic crash and concluded that the flight had been taken at unnecessary risk. And so, the 30-year career of the heroic and controversial Leigh-Mallory came to an abrupt end.

Life and times

Leigh-Mallory was 52 years old at the time of his death and had spent well over half his life in the military. Born on July 11, 1892, at Mobberley, Cheshire, he was the son of the local rector and a practising Christian all his life, growing up in prosperity with a large home and servants. He attended Cambridge and intended to become a barrister, but the outbreak of World War One changed his immediate plans.

Commissioned a 2nd lieutenant in the Lancashire Fusiliers, Leigh-Mallory trained as an officer and reached the Western Front in the spring of 1915. He was wounded at the Second Battle of Ypres and after recovering transferred to the Royal Flying Corps. He flew bombing and reconnaissance missions with No 7 Squadron and by November 1917 was in command of No 8 Squadron and received the Distinguished Service Order.

Remaining in the service after the war ended, Leigh-Mallory was promoted to wing commander in 1925 and attended the Army Staff College, Camberley, in 1930. He was elevated to air commodore in early 1936 while posted to Iraq, returning to Britain a year later to command No 12 Group in Air Chief Marshal Hugh Dowding's recently formed Fighter Command. Promotion to air vice marshal came in November 1938.

As war became imminent, Leigh-Mallory was one of four Fighter Command group leaders. He may well have felt slighted when Dowding appointed Air Vice Marshal Keith Park to lead No 11 Group as the Battle of Britain approached, realising that Park's squadrons around London and environs would do most of the fighting against the marauding Luftwaffe, while No 12 Group was intended largely to provide flank support in the industrial Midlands and protect the No 11 Group airfields.

At the same time, Leigh-Mallory and Air Vice Marshal Sholto Douglas advocated the concept of the Big Wing during the Battle of Britain. They asserted that massing three to five squadrons of fighters to intercept German air raids would inflict heavy losses at a distance from targets and offer the best prospect to neutralise the enemy threat. Dowding and Park disagreed. They reasoned that trained pilots and first-rate aircraft such as the Supermarine Spitfire and Hawker Hurricane were relatively scarce, favoured the deployment of individual squadrons to attack with more precision, and believed massed formations of fighters in combat would lead to heavier losses.

Leigh-Mallory and Park developed an enmity for one another and in league with Douglas, Leigh-Mallory actively sought the removal of Park from command. The ensuing rivalry distracted the senior RAF command at a critical time during the Battle of Britain, but when the Luftwaffe was defeated and the threat of an imminent invasion of the British Isles had subsided, Air Chief Marshal Charles Portal did remove Dowding and Park from command. Douglas became the head of Fighter Command and Leigh-Mallory took over No 11 Group.

Leigh-Mallory introduced the Big Wing concept with No 11 Group and though losses increased amid large fighter sweeps over enemy-controlled territory, he continued to advocate the concept. He succeeded Douglas as chief of Fighter Command in November 1942 and was promoted air marshal in January 1944, three months after being named to lead the Allied Expeditionary Air Forces for the Normandy invasion. His appointment was made largely on the basis of experience co-operating with army ground forces.

Subordinate to General Dwight D Eisenhower, Allied Supreme commander, Leigh-Mallory voiced his misgivings concerning the airborne phase of Operation Overlord. However, he successfully executed the Transportation Plan, intended to cripple the Germans' ability to move reinforcements by road and rail to reinforce defences in Normandy, and he was praised for his inter-service cooperation as Allied forces pushed inland from the D-Day landing beaches.

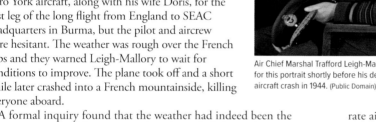

Above left: Leigh-Mallory pauses during activities at No 11 Group headquarters in Uxbridge, Middlesex. (Public Domain)

Above right: Leigh-Mallory addresses a group of pilots during a briefing in France in September 1944. (Public Domain)

Following a meeting at the Air Ministry in London, Leigh-Mallory exits the building. (Public Domain)

GENERAL BERNARD FREYBERG

Some British officers were miffed. The New Zealand soldiers they encountered rarely saluted. It was an annoying breach of military protocol, but when they approached the Kiwis' commanding officer, General Bernard Freyberg, he responded nonchalantly: "Just give them a wave and they will wave back."

Freyberg was British born but will forever be associated with New Zealand. By the time he came to command British and Commonwealth forces in the Mediterranean, including action in Crete, North Africa and Italy, he was well acquainted with the perils of combat. Wounded in the Great War, he held the coveted Victoria Cross, Britain's highest decoration for valour, and a remarkable three awards of the Distinguished Service Order (DSO). There was no question that Freyberg exhibited personal bravery – however, his tactical command skills sometimes led to criticism.

In Crete he failed to organise a counter-attack for 36 hours after the initial insertion of German airborne troops at Maleme airfield. At length, the island was lost and the Commonwealth forces under Freyberg's command there were either forced to evacuate or collected and sent into German captivity. Winston Churchill penned a critical letter to his adviser General Hastings Ismay, asserting that the slow response had contributed to the loss of the eastern Mediterranean island. Freyberg also absorbed some blame for the loss of Greece.

Nevertheless, Freyberg led the 2nd New Zealand Division capably in North Africa during the Second Battle of El Alamein and persevered at Monte Cassino during the desperate fighting against the Nazi Gustav Line. Freyberg did have the respect of Churchill, who called the general 'the Salamander' because of his ability to come through fire and survive.

General Bernard Freyberg was one of the most highly decorated general officers in the history of the British Army. (Creative Commons Archives of New Zealand via Wikipedia)

and he went on to participate in the abortive Dardanelles campaign in 1915. He was wounded more than once at Gallipoli and soon transferred to the British Army and the Queen's Royal West Surrey Regiment.

During the bloody Battle of the Somme in 1916, Freyberg played a key role in the capture of the village of Beaucourt and this action led to his Victoria Cross. He led his troops under heavy fire to take the town and capture 500 German prisoners. And out front as usual, Freyberg suffered two more combat wounds.

Promoted to brigadier at the end of the Great War, Freyberg remained in the military post-war and attended the Army Staff College, Camberley in 1920-1921. He represented New Zealand on the International Olympic Committee and was elevated to major general in July 1934 while posted to the War Office. Because of his many wounds, he was classified as unfit for active service in 1937. However, the coming of World War Two revived his field command opportunities and he received charge of the 2nd New Zealand Expeditionary Force and the 2nd New Zealand Division in 1939.

Freyberg was given command of all Commonwealth forces in Greece in the spring of 1941 and his concerns regarding a possible amphibious landing on Crete likely caused his delayed response to the German airborne assault there. Still, the situation was probably untenable from the start and he managed to maintain his reputation as a capable division-level tactician. Freyberg was a key leader in the resurgence of the British Eighth Army in North Africa. Wounded at Mersa Matruh in June, he returned to duty in time to perform outstanding service during the pivotal Second Battle of El Alamein. During the Italian campaign, he argued controversially for the bombing of the Abbey of Monte Cassino, believing the Germans had fortified the ancient monastery. The enemy did occupy the ruins of the structure after it was bombed.

In the autumn of 1945, Freyberg accepted the call to become Governor-General of New Zealand. He served in that capacity until 1952. He was appointed Deputy Constable and Lieutenant Governor of Windsor Castle upon his return to Britain the next year. He died on July 4, 1963, from complications of one of his many war wounds.

Freyberg wears a helmet on the front line during the fighting in Crete, May 1941. (Public Domain)

A military life

Bernard Freyberg was born in Richmond, Surrey and moved with his family to New Zealand at the age of two. He was a champion swimmer, attended Wellington College and established a dental practice while participating in the local Territorial Army unit's training.

In 1914, Freyberg travelled to the US, visiting San Francisco and then to Mexico. Rumours that he served under Mexican outlaw Pancho Villa are unsubstantiated, but no clear reason for his stay in North America is known. It is clear, though, that World War One compelled him to go to England. Churchill, then First Lord of the Admiralty, granted Freyberg a commission in the Royal Naval Volunteer Reserve

Above left: Freyberg in Italy in January 1944. He was an advocate for the bombing of Monte Cassino. (Public Domain)

Above right: Freyberg cuts the figure of the fighting commander in this portrait by artist Peter McIntyre. (Creative Commons Archives of New Zealand via Wikipedia)

GENERAL MILES DEMPSEY

Perhaps no other key senior commander during World War Two in Europe discharged his duties with less fanfare that General Miles Dempsey, commander of the British Second Army during the great campaigns of the conflict.

Dempsey was a quiet man who felt no need for the limelight and adulation sought by so many of his contemporaries. Nicknamed Bimbo, he discharged his duties capably and efficiently from the battlefields of France to the Italian campaign and back again. Dempsey was the handpicked subordinate of Field Marshal Bernard Montgomery, whose fame is everlasting in the wake of world war – and while Dempsey's service remains in the shadows to this day, his commander was quick to acknowledge the contribution of Second Army to the ultimate victory.

On May 8, 1945, Montgomery penned a handwritten letter of thanks to Dempsey. It read in part: "My Dear Bimbo, I feel that on this day I would like to write you a personal word of thanks for all you have done for me since we first served together in this war. As a Corps Commander in the Eighth Army and as an Army Commander in 21 Army Group, you have done your job in a way that is beyond all praise. No-one can ever have a more loyal subordinate than I have had in you. I want you to know that I am deeply grateful."

Dempsey had indeed earned the praise from Montgomery, leading British and Commonwealth troops in action against Axis forces on and off for six years. He displayed considerable understanding of both the strategic and tactical situations at any given time and proved adroit in the execution of combined arms warfare. Professional and dedicated, Dempsey deserves recognition as a quiet hero of World War Two.

Dempsey and staff pose with their mascot, Tiny, in France, in late 1939. (Public Domain)

Dempsey (right) and General Bernard Paget sit in the turret of a Crusader tank during 42nd Division manoeuvres. (Public Domain)

Tragedy and turning

Miles Dempsey was the youngest of three sons, born December 15, 1896 to an insurance broker and the daughter of an army major general. When the boy was six years old, his father committed suicide and the family moved from Cheshire to Crawley, Sussex. A good athlete, he played cricket and football at Shrewsbury School and attended officers training at Rugeley, reaching the rank of sergeant on the eve of World War One. In October 1914, he gained admission to the Royal Military Academy, Sandhurst and the following February was commissioned a second lieutenant of the Royal Berkshire Regiment.

Lieutenant Dempsey reached the Western Front with the 1st Battalion, Royal Berkshires, in June 1916. He commanded a platoon during the bloody Battle of the Somme a month later and survived heavy combat in which his battalion lost eight officers and scores of other ranks killed or wounded. As a company commander that autumn, he experienced heavy fighting again but emerged without injury. A staff appointment at headquarters of II Corps was followed by another field command, Captain Dempsey leading Company A, 1st Royal Berkshires during the Battle of Cambrai.

In the spring of 1918, the Germans launched their last desperate offensive in the west and Dempsey was one of 250 soldiers evacuated after being gassed.

He was brought back to England and underwent surgery to remove a hopelessly damaged lung.

General Miles Dempsey, commander of the British Second Army, sat for this portrait in April 1944. (Public Domain)

Following such a debilitating injury, he nevertheless returned to the Royal Berkshires and served until the armistice of November 11, 1918. He received the Military Cross for valour.

Between the wars

Remaining with the Royal Berkshires, Dempsey was posted to the army of occupation in Germany and in 1919 he resumed his athletic pursuits with lively cricket matches. By the autumn of 1920, the 1st Battalion was in the Middle East, posted to Iran and then moved to India, where Dempsey commanded an infantry company.

Returning to Britain for the first time in three years, the young officer assumed command of a company at Sandhurst, remaining until 1927 when he returned to Germany as an officer of the British Army of the Rhine and spent leisurely days visiting old battlefields and travelling around the countryside on a bicycle. He continued to play cricket, football and other sports in Germany and after his 2nd Battalion, Royal Berkshires, returned to Britain in 1928.

Attending the Army Staff College, Camberley in 1930-1931, Dempsey went on to a staff officer post with Military Secretary Major General Sidney Clive. In 1934, he was appointed brigade major of the 5th Infantry Brigade.

By October 1938, Dempsey's 1st Battalion, Royal Berkshires was assigned to 6th Brigade, 2nd Infantry Division. The following September, as World War Two broke out, it was deployed to

Dempsey (left) discusses troop dispositions in Sicily with staff officers, 1943. (Public Domain)

France with the British Expeditionary Force. At age 42, Dempsey was promoted brigadier, the youngest in the British Army and given command of the 13th Infantry Brigade.

Wartime command

On May 10, 1940, the German Army unleashed Case Yellow (Fall Gelb), ending months of relative inactivity on the Western Front, with an onslaught through the Ardennes Forest with armoured spearheads driving to the English Channel coast in mere days and threatening to cut off Allied forces to the north.

Dempsey's brigade fought a heroic delaying action at the River Scarpe during the withdrawal from the Dyle Line and at the end of the month, it held the line allowing the 3rd Division, commanded by General Montgomery, to withdraw to new positions. The retreat to Dunkirk followed and the brigade rendered critical service with the rear guard that allowed thousands of BEF troops to reach the evacuation beaches. The remnants of 13th Brigade reached safety in England in early June, with only 500 effectives remaining from an original complement of 3,000 soldiers.

Dempsey received the Distinguished Service Order, held a general staff liaison post to the Canadian Corps, attained major general rank and took command of the 46th Infantry Division in June 1941. Four months later, he took the 42nd Division as it transitioned from infantry to armour and developed a smooth training program for the change.

Montgomery had no doubt taken note of Dempsey's battlefield acumen in France and weeks after he took command of Eighth Army in Egypt, he called for Dempsey to join him as commander of the XIII Corps with the rank of lieutenant general. Arriving in Cairo in December 1942, Dempsey was thrown into the planning for the upcoming invasion of Sicily. He found flaws in the original planning, particularly with dispersed landing beaches that might not allow forces to mutually support one another. He expressed his concerns to Montgomery and the plan was revised in the spring of 1943.

When Operation Husky started, Dempsey's XIII Corps landed in the vicinity of Syracuse and achieved all its objectives slated for the first day. Soon enough, however, stiff opposition was encountered and a hard slugging match ensued before the island was secured in roughly six weeks of fighting. Dempsey and XIII Corps were withdrawn towards the end of the fighting in Sicily as planning for Operation Baytown, the Eighth Army crossing of the Strait of Messina and landing on the Italian mainland. When the corps landed, initial Axis opposition was light, but steadily the going got tougher. In 17 days, however, XIII Corps pushed northward 300 miles to link up with

Dempsey meets with King George VI and Field Marshal Bernard Montgomery in October 1944. (Public Domain)

US General Mark Clark's Fifth Army, which had come ashore at Salerno near Naples. Montgomery again noted Dempsey's strong performance as the Allied Fifth and Eighth Armies battled their way through rugged country up the Italian boot.

On the basis of proven combat experience and leadership, Montgomery chose Dempsey to command the Second Army, scheduled to land in Normandy on D-Day, soon after his own appointment to head 21st Army Group and Allied ground forces for the invasion. Subsequently, Dempsey assembled his staff and inter-service naval and air officers commanding to put together the plans for the landings at Gold, Juno and Sword Beaches. Six days after the successful landings, Dempsey moved Second Army headquarters to Normandy.

During the fight for control of Caen, Dempsey proposed a heavy assault to dislodge the German defenders of the crossroads and communications centre that had been a D-Day objective. He suggested a sledgehammer blow that was codenamed Operation Goodwood. The attack suffered heavy casualties and was only partially successful. Although there was some dismay among senior Allied officers and substantial criticism was levelled at Montgomery, Dempsey managed to stay out of the fray. Offensive operations in the hedgerow country of Normandy were difficult and Dempsey did effectively utilise heavy artillery and tactical air to soften enemy defences. However, progress was slow.

Dempsey crosses the River Rhine into the Nazi Fatherland in March 1945. (Public Domain)

Montgomery, though, chose to shoulder the responsibility for the pace of advance and to his credit never laid heavy criticism or blame on Dempsey.

Changes in corps command helped re-energise the British drive across northern France and Belgium. Dempsey had misgivings regarding the ability of XXX Corps to speedily execute the ground phase of Operation Market Garden in September 1944. However, he concluded that withdrawal of the most forward ground troops and the remnants of the 1st Airborne Division was the prudent course of action against unexpectedly stiff resistance, including two SS panzer divisions.

Dempsey was one of those officers who fostered good relations with Britain's American allies and he was not involved in the dust-ups that occurred with regularity as rival commanders jockeyed for pre-eminence. He executed his duties with skill and quiet fortitude.

On March 23, 1945, Second Army crossed the great River Rhine and rolled across the frontier of the Third Reich, capturing large numbers of enemy troops and occupying major cities of northern Germany. Dempsey negotiated the surrender of Hamburg and sent a delegation of German officers to Montgomery to conclude surrender terms with enemy forces in northwest Europe.

By August, Dempsey was named commander of the 14th Army in the China-Burma-India theatre. At war's end, he was responsible for the care of more than 700,000 Japanese prisoners. He replaced General William Slim as commander of Allied land forces in Southeast Asia in November. He was in charge of Middle East Command from April 1946 through the end of the year and retired from the British Army in 1947. Afterwards, Dempsey held numerous ceremonial posts. He died of cancer on June 5, 1969, aged 72.

GENERAL JACQUES-PHILIPPE LECLERC DE HAUTECLOCQUE

The tanks and troops of the French 2nd Armoured Division, detached from their corps command at the insistence of General Charles de Gaulle, liberated Paris, the City of Light, on August 25, 1944, ending four years of Nazi occupation. But it had not been easy.

Besides fighting the Germans, de Gaulle had personally travelled to the headquarters of General Dwight D Eisenhower, Supreme Commander of Allied Forces, demanding the release of the French division to take the capital and prevent lawlessness, destruction, and factional fighting rather than bypass the great city.

When the order was given, de Gaulle knew he could count on the commander of the 2nd Armoured to get the job done. General Jacques-Philippe Leclerc de Hauteclocque was young, fearless, and driven. He had proved himself time and again as a lieutenant of the Free French leader, who was familiar with the family name Hauteclocque when the young officer presented himself in London. Hauteclocque came from a noble family with a long line of soldiers, dating back to the Crusades, service to Napoleon and in World War One.

As the Germans overran France in the spring of 1940, Hauteclocque was chief of staff of the 4th Infantry Division, which retreated to the city of Lille and then prepared to surrender at the end of May. The young officer would have none of it, slipping to the south of France where his wife and children had fled. He then heard de Gaulle's famous BBC radio appeal of June 18 and became determined to reach London. He was given a false passport that stated he was a wine merchant named Leclerc and attempted to thread through German lines. Captured twice, he escaped both times, crossing Spain and Portugal and taking a ship to Britain. On July 25, he walked into de Gaulle's office. Immediately the Free French leader commissioned him as a major in the armed force he was assembling.

Remarkable fortitude

Hauteclocque kept Leclerc as his nom de guerre and to prevent German authorities from identifying his family members and exacting reprisals from those in occupied areas. He later changed his name officially from the original Philippe

General Jacques-Philippe Leclerc de Hauteclocque sits in a vehicle with the cane he used due to a horseback riding accident in the 1930s. (Public Domain)

Francois Marie de Hauteclocque to Jacques-Philippe Leclerc de Hauteclocque.

Born on November 22, 1902, Leclerc was a graduate of the French military academy at St Cyr, who had served with the French occupation forces in Germany after World War One and then in Morocco before returning to St Cyr as an instructor in the 1930s. Assigned to the 4th Infantry Division, he was determined to continue the fight against the Nazis after the fall of France and the decision to entwine his future with that of de Gaulle became the stuff of legend and defence of honour for the French people.

Leclerc was sent to French Equatorial Africa, where he organised Free French fighting units and conducted numerous raids from Chad into Italian Libya. Several of these were in co-operation with the British Long Range Desert Group, a clandestine force adept at hit-and-run raids. He executed a magnificent fighting march to the Libyan port of Tripoli and joined with the British Eighth Army during the decisive fighting in North Africa in 1943. Along the way, he was promoted several times, attaining the rank of major general.

An American liaison officer observed that Leclerc was 'a remarkable soldier, young, energetic, and absolutely adored by his officers and men'.

Leclerc's command, armed and supplied by the US and Britain, became the nucleus of the 2nd Armoured Division, which came ashore in Normandy on August 1, 1944, a component of General George S Patton, Jr's Third US Army. The 2nd Armoured Division fought at the Falaise gap, through the Normandy campaign, liberated Paris and then advanced into Alsace-Lorraine, liberating Strasbourg on November 23, 1944, fulfilling a pledge that Leclerc and his oldest soldiers had made to continue the fight until the French tricolour fluttered over the city's cathedral.

At the end of World War Two, the 2nd Armoured Division had pursued German forces into Bavaria, advancing to the famous village of Berchtesgaden near Hitler's Eagle's Nest. The performance of Leclerc's command had been admirable. He was named commander of the French Expeditionary Force in the Far East in July 1945.

After the war, Leclerc was dispatched to the restive French colony of Indochina in March 1946. Four months later, he became inspector general of forces in North Africa. He died November 28, 1947, when the aircraft he was aboard crashed in the Algerian desert. His body was returned to Paris and lay in state at the Arc de Triomphe. Following a state funeral, Leclerc was interred among other national heroes at Les Invalides and in 1952 posthumously promoted Marshal of France.

Above: Leclerc chats with some of the soldiers under his command. He was a beloved leader. (Public Domain)

Right: Leclerc stands to the left of General Charles de Gaulle during a meeting in Paris on the day of liberation, August 25, 1944.

A joyous crowd greets troops and tanks of the French 2nd Armoured Division during a victory parade in Paris. (Public Domain)

GENERAL ALPHONSE JUIN

arning the praise and confidence of General Charles de Gaulle, leader of the Free French forces in World War Two, was not an easy thing to do.

However, de Gaulle had known Alphonse Juin since their days as students at the prestigious French military academy at St Cyr. They had graduated together in 1912. Juin had subsequently proved himself a fine soldier and astute leader of men in the Great War, but with the fall of France in 1940, his allegiance to France was tested. After surrendering his 15th Motorised Division, he was taken prisoner by the Germans. Released at the request of Field Marshal Philippe Pétain, president of the collaborationist Vichy government, he was placed in command of all Vichy French troops in North Africa.

Juin was never a supporter of the Nazis and he denied their requests to use port facilities, railroads and other infrastructure in French North Africa in December 1941, although his orders were later countermanded. Juin's sympathies were with de Gaulle and the Allied cause and he demonstrated this with co-operation in the days following the Operation Torch landings in North Africa in 1942, working to minimise resistance to the Allied offensive and helping persuade Admiral Francois Darlan, head of the Vichy government there, to cease hostilities.

Tasked with organising and training a French army that would fight the Axis, Juin set to work, overcoming the doubts of some Allied officers regarding the loyalty of former Vichy soldiers. He gained the respect of American and British leaders and then planned and led the occupation of the island of Corsica in September 1943. Still, his most significant contributions to Allied victory were yet to come.

Marshal of France Alphonse Juin is shown in uniform in this 1952 image. (Public Domain)

Juin and other Allied officers view troops passing in review. Juin salutes with his left hand due to a war injury that rendered his right arm practically useless. (Public Domain)

Free French leader

Born in French Algeria on December 16, 1888, Alfonse Juin was well into his 50s with the outbreak of World War Two. He had experienced the varied cultures and exotic locales that were characteristic of metropolitan France and served many of his years in the army in French North Africa.

A decorated hero of World War One, he received the Legion d'Honneur for 'courage and power of decision' during the 1914 Battle of the Marne. He was seriously wounded at Soissons and lost most of the use of his right arm. After the war, he taught at Ecole de Guerre, the French War College, fought in the Rift War in 1923 and then held posts in Morocco and Algeria. He served as chief of staff to General Charles Nogues in Morocco and was promoted brigadier general in December 1938.

After the lengthy period of defeat, captivity and intrigue, an opportunity emerged. Juin was given command of the French Expeditionary Corps (FEC) and made Resident General of Tunisia in November 1943. A month later, General Dwight Eisenhower, commander of Allied forces in the Mediterranean, requested the FEC for combat in Italy. Although senior to American General Mark Clark, Juin subordinated to the Fifth Army commander, realising that co-operation would facilitate the earlier entry of the FEC into the fighting and sooner restore the honour of France.

Under Juin's command, the FEC proved an effective fighting force, playing a key role in the breach of the Nazi Gustav Line during Operation Diadem in the spring of 1944, prompting de Gaulle to later write: "Juin restored the French military command to honour in the eyes of the nation, the Allies, and the enemy." At the time, the FEC was truly a cross-section of the greater French realm, including Free French, Moroccan and Algerian troops and ethnic contingents from these areas, as well as the Levant.

Juin led the FEC beyond the liberation of Rome in June 1944, capturing Siena the following month and stabilising a 10-mile front along the River Arno. By August, Juin was selected by de Gaulle as General Chief of Staff of National Defence in Paris. He worked with Allied military leaders and helped de Gaulle to persuade Eisenhower to allow the French 2nd Armoured Division to liberate the French capital. A trusted adviser to de Gaulle, Juin joined him in the subsequent triumphal march through the City of Light.

After organising the armed fighters of the Free French Forces of the Interior into the 10th Infantry Division, Juin accompanied de Gaulle to the Soviet Union to confer with Premier Josef Stalin in December 1944. By then, numerous Allied officers had recognised him as the best French strategist and tactician of the conflict.

After World War Two, Juin offered sage advice as the French colonial empire began to fracture. Indochina was the epicentre of discord and he watched unable to prevent his government from embarking on four years of fruitless fighting that ended in disastrous defeat in 1954. He later held more posts in North Africa and was named at Eisenhower's request NATO Commander-in-Chief Land Forces Central Europe. In 1952, he was promoted Marshal of France.

Juin retired in 1962 and died five years later. He is interred at Les Invalides in Paris, the resting place of many of France's greatest heroes.

Above left: Juin stands with American General Mark Clark at Siena, Italy, July 1, 1944. (Public Domain)
Above right: Tough soldiers like this Moroccan Goumier fought under Juin's command in Italy. (Public Domain)

MARSHAL PIETRO BADOGLIO

On July 25, 1943, Italy's Fascist Grand Council voted to oust Benito Mussolini, 'Il Duce' or The Leader, who had wielded power since 1922. The pompous, arrogant Mussolini had dreamed of a restoration of the Roman Empire, but his delusional aspirations had been dashed in ignominious defeat during World War Two.

Hours after the Fascist Grand Council decision, Mussolini arrived at the Villa Savoia in Rome to meet with King Victor Emmanual III, who bluntly told the stern, bull faced dictator: "My dear Duce, it cannot go on any longer. Italy is in pieces. Surely you have no illusions as to how the Italian people feel about you at this moment. You are the most hated man in Italy; you have not a single friend left except for me."

The king went on to tell Mussolini that his choice as the new prime minister of Italy was Marshal Pietro Badoglio, a man who Victor Emmanuel believed would carry on with the Fascist government, but also one he knew to be of weak character. Badoglio had served in the Italian Army for half a century. He had fought in Italy's colonial wars as a young officer and led Italian forces in the brutal subjugation of Ethiopia in the mid-1930s. And now, he was thrust into the role of negotiator.

Allied forces had landed in Sicily and were completing the occupation of the island and all the world knew that soon enough, they would be coming ashore on the Italian mainland. The war had gone decidedly against Italy, but the country remained tethered to Nazi Germany by treaty and complicity in the aggression that had brought on this tremendous global conflict.

Badoglio began a dialogue with General Dwight D Eisenhower, commander of Allied forces in the Mediterranean theatre, but he seemed caught in the middle of a terrible dilemma. If he surrendered to the Allies while Italy was on the brink of invasion, he invited the Nazis to occupy the country and exact reprisals. If he remained in the Axis orbit, he risked the full wrath of the invading Allied armies.

In early September 1943, less than a week before Allied troops hit the beaches in Italy, Badoglio's government agreed to an armistice. The Italian armed forces were to switch sides and co-operate with the Allies, fighting against the former Nazi benefactors. All the while, though, Badoglio had been reassuring the Germans that Italy would remain faithful to its Axis partner. Then, within hours of the Allied landings, the Italian leader hesitated to formally announce the change to his armed forces and the Italian people.

Eisenhower was furious and made the announcement himself, forcing Badoglio's hand. During the weeks that followed, the Germans occupied much of Italy, disarming Italian soldiers and arresting those suspected to be in league with the pro-Allied faction of the government. The long campaign that followed found Italy to be a battleground to the end of World War Two and Badoglio remained head of the government for only nine months. However, he had left his mark on the nation and the course of the conflict.

March to the fall of Rome

Born September 28, 1871 into the family of a minor landowner, Pietro Badoglio graduated the Royal Military Academy in Turin in 1892. As a young officer, he participated in the late 19th century wars in Libya and Eritrea. During World War One, he received accolades and promotion to the rank of major after the capture of Monte Sabotino in the

Above left: Marshal Pietro Badoglio followed Benito Mussolini as Italian prime minister after negotiating with the Allies. (Public Domain)

Above right: Badoglio posed for this portrait in 1934. A year later he was leading troops in Ethiopia. (Public Domain)

summer of 1916. However, his career hung in the balance following the disaster that befell the Italian Army at the Battle of Caporetto. The stinging defeat was attributed in part to the poor performance of Badoglio, among many other contributing factors.

A court of inquiry was formed to investigate Badoglio's conduct at Caporetto, but before it could render a verdict, Benito Mussolini stepped in and closed the matter abruptly. Badoglio subsequently served as Mussolini's chief of staff from 1925 to 1940 and during that time he was promoted to field marshal and governor of Libya, then an Italian possession.

While commanding Italian forces in Ethiopia, Badoglio is believed to have been responsible, at least partly, for the use of mustard gas against the poorly armed and equipped Ethiopian troops, as well as civilians. He was never held to account for any war crime. In the wake of the victory in Ethiopia, the relationship with Mussolini began to erode. Badoglio remained in service to 'Il Duce' but took umbrage to the fact that the leader wanted all the credit for the African adventure. Badoglio then opposed the formal alliance with Nazi Germany but may also have given Mussolini false assurances of the Italian Army's capabilities. Its shortcomings were laid bare during the abortive invasion of Greece in 1940. Badoglio was deemed responsible and subsequently resigned as chief of staff.

After a brief term of nine months as prime minister, Badoglio was replaced by Ivanoe Bonomi and retired to his home in the Italian Piedmont in the summer of 1944. His assurances to the Western powers that he could assist in preventing the establishment of a communist regime in Italy helped avoid prosecution for war crimes in his later years. He died in 1956 at the age of 85.

Left: Badoglio meets with local officials during a visit to Italian colonies in North Africa. (Public Domain)

Right: Italian troops under the command of Badoglio parade through the Ethiopian capital of Addis Ababa. (Public Domain)

GENERAL JOHN P LUCAS

When General John P Lucas was informed that his US VI Corps was to execute Operation Shingle, the hazardous landings at Anzio on the Italian west coast, he had immediate misgivings.

"I felt like a lamb being led to the slaughter," he confided in the pages of his diary. "This whole affair has a strong odour of Gallipoli and apparently the same amateur was still on the coach's bench."

Lucas's references to Gallipoli and the 'same amateur' were directed at British prime minister Winston Churchill. In World War One, while serving as First Lord of the Admiralty, Churchill had advocated the ill-fated Dardanelles campaign that led to disaster at Gallipoli in 1915. And now, in early 1944, he was advocating another daring amphibious assault that was no doubt fraught with risk. Lucas never liked the Anzio plan; one intended to outflank and unhinge the stubborn German defences of the Gustav Line to the south and perhaps even capture Rome. If successful, the Eternal City would be the first Axis capital to fall to Allied forces.

Nevertheless, Lucas groused as the January 22 date for the landings approached. Just eight days prior, he wrote that the "Army has gone nuts again. The general idea seems to be that the Germans are licked and are fleeing in disorder and nothing remains but to mop up. The Hun has pulled back a bit but I haven't seen the desperate fighting I have during the last four months without learning something. We are not (repeat not) in Rome yet. They will end up putting me ashore with inadequate forces and get me in a serious jam. Then, who will take the blame?"

Perhaps Lucas was the wrong man for the wrong fight. In the event, the VI Corps came ashore at Anzio, completely surprising the Germans. But instead of driving on to Rome or moving inland to exert pressure on the Gustav Line against virtually no resistance, he chose to consolidate his beachhead. The swift German response subsequently kept the Anzio 'abscess' – or as Hitler described it, contained. The threat devolved into a four-month ordeal. Allied troops did not break out of the Anzio beachhead until a co-ordinated effort with those opposing the Gustav Line, Operation Diadem, was successfully executed in May 1944.

Churchill was downcast and commented on Operation Shingle: "I had hoped we were hurling a wildcat onto the shore, but all we got was a stranded whale." However, it must be admitted in Lucas's defence that he was ordered first to establish the beachhead and then 'advance on' the Alban Hills that controlled the approaches to Rome. In fact, Fifth Army commander General Mark Clark had warned Lucas not to 'stick his neck out'.

General John P Lucas commanded VI Corps during the disappointing Anzio operation. (Public Domain)

Thus, a less-than-aggressive commander, vague orders and an immediately efficient German response doomed Operation Shingle to disappointment. In turn, Lucas's prediction came true and in a way, it was a self-fulfilling prophecy and his lasting legacy.

Man and military

Born in Kearneysville, West Virginia, on January 14, 1890, John P Lucas was the son of a physician and a 1911 graduate of the US Military Academy at West Point. Commissioned a cavalry officer, he served several years in the Philippines and then participated in the 1916 punitive expedition against Mexican outlaw Pancho Villa. The young officer then commanded a signals battalion in the 33rd Infantry Division during World War One and was seriously wounded by a shell fragment near the French town of Amiens.

After recovering from his wound, Lucas held numerous staff and field posts and transferred to the field artillery. He became recognised as a solid officer, although promotion was slow in the inter-war army. Nevertheless, he gained the attention of General George C Marshall, the army chief of staff, who described him as an officer of 'military stature, prestige, and experience'. Indeed, Lucas had instituted vigorous and consistent training in his commands and became one of the few officers in the US Army of the period with any knowledge or training experience in amphibious operations. He was promoted brigadier general in 1940 and a year later took command of the 3rd Infantry Division with the temporary rank of major general.

Lucas commanded III Corps in the US and was then ordered to the Mediterranean, serving as a deputy to General Dwight D Eisenhower, the theatre commander. He briefly commanded II Corps. When the ineffective General Ernest Dawley was relieved of command in September 1943, Lucas took VI Corps and guided it during the early days of the Italian campaign. A month after the colossal failure of Operation Shingle, Lucas was, in turn, relieved of command of VI Corps. He later held posts in the US and as an advisor to the Nationalist government of China. He died suddenly at age 59, on December 24, 1949.

Right: Lucas poses in West Point uniform in 1911. (Public Domain)

Below: US and Canadian soldiers of the 1st Special Service Force are briefed prior to a patrol at Anzio. (Public Domain)

An M4 Sherman medium tank comes ashore at Anzio during Operation Shingle, 1944. (Public Domain)

GENERAL VASILY CHUIKOV

The Red Army victory at the Battle of Stalingrad was a turning point of World War Two. The German Sixth Army was surrounded in the city that bore the name of Soviet Premier Josef Stalin and annihilated.

The central figure in the drama that led to the great reversal of fortune was General Vasily Chuikov, a stalwart communist and determined foe of the Nazis. When he was summoned to a meeting of the Southwest Front on September 11, 1942, Chuikov was given command of the 62nd Army and informed that Stalingrad should be held to the last man. He was well aware of Stalin's firm order to take 'not one step back' and responded to his orders with steely resolve: "We will defend the city or die."

General Vasily Chuikov steeled the resolve of the Red Army defenders at Stalingrad. (Creative Commons Mil.ru via Wikipedia)

Military rise

Vasily Chuikov was born of peasant stock near Tula, in the Russian Empire on February 12, 1900. From the age of 12, he was working on a factory floor. He enlisted in the Red Army following the Russian Revolution and served with distinction during the civil war that followed. He graduated from the Frunze Military Academy and was later sent to China as a liaison and intelligence officer for two lengthy periods. He also served for a time with the Russian Far East command and managed to avoid incrimination during Stalin's bloody purges of the Red Army officer corps during the 1930s.

With the outbreak of World War Two, Chuikov led the 4th Army during the invasion of Poland. However, his next foray handling troops in combat conditions was less than spectacular as Finnish soldiers, often highly mobile ski troops, regularly took the measure of the invading Soviets during the Russo-Finnish War of 1939-1940. He commanded the 9th Army during the period and the Red Army learned valuable lessons regarding fighting in sub-zero temperatures and snow-covered terrain.

Chuikov began his second assignment in China in December 1940, assisting the Nationalists under Generalissimo Chiang Kai-shek in their war with Japan. He was recalled to Moscow in March 1942 to bolster the decreasing number of Red Army officers due to heavy casualties incurred while fighting the invading Nazis.

Destiny at Stalingrad

Chuikov arrived in Stalingrad on the same day as his fateful assignment and established his headquarters on a hilltop. He was already acquainted with the ferocity of the German enemy, his 64th Army having suffered heavy casualties as the advance of the 6th Army in the north and the 4th Panzer Army in the south was slowed. The Soviets were forced to abandon their outer defences and by early September the 62nd Army had lost half its strength. But Chuikov brought renewed determination and stern discipline to the defenders of Stalingrad. Desertion and cowardice would not be tolerated. Party commissars and secret police were constantly watching and those who shirked their duty were summarily executed.

The Red Army tactics were changed as Chuikov ordered his soldiers to stay close to the Germans, hugging the enemy and therefore reducing exposure to Luftwaffe bombing and strafing while also limiting the mobility of the enemy. Still, Red Army reinforcements were required to cross to the west bank of the great River Volga, exposing them to deadly air attack and artillery bombardment. Street-to-street and house-to-house fighting were commonplace. Close combat raged for control of a tank factory and a grain elevator. By early November, the Soviets maintained control of only 10 percent of Stalingrad.

However, Chuikov had instilled an iron will in his troops and wrote later: "Stalingrad will decide the fate of the motherland. The men understood this. The men were in such mood that if they had been wounded, even with a broken spine, they had tears in their eyes as they were being taken to the east bank. They would say to their comrades who had brought them out, 'I don't want to go. Better to be buried here'. They considered it shameful to go wounded to the other bank."

Chuikov's command held on by its fingernails and then in mid-November the Red Army unleashed Operation Uranus, the encirclement of 6th Army in Stalingrad. By early February 1943, the Germans had been starved and pounded into submission. Field Marshal Friedrich Paulus surrendered along with 22 of his subordinate generals and more than 90,000 soldiers destined for bitter captivity in Soviet POW camps.

After Stalingrad, Chuikov was given command of the 8th Guards Army, which fought through Belorussia and Ukraine, spearheading the Red Army drive to the Nazi capital of Berlin. He was twice honoured as Hero of the Soviet Union. After World War Two ended, he served as commander of Soviet occupation forces in Germany and commander of the Red Army Kiev District. He was promoted Marshal of the Soviet Union in 1955. He retired from military service in 1972 but remained a member of the Central Committee of the Communist Party until his death on March 18, 1982.

Right: Chuikov commanded the Soviet 62nd Army in the Battle of Stalingrad. (Creative Commons Andrey Mironov via Wikipedia)

Below: Chuikov peers towards enemy lines while Red Army artillery fires at German positions in May 1943. (Public Domain)

Chuikov and members of his staff direct the defence of Stalingrad in December 1942. (Creative Commons Mil.ru via Wikipedia)

GENERAL WALTER C SHORT

The Japanese attack on Pearl Harbor and other US military installations in Hawaii on December 7, 1941, not only crippled the US Pacific Fleet and Marine Corps bases scattered across the island of Oahu, but also devastated the US Army ground and air infrastructure.

General Walter C Short, a career military officer, was in command of the Hawaii Department at the time of the attack. Appointed by Army Chief of Staff General George C Marshall, Short took command on February 8, 1941. He was relieved of duty 10 days after the Japanese raid. Short had been responsible for the US Army's defensive dispositions in Hawaii as the prospects for war with Japan increased substantially.

Along with his naval counterpart, Admiral Husband E Kimmel, Short was held responsible for the lack of military preparedness on that fateful Sunday morning in December 1941.

General Walter Short shouldered blame for the unprepared state of defences in Hawaii prior to Pearl Harbor. (Public Domain)

Several official inquiries were convened to assess culpability for the disaster and the most influential of these was the Roberts Commission, which concluded that the defences against air attack were deficient. Short was found guilty of dereliction of duty, stripped of his command, demoted from his temporary rank of three-star lieutenant general to his permanent rank of two-star major general and forced to retire from the army on February 28, 1942.

In the aftermath of the debacle, Short asserted that his defensive preparations had been commensurate with the orders he received. With the awareness that a relatively large segment of the population of Hawaii was of Japanese ancestry, there was greater concern with sabotage than an outright attack by the Japanese military. Therefore, aircraft had been parked wingtip to wingtip so that they were more easily guarded. Air patrols and lookout stations were maintained.

When General Short testified before the US Congress in 1946, he further noted that the orders he received on November 27, 1941, just ten days prior to the Japanese attack, made no mention of the necessity to prepare for an enemy air raid. He also related that long-range air reconnaissance was the responsibility of Kimmel and the US Navy. Short requested a full court martial to present his case, but he never had his proverbial day in court.

Today, some historians conclude that a court martial might have cleared Short's name. Until the Pearl Harbor disaster, his record had been outstanding.

Road to ruin

Walter C Short was the son of a physician. Born in Fillmore, Illinois on March 30, 1880, he graduated from the University of Illinois in 1901, taught mathematics at the Western Military Academy for a year and then obtained a commission in the army.

Short served with distinction in the Philippines and took part in the 1916 punitive expedition against Mexican outlaw Pancho Villa. During World War One, he was a staff officer with the 1st Infantry Division and assistant chief of staff of Third Army. Between the wars, he served on the War Department general staff, with the Far Eastern Section of Military Intelligence and then attended the Army War College, later returning as an instructor.

Promotions were steady for Short and this was somewhat remarkable for the peacetime army. He commanded the 1st Infantry Division and was leading I Corps until his appointment to the Hawaii Department in early 1941.

Short's treatment after Pearl Harbor remains controversial to this day and some observers consider both Short and Kimmel to be scapegoats. Through the years, additional information relating to his circumstances has surfaced, including the fact that some intelligence reports related to the movement of Japanese military forces prior to the attack were withheld from the senior army and navy commanders in Hawaii due to security concerns.

However, historian Gordon Prange, co-author of the books At Dawn We Slept and Pearl Harbor: The Verdict of History, wrote: "One may sympathise with Short, understand his motives and agree that Washington DC did not give him all the facts in its possession. But these things cannot mitigate the fact that Short failed in the event for which his whole professional life had been a preparation."

On May 25, 1999, after reviewing available information, the United States Senate passed a resolution to exonerate both General Short and Admiral Kimmel. The vote was narrow, 52-47, and the resolution was non-binding. The action came 50 years after General Short's death in Dallas, Texas, at the age of 69.

Short, commander of the Hawaii Department on December 7, 1941, wears the temporary rank of lieutenant general. (Public Domain)

A Boeing B-17 Flying Fortress bomber lies destroyed at Hickam Field after the Japanese attack of December 7, 1941. (Public Domain)

Installations at Wheeler Army Airfield on the island of Oahu burn after being attacked by Japanese planes on December 7, 1941. (Public Domain)

GENERAL ARTHUR PERCIVAL

General Arthur Percival walks alongside the Union Jack toward ignominious surrender at Singapore, February 15, 1942. (Public Domain)

Left: In the largest capitulation in British military history, Percival surrendered the British and Commonwealth garrison at Singapore. (Public Domain)

The fall of Singapore was a catastrophe for Great Britain. Not only was the prestige of the empire dealt a severe blow, but the scope of the Japanese victory in the early days of World War Two in Asia and the Pacific was startling.

To this day, historians continue to scrutinise the events leading up to the lightning fast Japanese conquest of the Malay Peninsula and the surrender of the British bastion that at times had been thought virtually impregnable. Some point an accusatory finger at the lack of leadership and fortitude in the defence under the command of General Arthur Percival, while others argue that the priorities of British leaders, particularly prime minister Winston Churchill, lay elsewhere, leaving Singapore neither properly garrisoned nor supplied while the plan of defence was flawed from the beginning.

Regardless, the Japanese were resolute in their pursuit of victory, landing the 25th Army, 50,000 strong, at multiple points on the coast of Malaya and Thailand on December 8, 1941. General Tomoyuki Yamashita earned the nickname 'Tiger of Malaya' during the ten-week onslaught that brought the Japanese to the doorstep of Singapore and compelled Percival to surrender on February 15, 1942. In the days that followed, around 80,000 British and Commonwealth soldiers were marched into brutal Japanese captivity, starved, beaten and ravaged by disease. Percival was among them.

After enduring more than three years in Japanese prison camps from Singapore to Formosa and then Manchuria, Percival was liberated in September 1945 after being held along with other high profile Allied officers, including American General Jonathan Wainwright, who had surrendered the Philippines in the spring of 1942. He was present at the signing of the Japanese surrender documents in Tokyo Bay on September 2, 1945 and General Douglas MacArthur presented him with one of the pens used during the ceremonies.

A military man

Arthur Percival was born in Hertfordshire on December 26, 1887, the son of the land agent of the Hamel's Park estate. More successful in sporting activities than academics, he was only an average student. He was working as a clerk in the office of an iron merchant when World War One erupted and enlisted in the army.

Although Percival's military career began with the lowly rank of private, promotion came quickly. Within three months, he was a captain. Wounded during the 1916 Battle of the Somme, he received the Military Cross, Croix de Guerre and then the coveted Distinguished Service Order. After the Great War, he remained in the army and served with the British Military Mission at Archangel during the Russian Civil War. By 1920, he was in Ireland amid continuing violence there.

Percival's record had been impressive thus far and promotions were steady. Prime minister David Lloyd George personally recommended him to attend the Staff College, Camberley and he completed the course in 1924. The influential General Sir John Dill became his mentor through years posted in Africa, to the Royal Naval College and with the Cheshire Regiment. He was elevated to colonel in 1936. In the same year, he became chief of staff to General William G S Dobbie, General Officer Commanding, Malaya.

A year later, Percival returned to Britain as a brigadier and staff officer at Aldershot. However, his career was already intertwined with the fate of Singapore. During his initial posting there, Percival had made observations regarding the defences and noted Singapore's vulnerability to an attack not from the sea, but from the landward side. His comments were prophetic.

When the Japanese came, it was indeed by land. Yamashita and his troops, though flush with victory during their rapid advance along the Malay Peninsula, were exhausted, their supplies depleted. Still, they executed amphibious landings across the narrow Johor Strait, breached outer defences and seized the supply depot at Bukit Timah and the reservoirs that held the supply of potable water for Singapore island. Yamashita then bluffed Percival to the negotiating table, threatening a heavy artillery bombardment and a renewal of vigorous offensive operations if the British did not surrender.

Percival gave in and the image of his march to the capitulation while a staff officer shoulders the Union Jack is emblematic of the largest capitulation of troops in British military history. After his repatriation, Percival returned to Britain and retired in 1946 with the honorary rank of lieutenant general, although his pay was at the lower permanent rank of major general. He was never offered a peerage. However, he earned praise for his conduct while a prisoner of war and for his advocacy and support of former POWs. He was honoured as lifetime president of the Far East Prisoners of War Association.

During his later years, Percival worked with numerous charitable organisations. He died on January 31, 1966, aged 78.

Right: Percival arrives to take command of British forces at Singapore in 1941. (Public Domain)

Below: A group of Japanese officers surround Percival following the surrender of Singapore. (Public Domain)

GENERAL ROY URQUHART

Operation Market Garden was a daring venture. If successful, the combined airborne/ground offensive might have ended World War Two by Christmas 1944.

However, it was not to be. The thrust concluded in failure – and a costly failure it was. The brainchild of General Bernard Montgomery, commander of Allied 21st Army Group, Market Garden involved the insertion of three airborne divisions, the British 1st and the American 82nd and 101st, to seize key bridges in Nazi-occupied Holland. The paratroopers were to hold the spans until relieved by the ground advance of XXX Corps up a single road to the town of Arnhem, where the bridge across the Neder Rhine would be the gateway to an assault into the Ruhr, Germany's industrial heartland.

In the event, the 1st Airborne suffered tremendous losses as the tanks and panzergrenadiers of two SS panzer divisions, sent to the vicinity of Arnhem to rest and refit after fighting in Normandy, proved too powerful for the lightly armed paras, marooned well beyond the limits of endurance of ordinary men.

General Robert Elliot 'Roy' Urquhart, arriving by glider, took approximately 10,000 men into action in and around Arnhem, and when the remnants of the 1st Airborne Division were withdrawn only about 2,000 were left. Urquhart had faced an uphill battle from the start and just about everything that could go wrong did. Nevertheless, he had done all that valour and devotion to duty could do in dire circumstances. While his Red Devils fought the Germans for nine days and a single battalion actually reached the Arnhem bridge only to be decimated, Urquhart had spent some desperate hours separated from his command and hiding in the attic of a house.

Though Market Garden was a severe defeat, the courage displayed by Urquhart and the 1st Airborne have become legendary.

Ground to air

Roy Urquhart was born in Shepperton, Middlesex, on November 28, 1901. He was the son of a Scottish physician and attended St Paul's School in London and the Royal Military Academy, Sandhurst. He received a commission as a second lieutenant in the Highland Light Infantry in 1920 and two years later was promoted to lieutenant. Five years followed before he was elevated to captain in the peacetime inter-war British Army. He served in Malta with the Highland Light Infantry's 2nd Battalion from 1933-1936, attended the Staff College, Camberley, for a year and then returned to his unit, which had been ordered to Palestine during the unrest of the Arab Revolt. Promotion to major and posting to India followed in 1938 and the next spring Urquhart became Deputy Assistant Quartermaster General of the Indian Army.

Posted briefly to North Africa in 1941, Urquhart returned to Britain and the staff of the 3rd Division. Promoted to lieutenant colonel, he commanded the 2nd Battalion, Duke of Cornwall Light Infantry and then was assigned to the staff of the 51st Highland Infantry Division before its deployment to North Africa in mid-1942. He commanded the 231st Infantry Brigade with the rank of brigadier for a brief period during Operation Husky, the Allied invasion of Sicily and the early days of the Italian campaign before returning to Britain as a staff officer with XII Corps.

British soldiers of the 1st Airborne Division gather equipment after their gliders have landed in the opening phase of Operation Market Garden. (Public Domain)

Right: Colonel John Frost led 2 Para to the bridge at Arnhem and put up a ferocious fight against German panzers. (Public Domain)

Meanwhile, General George Hopkinson, commander of the 1st Airborne Division, was killed in Sicily and General Frederick 'Boy' Browning, commanding I Airborne Corps, was in need of a replacement. Urquhart had been praised for his skilful command of the 231st Brigade and he was chosen to lead the airborne division. Urquhart was taken aback. Always a foot soldier, he had no experience with the airborne and was prone to air sickness.

Some observers were sceptical of the appointment and expected the worst, but Colonel John Frost, commander of 2 Para at Arnhem and captured by the Germans during Market Garden, later noted: "The division was spread all over Lincolnshire. We saw Urquhart less than we would have liked. But Urquhart soon had our full respect and confidence. In fact, there have been few generals who have been so heavily tested and passed that test."

After such heavy losses during Market Garden, the 1st Airborne Division saw no further combat during World War Two. When hostilities ceased, Urquhart brought the division to Norway to handle the repatriation of German prisoners and the reestablishment of the Norwegian government. He retired in 1955 after holding divisional commands and then serving as General Officer Commanding Malaya Command and leading British troops in Austria.

General Urquhart, who died on December 12, 1988 at age 87, served as an adviser during the filming of the motion picture A Bridge Too Far, relating the story of Market Garden. He was portrayed on screen by noted actor Sean Connery.

Left: Urquhart in front of his Market Garden headquarters, September 22, 1944. (Public Domain)

Right: After surrendering in Arnhem, British airborne soldiers prepare to march into captivity. (Creative Commons Bundesarchiv Bild via Wikipedia)

GENERAL HENRY D G CRERAR

The prolonged offensive in Normandy following the D-Day invasion of June 6, 1944 finally showed signs of a great Allied victory by August. The fighting in the hedgerow country, or bocage, had been costly. And for the British 21st Army Group, the capture of Caen – set for D-Day – had taken weeks against tough, fanatical resistance, particularly from German SS panzer divisions.

However, by late summer, the Allies had achieved the upper hand and the jaws of a large encirclement were closing. German Army Group B, including elements of the 7th Army and 5th Panzer Army, were in the net near the French town of Falaise. When the Battle of Falaise was over, the Germans had lost 50,000 prisoners, 10,000 dead and 500 irreplaceable tanks, self-propelled artillery pieces and field guns.

Even so, the victory at Falaise was short of what it might have been. Historians debate the swiftness of the Allied manoeuvre to close the jaws of the trap and three of the figures under scrutiny are General Bernard Montgomery, commanding 21st Army Group, General Omar Bradley, commanding 12th Army Group, and General Henry D G 'Harry' Crerar, commander of the Canadian 1st Army under Montgomery. While the alacrity of the movement toward Falaise seems to be the root of the controversy, the delayed closure led to the escape of thousands of German soldiers to continue the fight. General George S Patton, Jr complained bitterly that orders to halt his spearheads at Argentan stymied his ability to slam the door on the Germans. Meanwhile, Montgomery, Bradley and Crerar have been criticised for the 'slows'.

Crerar was the commander of the Canadian 1st Army throughout 1944-1945, serving as the senior Canadian field general of World War Two. Besides his involvement at Falaise, he led the Canadian effort to capture several French ports on the coast of the English Channel and in the bitter weeks-long battle to clear the estuary of the River Scheldt and open the port of Antwerp in Belgium. The Canadians were also heavily involved in the fighting in the Netherlands in the waning weeks of the war, and the campaign in the region of the Lower Rhine was gruelling.

Canada to conquest
Crerar was born in Hamilton, Ontario, on April 28, 1888, the son of a businessman and barrister. He graduated from the Royal Military College of Canada in Kingston, Ontario in 1909. During World War

General Harry Crerar, commander of the Canadian First Army, was his country's highest ranking field commander of World War Two. (Public Domain)

One, he served as an artillery officer and received the Distinguished Service Order for action at Vimy Ridge.

Recognised as a superb administrator, Crerar held numerous staff positions within the Canadian Army in the 1920s and 1930s, including attaché to the British War Office and director of military intelligence and operations. He also held an administrative position under General A G L McNaughton, chief of the army general staff.

With the outbreak of World War Two, Crerar served in a liaison role in Britain and became chief of the general staff in 1940 with responsibility for training more than 100,000 Canadian soldiers of the I Corps, while also issuing the fateful order that sent thousands of soldiers to Hong Kong in support of the British defences there. Meanwhile, Crerar itched for a combat command and took charge of I Corps in the Mediterranean in 1942.

After leading I Corps through Sicily and into the Italian campaign, Crerar returned to Britain to organise the 1st Army for Operation Overlord, the D-Day landings. At various times, the ranks of 1st Army also included Belgian, Dutch, American, Polish, French and Czech soldiers. While Crerar has been the subject of scrutiny at the tactical level along with Montgomery and Bradley for their apparent lack of haste at Falaise, he is primarily remembered for his organisational and training skills, as well as capably executing his duties in command of a force that exceeded half a million troops at its peak strength. Reviews of his overall performance remain mixed.

In the process, Crerar strove to maintain the highest degree of autonomy for Canadian forces during World War Two. He was considered somewhat aloof by his contemporaries and a demanding superior by those staff officers close to him. He shunned the spotlight and retired from active service in October 1946. Crerar died on April 1, 1965, at the age of 76.

Crerar consults a map near the open door of a light aircraft in 1945. (Public Domain)

Crerar greets Canadian prime minister William Mackenzie King in April 1944. (Public Domain)

Crerar (second from left) and General Bernard Montgomery (third from left) join other officers at a field headquarters in February 1945. (Public Domain)

ADMIRAL CHESTER W NIMITZ

In the wake of the Japanese attack on Pearl Harbor, December 7, 1941, the US Pacific Fleet was in shambles. Eight battleships had either been sunk or heavily damaged, along with many other cruisers, destroyers and auxiliary ships. More than 2,403 Americans, military and civilian, had been killed and the United States was suddenly at war.

Not only had the Japanese struck the anchorage of the Pacific Fleet, but other military installations across the island of Oahu in the Territory of Hawaii had been devastated. The Japanese had also mounted attacks against the US outpost at Midway Atoll in the Philippines and against the British in Malaya. The situation was bleak and the forces of Imperial Japan appeared poised to extend control over much of Asia and the Pacific.

Three weeks after the attack on Pearl Harbor, Admiral Chester W Nimitz arrived on the scene. Recovery work had already begun, but the task before the new Pacific Fleet commander was daunting. Nimitz's flag was raised aboard the submarine USS *Grayling* for two reasons. First, Nimitz had spent much of his navy career as a submariner and second because there were no dry battleship or other surface warship decks that could accommodate his staff.

Nimitz took stock of the situation and noted that for all the devastation wrought, the Japanese had failed in key areas to strike a death blow to the American military presence in the Pacific. Repair and machine shops were untouched, oil reserves and tanks that held precious fuel were virtually unscathed and the three American aircraft carriers that were to become the primary offensive weapons of the growing conflict were at sea. They had escaped intact. These positive aspects of the tough times provided a starting point on the long, difficult road to Tokyo Bay and victory four years later.

The admiral set about restoring morale and organising salvage

Above left: Admiral Chester Nimitz was Chief of Naval Operations when he posed for this portrait. (Public Domain)

Above right: Nimitz wears the uniform of a midshipman at the US Naval Academy in this 1905 photo. (Public Domain)

operations at Pearl Harbor while developing plans to confront the Japanese as rapidly as possible and wherever the US Navy could strike back. With determination, strong will and accepting the principle of the calculated risk, Nimitz commanded an incredible resurgence.

Land or sea

Ironically, the leader of the US Pacific Fleet in World War Two was born far from the sea, in Fredericksburg, Texas, on February 24, 1885. Six months earlier, his frail father, always in poor health, had died and perhaps the greatest influence on the boy was his grandfather, Charles Henry Nimitz, a German-born former merchant sailor. The old man told captivating yarns of his seafaring years, but young Chester was

Left: Nimitz presents the Navy Cross to sailor Dorie Miller at Pearl Harbor in 1942. (Public Domain)

Below: While Nimitz was in command, the destroyer USS *Decatur* ran aground in the Philippines. (Public Domain)

Nimitz signs surrender documents aboard the battleship USS *Missouri* in Tokyo Bay. (Public Domain)

not as excited by them as others, even when the former sailor made improvements to the family business, a hotel, to make the façade resemble a sailing ship.

Chester's interest in the sea came somewhat by accident – or perhaps fate – when his aspirations to obtain an appointment to the US Military Academy at West Point, New York, were dashed. He was only 15 years old when his local congressman broke the news that no slots were available at West Point. Still, there was another option, the politician said. Young Chester could, if he chose, sit for a written examination and compete for the single available position at the US Naval Academy at Annapolis, Maryland. Chester recognised the simple fact that a poor boy's best opportunity for a free education, a career and adventure lay with the navy. His score was top and Chester graduated from the academy ranking seventh in the class of 1905.

Upon graduation from Annapolis, Nimitz was obligated to spend two full years on sea duty with a cruise to the Far East aboard the battleship USS *Ohio*. His impressions of life aboard ship were not particularly glowing, and he wrote: "I got frightfully seasick and must confess to some chilling of enthusiasm for the sea."

Nevertheless, he had earned an ensign's commission by 1907 and took command of the gunboat USS *Panay*, which itself was the subject of an international incident 30 years later when sunk by Japanese warplanes on the River Yangtze in China. He moved on to command the Bainbridge-class destroyer USS *Decatur* and narrowly avoided the end of his naval career when the vessel ran aground. On

This image of Admiral Chester Nimitz hangs in the National Portrait Gallery. (Creative Commons Billy Hathorn via Wikipedia)

the night of July 7, 1908, *Decatur* sailed into Batanas Harbour, south of the Philippine capital of Manila, with 22-year-old Ensign Nimitz in command. It was highly unusual for an officer of such youth and inexperience to hold such a post.

As *Decatur* sailed into the shallows, Nimitz only estimated the ship's location rather than taking specific bearings. He complicated the situation by failing to verify the direction of the tides. The destroyer ran aground on a muddy bank and stuck fast, freed by a small steamboat the next day. Nimitz was embarrassed and in hot water. He was charged with 'culpable inefficiency in the performance of duty' and hauled before a court martial.

During the proceedings, the young officer impressed the court by taking full responsibility for his shortcomings. Nimitz was found guilty of a lesser charge 'neglect of duty' and received a public reprimand. He had stood tall when accused and his clean record prior to the incident provided the opportunity for leniency, as did the poor quality of available navigational charts for the harbour. Eighteen months later the incident appears to have been largely forgotten. Nimitz received promotion to lieutenant, passing over the intervening rank of lieutenant junior grade.

Transfer to the Atlantic Fleet followed and Nimitz became engaged in the development of the submarine, a new weapon of war with fantastic potential. He spent the next five years working with submarine development and showed personal bravery when he saved the life of a drowning sailor while serving aboard the USS *Skipjack*. Nimitz received the Silver Lifesaving Medal for the rescue and worked to become an expert on the maintenance and upkeep of the diesel engines that provided propulsion for the submarines. In time, he was recognised as the foremost authority on the diesel engine in the US Navy and assigned to work on the construction

The nuclear-powered aircraft carrier USS *Nimitz* under way in the Pacific Ocean. (Public Domain)

of engines for the fleet oiler USS *Maumee* in early 1913. He later went to Ghent, Belgium, and Nuremberg, Germany, to observe the construction of diesel engines there. After seeing to the installation of the diesels aboard *Maumee*, Nimitz became the ship's executive officer.

As the United States entered World War One, Nimitz was a staff officer with the US Atlantic Submarine Command, working in September 1918 with the office of the Chief of Naval Operations and the board of submarine design. During the years between the wars, he supervised the construction of the submarine base at Pearl Harbor and then served as the executive officer aboard the battleship USS *South Carolina* and the cruiser USS *Chicago*. He attended the Naval War College prior to establishing the Naval Reserve Officer Training Corps programme at the University of California, Berkeley. The establishment of such preparatory programmes proved critical in providing qualified junior naval officers during World War Two. He also taught naval science and technology at the university.

At long last, his talents recognised at a high level, Nimitz was given a prestigious sea command. In 1933, he was named skipper of the cruiser USS *Augusta*, flagship of the US Navy's Asiatic Fleet.

The world stage

After the debacle at Pearl Harbor, President Franklin D Roosevelt chose Admiral Nimitz to take command of the shattered Pacific Fleet, replacing Admiral Husband E Kimmel. When he received word of the new assignment, Nimitz was serving as chief of the US Navy Bureau of Navigation.

When he arrived at Pearl Harbor on December 31, 1941, Nimitz was aghast at the devastation but realised that the United States had to strike back at Japan as soon as possible. An old submariner, he knew that the submarine fleet offered the most immediate means of doing so. He further decided that his command headquarters would remain in Hawaii, as close to the Pacific combat zones as possible but without going to sea and engaging in tactical command.

Nimitz proved innovative in his outlook, open minded and focused, with a solid grasp of the strategic picture. He relied on subordinate commanders close to the action to make tactical decisions based on immediate combat conditions. At the time, his career had spanned 35 years of naval service.

Shortly after arriving in Hawaii, Nimitz was named commander of Allied Forces, Pacific Ocean Areas, reflective of his responsibilities across the vast expanse of the ocean. During the first weeks of the Pacific War, he assumed offensive operations.

On February 1, 1942, just seven weeks after Pearl Harbor, Nimitz's carriers were in action against the Japanese. Under the command of Admirals Frank Jack Fletcher and William F 'Bull' Halsey, aircraft flying from the decks of the aircraft carriers *Enterprise* and *Yorktown* began a series of raids against Japanese installations in the Gilbert and Marshall Islands. Although the

Nimitz wears the five-star rank of fleet admiral in1945. (Public Domain)

Left: Nimitz (left) and William F Halsey confer at Espiritu Santo in the Pacific in 1943. (Public Domain)

Below: During a July 1944 meeting with President Franklin Roosevelt and General Douglas MacArthur, Admiral Nimitz points to a location on a map. (Public Domain)

objectives of these early US Navy carrier raids were limited, their impact was in fact substantial. Not only did they demonstrate American resolve to assume the offensive in the Pacific as early as possible, but they also laid bare the inherent difficulties the Japanese faced in defending a far-flung island perimeter across thousands of miles of ocean.

On April 18, 1942, Lieutenant Colonel Jimmy Doolittle led the famed raid on the Japanese capital of Tokyo, shocking the enemy's Imperial General Staff. The Japanese decided to expand their defensive perimeter in the Pacific and mounted offensives against key locations. The result was a severe test for Nimitz, but embedded was the opportunity to reverse the course of the war in favour of the US. Nimitz showed himself a master of the calculated risk in two decisive actions that occurred that spring.

During the Battle of the Coral Sea in May, American carrier aircraft blunted the Japanese drive to capture Port Moresby on the island of New Guinea, which might have been used as a staging area for an invasion of Australia. Coral Sea was the first naval battle in history in which opposing surface forces never came within sight of each other. The US lost the aircraft carrier *Lexington*, but the Japanese lost the light aircraft carrier *Shoho*, while the fleet carriers *Shokaku* and *Zuikaku* were damaged and lost many experienced air crew. Tactically, the sea fight was a draw, but the withdrawal of the Port Moresby invasion force made Coral Sea a strategic American victory.

At the same time, US Naval Intelligence was reading large portions of coded Japanese radio traffic and confirmed that the enemy intended to strike the US naval base at Midway, about 1,300 miles west of Hawaii. Although his forces were at a distinct numerical disadvantage, Nimitz was obliged to defend Midway. Japanese occupation of the atoll would present an unacceptable threat to Hawaii itself.

The aircraft carrier *Yorktown* had been severely damaged at Coral Sea but limped back to Pearl Harbor, apparently in need of repairs that would take months to complete. Nimitz informed the dock workers that they had 72 hours to prepare the carrier for sea once again. Remarkably, *Yorktown* did sail into harm's way on Nimitz's schedule. The situation was desperate and the commander had ordered two task forces to rendezvous off Midway and ambush the approaching Japanese.

Task Force 17 was commanded by Admiral Fletcher aboard *Yorktown*. However, Admiral Halsey was hospitalised with a raging skin disorder and when Nimitz asked his recommendation for a replacement, Halsey quickly responded: "Ray Spruance." Although Spruance had virtually no experience with carriers or naval aviation, he put to sea in command of Task Force 16, including the carriers *Hornet* and *Enterprise*.

The resulting Battle of Midway proved to be the turning point of World War Two in the Pacific. Nimitz had staked everything on the outcome of the battle and in the event US carrier-based dive bombers dealt a heavy blow to Japanese aircraft carrier superiority in the Pacific. They sank four enemy carriers, *Akagi, Kaga, Soryu,* and *Hiryu*. In turn, the *Yorktown* was sunk. However, the Japanese landing force intended to seize Midway was turned back. After the epic battle, the United States had wrested the initiative from the Japanese, who were forced to wage a defensive and largely reactionary war of attrition. They were doomed to fail and again the prescience of Admiral Nimitz had been the catalyst for decisive victory.

By August 1942, the US armed forces had assumed the offensive on land as well. Forces under Nimitz's strategic command landed on the island of Guadalcanal in the Solomons chain and wrested control of the island and its vital airstrip, Henderson Field, from the Japanese in six months of bloody struggle. US Marines and army troops fought for the island while a series of naval battles swirled off the coast of Guadalcanal. In the end, the Japanese withdrew after expending resources that were irreplaceable.

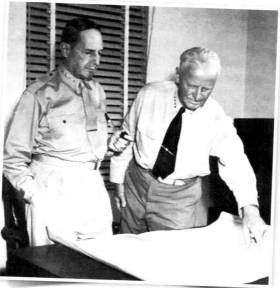

Above left: Artist Andrew Lamb painted this portrait of Nimitz in 1960. (Public Domain)

Above right: Nimitz and General Douglas MacArthur confer on Pacific War strategy. (Public Domain)

At the same time, Nimitz and General Douglas MacArthur, commander of Allied forces in the South Pacific, differed on the most efficient path toward final victory. While Nimitz favoured an advance to the Japanese-held island of Formosa and then the home islands while bypassing the Philippines, MacArthur had pledged to return to the Philippine Islands after evacuating from there in 1942. He believed that his oath and the American obligation to liberate its own territory were more pressing. President Roosevelt approved MacArthur's plan and two distinct operations continued across the Pacific Ocean. Nimitz was promoted to the five-star rank of fleet admiral in December 1944.

While MacArthur fought through New Guinea and landed forces in the Philippines in early 1945, Nimitz and his naval might along with the Fleet Marine Force and a strong commitment of army divisions moved on to assault more islands in the Pacific. A major Marine landing occurred at Iwo Jima in February. The bloody fight there led to the iconic image of Marines raising the US flag atop embattled Mount Suribachi, a 550-foot extinct volcano that dominated the island. The image by photographer Joe Rosenthal was published worldwide and amid the heavy losses, Admiral Nimitz commented that at Iwo Jima, 'uncommon valour was a common virtue'.

At long last, the inevitable trek toward the Japanese home islands was underway and naval support facilitated the US Marine and army landings on islands across the expanse of the Pacific, including the Gilbert, Marshall and Marianas Islands. At sea, the Imperial Japanese Navy suffered terrible defeats in 1944 at the Philippine Sea and Leyte Gulf, with the US fleet engaged under the command of Spruance and Halsey respectively.

Final battle

In April 1945, the US armed forces embarked on the final major battle of World War Two with landings on the island of Okinawa. While the Marines and army troops battled for control of the island, the supporting naval vessels offshore endured a storm of Japanese kamikaze suicide attacks and suffered mightily, earning the nickname of the 'fleet that came to stay'. Nimitz lamented the losses taken off Okinawa but praised the fortitude of his navy personnel.

When the Japanese surrender ceremonies took place aboard the battleship USS *Missouri* in Tokyo Bay on September 2, 1945, Admiral Nimitz represented the United States and signed the instrument of surrender. At the end of the year, he succeeded Admiral Ernest J King

Nimitz stands with Fleet Admiral Ernest J King and Secretary of the Navy James Forrestal in 1945. (Public Domain)

Nimitz poses with Admiral Ray Spruance, Admiral Marc Mitscher and Admiral Willis Lee in February 1945. (Public Domain)

The devastation at Pearl Harbor was tremendous when Nimitz took command of the US Pacific Fleet in December 1941. (Public Domain)

Above left: Nimitz relaxes with his dog Dyna at his home in California in 1954. (Public Domain)

Above right: Nimitz stands with Admiral Ray Spruance and General Simon Bolivar Buckner Jr during operations at Okinawa. (Public Domain)

Golden Gate Cemetery for other officers, I earnestly request that Admiral Raymond A Spruance, USN (Retired) and Admiral R K Turner, USN (Retired) upon their deaths be given grave sites adjoining those which have been reserved for Mrs Nimitz and me…"

Spruance, of course, had commanded naval task forces in pivotal battles of World War Two. Turner had commanded multiple amphibious landing operations in the Pacific. And then, Admiral Charles Lockwood, another close friend and commander of the Pacific Submarine Force, was later included in the request. The four titans of World War Two in the Pacific rest side by side today along with their wives at the Golden Gate Cemetery. They lie near the graves of many American military personnel who gave their lives during the costly conflict. The burial sites are along the first row beside a street appropriately named Nimitz Drive.

Admiral Chester Nimitz was further honoured with the christening of the nuclear-powered aircraft carrier USS *Nimitz*, one of the largest ships in the world at the time, on May 13, 1972. Nimitz remains one of the greatest naval heroes in US military history, a skilled naval strategist, a true diplomat in high-level negotiation and the architect of Pacific naval victory.

as Chief of Naval Operations. During two years as the top naval officer, he was a staunch advocate for the development of nuclear propulsion systems, a major step in the modernisation of the post-war US Navy. He later held a post as special assistant to the Secretary of the Navy and then as an envoy for the fledgling United Nations and as a regent of the University of California.

In his later years, Nimitz lived quietly with his wife, Catherine, in naval quarters at San Francisco, California, while technically officers of five-star rank never fully retired. He died at on February 20, 1966, from a stroke and complicating pneumonia, four days before his 81st birthday. He had already made provision for his final resting place. Rather than Arlington National Cemetery, the best known shrine to America's heroes, Nimitz chose to be interred at the Golden Gate National Cemetery in San Bruno, California. It was fittingly near the Pacific Ocean, with which his life had been so intertwined.

During his long, distinguished career, Nimitz had cemented lasting friendships and developed mutual respect for a close group of fellow officers. Prior to his death, he invited other prominent naval officers of the Pacific War to be buried nearby upon their deaths. It was an unusual request and he wrote for permission in September 1952.

"While I fully understand and appreciate the decision of the Quartermaster General to make no grave site reservations in the

Nimitz looks towards the stern of the submarine USS *Nautilus* while standing in the conning tower. (Public Domain)

Nimitz sits with General MacArthur and President Roosevelt aboard the cruiser USS *Baltimore* in July 1944. (Public Domain)

Nimitz rides in the passenger seat of a Jeep on the island of Guam in the Marianas, 1944. (Public Domain)

ADMIRAL ISOROKU YAMAMOTO

The crewmen aboard the Imperial Japanese Navy aircraft carrier *Akagi* listened intently, having snapped to attention on the flight deck at 9pm on December 6, 1941.

When the loudspeaker crackled, the assembled men recognised the voice of the most senior officer aboard, Admiral Isoroku Yamamoto, Commander-in-Chief of the Combined Fleet. Earnestly serious, Yamamoto stated: "The rise and fall of the empire depends on this battle. Everyone will do his duty to the utmost." He was paraphrasing words spoken decades earlier when the Japanese Navy had won the great victory over the Russian Baltic Fleet at Tsushima in 1905. Togo, in turn, had echoed a message delivered by the British Royal Navy hero Admiral Horatio Nelson before the victory at Trafalgar in 1805.

Such was the gravity of the monumental military step that Imperial Japan was about to take. Within hours, the nation would be at war with the United States as its carrier-based naval aircraft savaged the US Pacific Fleet anchorage at Pearl Harbor and other military installations on the island of Oahu in the Territory of Hawaii. The significance of the moment was lost to no-one and the messenger was the 57-year-old heart and soul of the Imperial Japanese Navy.

Admiral Yamamoto had come to such a time and place despite his vigorous opposition to war with the United States. He had travelled extensively in the country as a young naval officer and studied at Harvard University. He knew the American spirit and people well and he had agonised over the future of his homeland. Nevertheless, duty had compelled him to act.

Bound by duty

Isoroku Yamamoto stood only 5ft 3in tall. Yet, he was a towering figure among the senior commanders of the Imperial Japanese Navy on the eve of World War Two. He was often stoic but possessed of a good sense of humour, well respected as a veteran officer and was known as

Above left: Admiral Isoroku Yamamoto, Commander-in-Chief of the Imperial Japanese Navy Combined Fleet, was the architect of the attack on Pearl Harbor and later led his forces to ruin. (Public Domain)

Above right: Yamamoto stands beside his friend and fellow naval officer Teikichi Hori in 1915. (Public Domain)

Admiral Heihachiro Togo stands aboard his flagship, the battleship *Mikasa*, at the Battle of Tsushima in 1905. As a young ensign, Isoroku Yamamoto was seriously wounded in the battle. (Public Domain)

a risk taker in poker, bridge and other card games. He was a passionate patriot and fluent in English.

As Japan and the United States confronted one another across the expanse of the Pacific Ocean, Yamamoto warned against going to war – a war he sincerely believed that Japan could not win. He had seen the industrial might of the United States first hand. While many Japanese believed the American people were amoral, prone to hedonistic lifestyles and basically without the power or the will when confronted with adversity, he disagreed vehemently.

Yamamoto once visited with students at his former middle school in the city of Nagaoka and he spoke frankly to the assembled youngsters. "Most people think Americans love luxury and that their culture is shallow and meaningless," he said to them. "It is a mistake to regard America as luxury loving and weak. I can tell you Americans are full of the spirit of justice, fight and adventure. Do not forget American industry is much more developed than ours and unlike us they have all the oil they want. Japan cannot beat America. Therefore, she should not fight America."

Despite his personal misgivings, when the course for war appeared inevitable Yamamoto committed himself to the effort. He was of the opinion that the only real prospect to defeat the United States in armed conflict and to avoid devastating losses in a prolonged war would be to strike a decisive blow against US naval power in the Pacific. From there, he reasoned, Japanese forces should pursue a rapid succession of dramatic victories. The lightning strikes would sap American morale and hopefully compel the US to seek peace terms. Even then, Yamamoto harboured no illusions.

"Should hostilities break out between Japan and the United States, it is not enough that we take Guam and the Philippines or even Hawaii and San Francisco," he wrote in January 1941. "We would have to march into Washington and sign the treaty in the White House. I wonder if our politicians who speak so lightly of a Japanese-American war have confidence as to the outcome and are prepared to make the necessary sacrifices."

While serving as naval attaché in Washington DC, in 1925, Yamamoto sits at left with Secretary of the Navy Curtis Wilbur, Captain Kiyoshi Hasegawa and Admiral Walter Eberle. (Public Domain)

he developed his love of card games and a penchant for gambling that would last his lifetime. When both his father and mother died that year, Isoroku was adopted by the Yamamoto family, which took great pride in a long tradition of naval service. Such was a common practice for those families whose surname might be extinguished in the absence of a male heir.

Steady command climb

In December 1915, Yamamoto was promoted to lieutenant commander. He was prone to numerous affairs with geishas and had a voracious sexual appetite, but in August 1918, he married housemaid Reiko Mihashi. The couple had two daughters, but their relationship was essentially loveless, never warm or strong, and separation was soon to come.

In the spring of 1919, Yamamoto was ordered to the United States as a 'special student in English' at Harvard University in Boston, Massachusetts. He also studied economics and toured the countryside regularly. He was impressed with the vastness of the US and marvelled at its enormous industrial capacity. In the process, Yamamoto became an authority on the petroleum industry, but he declined to accept job offers from major oil companies.

His country first

Yamamoto's patriotism overshadowed his personal perspective on the prospects for victory and his devotion had its roots in a naval career that had extended nearly 40 years by the mid-1930s. Culturally, he was bound to place the future of the nation above his own desires or reasoning.

Born Isoroku Takano in Nagaoka on April 4, 1884, Isoroku was the seventh child of schoolmaster Sadayoshi Takano, a member of the samurai class but one of modest means, certainly not wealthy. The boy's name translates literally as '56' in reference to the age of his father when he was born. Childhood was difficult and somewhat spartan, with plenty of work to do. Nevertheless, the boy received an excellent education from the time he was able to focus his attention on a variety of concepts and ideas. He was fascinated by American and British culture, read voraciously and received some instruction in school subjects and religion from Christian missionaries. As he grew, the barrel-chested boy became a fine athlete, excelling in gymnastics. He often took great delight in performing gymnastic stunts for friends.

At the age of 16, Isoroku applied for admission to the Imperial Japanese Naval College at Etajima, scoring second on the entrance examination among 300 applicants. Life at Etajima was empty of personal pleasure. Smoking or drinking of alcohol were not allowed and the consumption of sweets was forbidden as well. No fraternisation with women was tolerated and the final year of academy education was spent aboard ship. Graduating seventh in the class of 1904, Isoroku received his commission just as his country was going to war with Imperial Russia. During the 19-month Russo-Japanese War, the Japanese military stunned the world with a decisive victoryo. For the first time in history, an Asian nation had defeated a traditional European power. The great victory had come on both land and sea.

Midshipman Isoroku Takano was present at the pivotal naval Battle of Tsushima in May 1905. The Japanese fleet under Togo thoroughly defeated the Russian Baltic Fleet, which had sailed virtually around the world to meet its ignominious fate. However, young Isoroku was nearly killed in the battle while aboard the cruiser *Nisshin*. A shell burst knocked him unconscious and hot shrapnel slammed into his thigh, slicing off a chunk the size of an orange. The index and second fingers of his left hand were severed. After two months in hospital, he was promoted to the rank of ensign in August 1905 and assigned to naval headquarters in Tokyo.

In 1913, Isoroku received a coveted appointment to the Naval Staff College and he displayed tremendous insight and energy during the academic pursuits, distinguishing himself from the other officers. During this period, he discovered that he could not tolerate alcohol well and decided to refrain from drinking. However, at the same time

Yamamoto and his staff pose on the flight deck of the aircraft carrier *Akagi* on December 24, 1941. (Public Domain)

The officer honed his skills in the English language. He was amazingly energetic, usually sleeping just three hours a night. The addictive side of his personality continued at times to hold sway and he indulged his love of gambling with lengthy poker games. He returned to Japan in 1921 and received promotion to the rank of commander.

Achieving high command

Yamamoto was a captain within three years and he received his first major assignment, as executive officer of the air training school at Kasumigaura. He had already familiarised himself with the use of aircraft during World War One and carrier aviation was a new frontier among the major navies of the world. He carried out his duties during the day and studied flying during the evenings. Impressively, he earned his pilot's wings at the age of 40.

Yamamoto then commanded the cruiser *Isuzu* and the aircraft carrier *Akagi* before returning to Washington DC in 1926 as naval attaché.

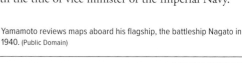

He gathered practical information on the strengths and weaknesses of the US Navy and insights on the world perspective of its officer corps. Promoted to rear admiral in late 1929, he served as a delegate to the London Naval Conference the following year. He became convinced that aircraft carriers and their strike capability would supplant the battleship as the foremost naval weapon in future conflicts. In 1933, he took command of the 1st Carrier Division and two years later he was promoted vice admiral along with the title of vice minister of the Imperial Navy.

Yamamoto reviews maps aboard his flagship, the battleship Nagato in 1940. (Public Domain)

Convinced of the future prowess of the aircraft carrier, Admiral Yamamoto opposed the construction of new battleships and gained the animosity of several old line officers who could not grasp the concept of naval air power. He told them that battleships were 'like elaborate religious scrolls which old people hang in their home' and often quoted an ancient proverb to his adversaries: "The fiercest serpent may be overcome by a swarm of ants." Obviously, he was alluding to the probability that aircraft armed with bombs and torpedoes could attack and sink the largest battleship. His theories were proved correct during the course of the Pacific War.

Nevertheless, as chief delegate to the second London Naval Conference in 1935, Yamamoto used superb negotiating skills and measured, calculated risk management to achieve parity with other powers for the Japanese navy in terms of capital ships.

Thus, earlier restrictions were ended and he had salvaged to a degree his relationships with some members of the battleship faction. The achievement brought acclaim and served as a springboard for Yamamoto's own recommendations to improve training and modernise the fleet. Through it all, he continued to lobby for a stronger commitment to naval aviation, believing that the carrier was the future of naval warfare.

The radical element

Even as his policies transformed the Imperial Japanese Navy into one of the most modern and efficient in the world, Yamamoto was troubled by a rising wave of militarism in Japan. Assassinations of public figures were becoming almost commonplace in the 1930s and an extremist threat to kill Yamamoto prompted him to take an extended

Yamamoto in 1942 as the tide of war turned against Japan. (Public Domain)

Yamamoto salutes a Japanese plane taking off from Guadalcanal in January 1942. Seven months later US ground forces landed on the island and captured the airfield. (Public Domain)

deployment at sea in the summer of 1939. Afterwards, he spent increasingly longer periods of time aboard his flagship, the battleship *Nagato*, as a safeguard against would-be assassins.

Yamamoto opposed Japan's entry into the Tripartite Pact of 1940 with Nazi Germany and

Below: US carrier-based dive bombers plummet toward Japanese warships during the Battle of Midway. The action was a catastrophe for the Imperial Japanese Navy. (Public Domain)

Fascist Italy. His vocal denunciation of the treaty and opposition to the growing influence of the Japanese Army in government alienated many politicians and military officers, particularly younger men who envisioned Japan as the dominant power in the Pacific and on the Asian mainland while advocating territorial expansion – through military means if necessary.

Despite the fact that Yamamoto's continuing cautions against war with the United States placed his life in jeopardy, he remained resolute and unafraid in dissent amid growing talk of hostilities. At the same time, the admiral pushed an intense training regimen in the Imperial Navy and his carrier air forces were becoming more proficient in their tactics. With growing confidence in the offensive capability of the fleet, he commented: "I think an attack on Hawaii may be possible now that our air training has turned out so successfully."

Pre-emptive strike

Yamamoto was promoted full admiral in November 1940 and in the same month word was received of the successful British attack against the Italian Fleet anchored in the harbour of Taranto. It had been executed by a mere handful of carrier-based Fairey Swordfish torpedo bombers of the Royal Navy Fleet Air Arm. The Italian warships were at anchor and presumed safe, but the obsolete biplanes had swept into the harbour and crippled three Italian battleships and other vessels with torpedoes.

Japanese war planners had already been evaluating the prospects for a successful air raid on Pearl Harbor and other US installations in Hawaii and the British triumph energised the process while carrier air training proceeded with renewed vigour. Still, as late as the autumn of 1941, Yamamoto hoped that Japan would avoid war. However, in October General Hideki Tojo, a hard line militarist whose Kwantung Army troops had already seized the province of Manchuria in China and fought a hot and cold land war with Japan's vast neighbour since 1931, was elevated to the office of prime minister.

Yamamoto became resigned to the fact that Japan was headed toward war with the United States. He committed himself and his navy to preparedness and he tirelessly advocated for approval of the pre-emptive attack on Pearl Harbor. Realistically, he noted: "If I am told to fight regardless of the consequences, I shall run wild for the first six months or a year, but I have utterly no confidence for the second or third year."

There was substantial opposition to the Pearl Harbor plan. Ironically, many of those officers who were quite willing to go to war with America argued that such an operation was too risky. True enough, it was a high-risk versus high-reward venture, but going to war against

The hulk of the Japanese aircraft carrier *Hiryu*, one of four Japanese carriers sunk during the Battle of Midway, drifts before sinking on June 5, 1942. (Public Domain)

The last image of Admiral Yamamoto taken alive, was made at the island of Rabaul on April 18, 1943. Hours later his aircraft was shot down by American fighter planes. (Public Domain)

Prime minister Hideki Tojo bows before a portrait of Yamamoto after his ashes had been returned to Japan in May 1943. (Public Domain)

the economic and industrial colossus that was the United States was risky in itself.

War games indicated that the imperial fleet would lose at least two aircraft carriers and one senior officer asserted that attacking Pearl Harbor would only raise the ire and indignation of the United States. He asserted that a direct attack on the Dutch East Indies would be the best option for a bold stroke, securing the vital natural resources of the region for future military operations. If the US Navy ventured out to oppose the thrust toward the Indies, then the modern samurai of Yamamoto's vaunted naval air force could deal with the Americans as he envisioned.

Yamamoto listened intently, negotiated and finally threatened to tender his resignation if the plan to attack Pearl Harbor was not allowed to move forward. It was enough to tip the scales in Yamamoto's

Crowds of civilians and military personnel line the streets during Yamamoto's funeral procession in June 1943. (Public Domain)

favour and the great endeavour was approved. As a footnote, Yamamoto told other officers that the Japanese Navy could seize the Dutch East Indies and move offensively against other strategically valuable targets in Asia and the Pacific while the US Navy was still reeling from the massive strike at Pearl Harbor.

Fleeting success

In the event, two waves of Japanese carrier-based attack aircraft wrought destruction at Pearl Harbor on December 7, 1941 and the US Pacific Fleet was indeed a shambles when the raid was over. When news of the great success was revealed to the people, celebrations erupted in the streets of major Japanese cities. Yamamoto was hailed a national hero, the greatest military mind and naval strategist in the island nation since Togo. Nevertheless, the American aircraft carriers, primary targets of the raid, were unscathed. All of them were at sea at the time of the attack. Further, repair and maintenance facilities and oil and fuel storage depots were left alone, virtually undamaged. Though 2,403 Americans had been killed, these were shortcomings that would later haunt the Japanese in their bid for hegemony in Asia and the Pacific.

For the time, though, Yamamoto reigned supreme among the warlords of Japan. He technically reported to the naval general staff but functioned virtually independently and without direct interference from other senior officers. Just as he predicted, Japanese forces on land, sea and air did 'run wild' for several months, inflicting stinging defeats on Allied naval forces in the Dutch East Indies and the Indian Ocean and capturing large swaths of territory. Three days after Pearl Harbor, Japanese planes caught the British battleship *Prince of Wales* and the battlecruiser *Repulse* in the open without air cover and sank them both. Japanese troops captured Hong Kong on Christmas Day 1941, swept down the Malay Peninsula and took Singapore on February 15, 1942 and marched to victory in the Philippines that spring.

Still, all was not well. American carrier planes raided Japanese installations on Marcus and Wake Islands in February 1942. While these were only pinpricks, the implication was clear. American aircraft carriers were operating and still posed a threat. Then, in April 1942, the daring Doolittle Raid on Tokyo raised further alarm. Even the home islands and Tokyo itself were vulnerable to air attack. Further concerns were raised when an invasion force intended to land at Port Moresby on the island of New Guinea was turned back during the Battle of the Coral Sea in early May.

Pacific crossroads

Yamamoto decreed that the most effective immediate response to the American resurgence was to extend the defensive perimeter of the empire to provide additional security. The most logical objective was tiny Midway Atoll, consisting of two islets, Sand and Eastern, located 1,300 miles

Right: Yamamoto in full dress uniform. His predictions of the course of World War Two in the Pacific were uncannily accurate. (Public Domain)

Below: Yamamoto sits second from left with other family members in this 1931 photo. (Public Domain)

Left: Yamamoto as a young officer in 1905 prior to the Battle of Tsushima in which he was seriously wounded. (Public Domain)

Right: Battle damage to the Japanese cruiser *Nisshin* inflicted during the Battle of Tsushima. Yamamoto was wounded by the blast. (Public Domain)

northwest of Hawaii. Ever the gambler, Yamamoto conceived a complex plan to lure the American aircraft carriers into battle and eliminate them while also seizing Midway. Japanese occupation of the atoll would pose a direct threat to Hawaii. During the first week of June 1942, the Battle of Midway ended in disaster for the Imperial Japanese Navy. The loss of four aircraft carriers, nearly 250 aircraft and over 3,000 dead – including veteran pilots and crewmen – was a staggering blow.

Again, eerily true to Yamamoto's prediction, the Imperial Japanese Navy had shot its offensive bolt around six months after Pearl Harbor. In the wake of the Midway disaster, Yamamoto retained his senior command role, but the Imperial Navy was compelled to fight a defensive war, one of attrition and one it could not hope to win. While American industry reached a wartime footing and produced new and better warships at an alarming rate, Japanese wartime production was much slower. American submarines sent merchant shipping to the bottom of the sea with startling regularity as the war dragged on and natural resources dwindled.

In August 1942, US forces landed on Guadalcanal in the Solomon Islands and while bitter fighting occurred on land, numerous sea battles also took place. Japan's fighting strength was slowly eroded in successive actions on the periphery of the empire's defensive cordon. Yamamoto realised that his worst fears were becoming reality and he contemplated his own death. In late summer he wrote to a colleague: "I sense that my life must be completed in the next 100 days."

Yamamoto grew melancholy. He bore the weight of these setbacks with true dignity, but perhaps motivated by a proverbial death wish, moved his headquarters from the relative safety of Truk in the Caroline Islands to Rabaul on the island of New Britain in the Bismarck Archipelago. Rabaul was significantly closer to American airfields in the region, but on April 18, 1943, he boarded a Mitsubishi G4M Betty bomber, embarking on a morale-building inspection tour of bases in the northern Solomons.

When American cryptanalysts read radio traffic indicating that Yamamoto would be vulnerable in the air, a plan was hatched to eliminate the mastermind of Pearl Harbor, the personification of America's arch enemy. A squadron of US Army Air Forces Lockheed

Yamamoto sits second from right on the second row with former classmates from the Japanese Naval Academy. (Public Domain)

P-38 Lightning fighters was detailed to shoot down the Admiral's plane. While several fighters went after Yamamoto's bomber, others engaged his escort of Mitsubishi A6M Zero fighters. Amid the swirling dogfight, the Betty was set ablaze and plunged into the jungle on the island of Bougainville.

A search party located Yamamoto's body, still strapped into his seat in dignified repose. He wore white gloves as his left hand maintained a tight grip on the hilt of his sword. His right hand rested atop the left. Struck in the head by a machine-gun bullet, he was probably dead before the plane ripped through the jungle canopy and crashed.

As the people of Japanese mourned their great and prophetic hero, Yamamoto's ashes were placed in two urns, one to be deposited alongside Admiral Togo at Tamabuchi Cemetery in Tokyo and the other with the ashes of his father in Nagaoka.

Perhaps it was somewhat fitting that Yamamoto, the visionary architect of the Pearl Harbor attack, did not live to see the destruction wrought on Japan and his country's unconditional surrender in 1945.

The wreckage of Yamamoto's aircraft where it crashed in the jungle on the island of Bougainville in April 1943. (Public Domain)

Right: This American propaganda poster features Admiral Yamamoto as the face of the Japanese enemy during World War Two. (Public Domain)

"I am looking forward to dictating peace to the United States in the White House at Washington" — ADMIRAL YAMAMOTO

What do YOU say, AMERICA?

ADMIRAL WILLIAM F HALSEY

"Where is – repeat where is – Task Force 34? The world wonders." Admiral William F Halsey, Jr read the message from Admiral Chester Nimitz, US Navy Commander-in-Chief Pacific Ocean Areas, with consternation, throwing his cap to the deck of the battleship USS *New Jersey*.

Halsey was in the middle of the Battle of Cape Engaño, one of several engagements that took place during the great Battle of Leyte Gulf in October 1944. Halsey had chased the Japanese decoy force under Admiral Jisaburo Ozawa far to the north of the landing beaches and vulnerable supply ships off the coast of the Philippine island of Leyte. Lured away by the promise of an opportunity to destroy Japanese aircraft carriers that had virtually no aircraft to launch, he left the Leyte area defended only by clusters of tiny escort carriers, destroyers and destroyer escorts whose primary roles had been air support for the US troops ashore and anti-submarine patrols.

In the event, the Japanese task force that nearly decimated the defenders turned away on the brink of victory. Halsey has been roundly criticised for his decision at Leyte Gulf but defended it after the war. Undoubtedly, he would have experienced a much harsher historical rebuke had the situation turned out differently at Leyte. In Halsey's defence, he had waited his entire professional life for such an opportunity and the destruction of Japanese aircraft carriers had always been a priority. Further, there was some confusion regarding the disposition of Task Force 34, a contingent of battleships that would have provided the necessary security for the landing forces and support vessels, which could have been detached from Halsey's overall Task Force 38 command.

Halsey had misunderstood the tenor of Nimitz's message that day – the phrase 'the world wonders' was intended only as padding and to confuse potential Japanese interceptors of the transmission. But it was inadvertently retained in the body of the communication and taken as a stinging rebuke.

William F 'Bull' Halsey was one of only four naval officers to attain the five-star rank of fleet admiral. (Public Domain)

Still, during the Battle of Leyte Gulf, the US Navy decimated the Japanese warships sent to disrupt the landings at Leyte and Halsey continued in command of Task Force 38, alternating with Admiral Raymond A Spruance. The two seagoing admirals took turns leading the ships in offensive campaigns. While one engaged the enemy, the other was planning the next naval move. Halsey's command was called the Third Fleet and its combat nucleus Task Force 38. With Spruance in charge, it was the Fifth Fleet and Task Force 58.

At the time of the Battle of Leyte Gulf, Admiral Halsey was 62 years old. The son of a career navy officer, he had built a reputation as a pugnacious, quick-tempered commander who was looking for a fight, an opportunity to deliver a crushing blow to the Japanese. Halsey earned the nickname 'Bull', perhaps the most fitting of such monikers ever bestowed in the US Navy.

To the sea

William F Halsey Jr was born on October 30, 1882, in Elizabeth, New Jersey. His father, Captain William F Halsey Sr, spent nearly 40 years in the US Navy. Initially frustrated while waiting for an appointment to the US Naval Academy at Annapolis, Maryland, the son enrolled at the University of Virginia to study medicine and then hopefully join the navy as a physician. After a year, the appointment came through at long last and Halsey excelled in football, graduating from Annapolis in 1904. He sailed around the world with the fabled Great White Fleet from 1907-1909 and commanded torpedo boats afterwards, receiving promotion from ensign directly to lieutenant and bypassing the rank of lieutenant junior grade.

During World War One, Halsey commanded torpedo boats and destroyers on Atlantic convoy escort duty. By the end of the war, he had been promoted lieutenant commander and received the Navy Cross for heroism.

From 1921 to 1924, Halsey served as a naval liaison officer in Germany, Norway, Denmark and Sweden. He then returned to sea duty and commanded destroyers before serving as executive officer of the battleship USS *Wyoming* and as commander of the naval academy station ship Reina Mercedes. During two more years at sea, he was promoted captain and commanded Destroyer Division Three. He then completed the Naval War College.

Halsey was always ready for adventure and at age 52 earned his pilot's wings. In 1938, he was promoted rear admiral. A true advocate

A Douglas SBD Dauntless dive bomber flies over the aircraft carriers USS *Enterprise* and USS *Saratoga* in December 1942. Halsey commanded both of these warships. (Public Domain)

Halsey wears a US Navy pith helmet in the sweltering Pacific sun. (Public Domain)

Admiral Chester Nimitz (left) confers with Halsey in early 1943. (Public Domain)

for the potential of naval aviation, he commanded the aircraft carriers *Saratoga, Yorktown* and *Enterprise* during the 1930s and with the US entry into World War Two, he was far and away the most experienced carrier commander in the US Navy. (Public Domain)

World war and will

When the Japanese attacked Pearl Harbor on December 7, 1941, Halsey was at sea aboard USS *Enterprise*, returning from the delivery of fighter planes to Wake Island. Enterprise had been scheduled to reach Hawaii on December 6, but bad weather fortuitously delayed the carrier's return.

When he viewed the wreckage of the Pacific Fleet and the destruction of raid, Halsey's blood boiled. He vowed to avenge the attack, set out to do so swiftly and remarked: "Before we're through with them, the Japanese language will be spoken only in hell." In the weeks following Pearl Harbor, Halsey commanded Task Force 8 aboard *Enterprise* and carrier-based aircraft struck Kwajalein, Taroa and Wotje in the Marshall Islands, inflicting damage on Japanese outposts, damaging an enemy cruiser and destroying 15 Japanese planes. He led further raids in company with USS *Yorktown*, under Admiral Frank Jack Fletcher, against targets in New Guinea and Marcus Island. The raids were indicative of Halsey's fighting spirit.

In December 1944, Halsey (right) discusses strategy with Admiral John S McCain. (Public Domain)

Halsey dines with crewmen aboard the battleship USS *New Jersey* in November 1944. (Public Domain)

Halsey, however, was not finished. By early April 1942, he was in command of the navy task force that brought Lieutenant Colonel Jimmy Doolittle and his intrepid group of US Army air raiders within striking distance of the Japanese capital of Tokyo. When the US task force was discovered short of its intended launch point, Halsey weighed in on the decision to launch Doolittle's bombers. The resulting raid made history, bolstering morale at home and throwing a scare into the Japanese high command that altered the course of World War Two.

Although he missed the epic Battle of Midway due to hospitalisation with a skin ailment, Halsey picked his own replacement, praising Admiral Raymond A Spruance, who turned out to be an excellent choice. When he recovered sufficiently, Halsey was given the tough assignment of re-energising the American campaign to secure the island of Guadalcanal in the Solomons. Replacing Admiral Robert L Ghormley, he committed sufficient surface assets to fend off the Japanese in a series of pivotal naval battles that took place in the vicinity of Guadalcanal and provided support for the Marines and army troops fighting on land. Halsey's command presence and perseverance facilitated the victory at Guadalcanal, the first land triumph of the Pacific War for US forces.

When Halsey led Task Force 38 into battle at Leyte Gulf, his hot temper and impetuosity got the better of him. His move jeopardised the safety of the transports and supply vessels off the Leyte coast and in turn the entire invasion of the Japanese-held Philippine Islands. When he became aware of the threat to the landings, Halsey detached some heavy forces toward San Bernardino Strait, but they did not participate in the primary action off the island of Samar. Meanwhile, his carrier-based aircraft pummelled Ozawa, sinking four aircraft carriers and decimating the enemy decoy force. Among the Japanese aircraft carriers sent to watery graves was *Zuikaku*, the last survivor of the carrier force that had attacked Pearl Harbor in 1941.

It should also be mentioned that the absence of unity of command among the American naval forces at Leyte Gulf contributed to the near disaster. Halsey reported to Nimitz in far-off Hawaii, while Admiral Thomas Kinkaid's Seventh Fleet, including the escort carriers and small ships off Leyte, were subordinate to General Douglas MacArthur. Such

Halsey stands second from left as Admiral Nimitz signs the instrument of surrender in Tokyo Bay, September 2, 1945. (Public Domain)

a structure contributed substantially to the confusion surrounding the naval dispositions.

Halsey spent much of his remaining career defending his command decisions at Leyte Gulf. In an article he wrote for the May 1952 edition of the Naval Institute Proceedings magazine, he plainly stated: "If the two fleets had been under the same command with a single system of operational control and intelligence, the Battle for Leyte Gulf might have been fought differently and with better coordination. My decision was to strike the Northern Force. Given the same circumstances and the same information as I had then, I would make it again."

Typhoon troubles
Even as the criticism of the Leyte operation simmered, controversy found Halsey once again. In December 1944, the Third Fleet was on station in Philippine waters when meteorologists issued an alert that a major typhoon was approaching. Reports about the storm were somewhat contradictory however and Halsey chose to remain in the same location rather than sailing out of harm's way.

The most vulnerable of Halsey's ships were the destroyers, which were in need of refuelling and would obviously pitch and roll more profoundly in the heavy weather. "We were completely cornered," Halsey reported as he realised the severity of the situation. "The consideration then was the fastest way to get out of the dangerous semi-circle and to get to a position where our destroyers could be fuelled." He sent a warning to all ships and weather stations, but the fleet was already in the crosshairs of the typhoon.

The storm hit with devastating effect, sinking three US Navy destroyers and damaging several other ships, while 146 aircraft were lost and 802 seamen were killed. A court of inquiry was subsequently convened and it concluded that Halsey had made an error in judgment. However, he was not formally reprimanded. A second typhoon struck the Third Fleet in the spring of 1945 and a second court of inquiry held Halsey responsible for the losses incurred, recommending the admiral be re-assigned. At the time, Halsey was one of the heroes of the Pacific War and the outcome of the conflict was a foregone conclusion. Tarnishing the reputation of such a towering figure when the Allies were on the brink of victory would remove some of the lustre from the achievement. Again, no action was taken.

Halsey was present on the deck of the battleship USS *Missouri* when the Japanese formally surrendered, ending World War Two in the Pacific, September 2, 1945. He received his fifth star, signifying the rank of fleet admiral, on December 11, becoming one of only four officers in the history of the US Navy to reach the pinnacle of command. He served on special duty with the office of the Secretary of the Navy and retired from active service in 1947.

In his later years, Halsey served as an executive with subsidiaries of International Telephone and Telegraph. He died of a heart attack on August 16, 1959, aged 76.

Although Halsey was prone to taking risks and was perhaps most responsible for the near catastrophe at Leyte Gulf and culpable in the pair of typhoon incidents, he is remembered also for rendering decisive leadership and displaying courage at critical times during the Pacific War. His aggressiveness, in the final analysis, was both an asset and a liability.

Halsey wears the rank of full admiral. Note the naval aviator's wings on his uniform. (Public Domain)

Left: Halsey strikes a stern pose in this portrait from late in his career. (Public Domain)

Below: The aircraft carrier USS *Langley* heaves in the rough seas during the typhoon of December 1944. (Public Domain)

ADMIRAL RAYMOND A SPRUANCE

The Battle of Midway, fought during the first week of June 1942, was the turning point of World War Two in the Pacific. And the most significant tactical decisions during the battle that led to a resounding victory for the US Navy were made by Admiral Raymond A Spruance.

Spruance had no prior experience with naval carrier-based aviation, but he took command of Task Force 16, including the precious aircraft carriers *Enterprise* and *Hornet*, just days before the pivotal battle. Spruance was to rendezvous with Task Force 17, under Admiral Frank Jack Fletcher, aboard the carrier *Yorktown*, at Point Luck, in the open sea and seek an opportune time to strike a telling blow against Japanese forces intent on seizing Midway Atoll, 1,300 miles west of the Hawaiian Islands.

US Naval Intelligence had determined that the Japanese were intent on taking Midway and their superiority in naval strength was significant. However, Admiral Chester W Nimitz, commander of the US Pacific Fleet, had no choice but to defend the tiny atoll or possibly see Hawaii under threat of imminent Japanese invasion. Nimitz, therefore, put everything on the line, committing his three available carriers and hoping that the element of surprise would assist in fending off the enemy.

In truth, it was a desperate situation and Nimitz needed his most capable and experienced carrier commanders available for the coming battle. However, the pugnacious Admiral William F 'Bull' Halsey was hospitalised with a skin infection and unable to participate in the looming fight. So, when Nimitz visited his sickbed and asked Halsey who should command Task Force 16, Bull Halsey did not hesitate and shot back: "Ray Spruance." After all, Spruance had commanded the cruiser screening force that sailed with Halsey's carriers during earlier operations in the opening weeks of the Pacific War and Bull had complete confidence in his cohort.

As the Battle of Midway unfolded, Spruance made the critical decisions that led to carrier-based aircraft inflicting grievous damage on the superior Japanese carrier force. He ordered his carriers to launch their planes after the Japanese were sighted. Dive bombers from *Enterprise*, *Hornet*, and *Yorktown* sank four enemy aircraft carriers and altered the naval balance of power in the Pacific. When *Yorktown* was subsequently damaged by Japanese planes, Fletcher, although senior, yielded tactical control of the American surface forces to Spruance.

Spruance and officers of the US Navy and Marine Corps stand on the island of Kwajalein after its capture in February 1944. (Public Domain)

Weighing the possibility of inflicting further damage on the Japanese or placing the unscathed *Enterprise* and *Hornet* at further risk, Spruance made the prudent call to retire. The Japanese turned away, their mission ending in disaster. *Yorktown* was sunk by a Japanese submarine, the major US loss of the historic sea fight.

Admiral Spruance went on to command Task Force 58 during the course of the Pacific War and led the US forces in the great victory at the Battle of the Philippine Sea in June 1944.

To the toughest test

Ray Spruance was born in Baltimore, Maryland, on July 3, 1886 and spent his boyhood years in Indianapolis, Indiana. He was a 1907 graduate of the US Naval Academy at Annapolis, Maryland and was commissioned an ensign after the two years of compulsory sea duty. He served aboard the battleships USS *Iowa* and USS *Minnesota* during the famed world cruise of the Great White Fleet during the administration of President Theodore Roosevelt.

During World War One, Spruance was an assistant to the inspector of machinery at Newport News Shipbuilding and Dry Dock Company in Virginia. By the end of the Great War, he had served aboard the battleship USS *Pennsylvania* and as an engineer officer at the New York Navy Yard. He reached the rank of rear admiral in December 1939, commanding the Tenth Naval District in San Juan, Puerto Rico, the Caribbean Sea Frontier and then Cruiser Division Five by September 1941.

As the US Navy responded to the devastation of the Japanese attack on Pearl Harbor, Spruance flew his flag aboard the heavy cruiser USS *Northampton* and shepherded Halsey's carriers during early air strikes against Japanese installations in the Gilbert and Marshall Islands. During these hit-and-run raids, Spruance earned Halsey's praise and respect as a capable naval officer. In April 1942, he commanded the cruiser escort for *Enterprise* and *Hornet* as the carriers travelled into dangerous waters of the western Pacific to deliver the Doolittle Raiders on their one-way mission to bomb the Japanese capital of Tokyo.

The wider war

When he was handed command of Task Force 16 for the Midway battle, Spruance was also given Halsey's staff cadre, a competent group of experienced naval aviation officers. Nevertheless, the

Above left: Admiral Raymond A Spruance was a hero of the pivotal Battle of Midway in June 1942. (Public Domain)

Above right: Spruance stands with Admiral Chester Nimitz in this wartime image. (Public Domain)

decisions to launch planes at a given time and place, the flexibility to assume tactical command of the entire naval fighting force and the discernment to withdraw after a stunning victory rather than remain in harm's way or engage in a fruitless pursuit, had validated the capability of Spruance, a cool and calm leader even when in the crucible of a heated battle.

Following the Midway triumph, Spruance was an aide to Nimitz, who had been named Commander-in-Chief Pacific Ocean Areas and a well-deserved promotion to Deputy Commander followed in September 1942. In August 1943, Spruance was given command of Central Pacific Force and he led Operation Galvanic, the offensive to seize Tarawa and Makin Atolls in the Gilbert Islands in November 1943, involving US Navy, Marine Corps and US Army assets. The landings at Tarawa and Makin were the first US amphibious operations against contested beaches in the Pacific War.

Through the balance of the year, Spruance directed further operations in the Gilberts and Marshalls along with the devastating air strikes against the major Japanese base at Truk in the Caroline Islands. Halsey recovered sufficiently to resume command and replaced Admiral Robert L Ghormley during the critical land and sea fight for the island of Guadalcanal in the Solomons.

In the spring of 1944, the Central Pacific Force was redesignated as the Fifth Fleet and Admiral Nimitz implemented a system to maximise its utilisation. American naval power had grown significantly with the nation's industrial might on a war footing and the availability of such strength enabled the combat element of Fifth Fleet to operate almost continually. Nimitz named Spruance to command the strike force, alternating with Halsey. While one admiral was at sea with the carriers, the other could be planning the next offensive move. The combat

During change of command ceremonies at Pearl Harbor, Spruance addresses the assembly, November 1945. (Public Domain)

Torpedo bombers are prepared for take-off from the deck of the aircraft carrier USS *Enterprise* during the Battle of Midway, June 4, 1942. (Public Domain)

Spruance (far left) meets Marine General Holland Smith (second from left) at Orote Field on the island of Guam. (Public Domain)

element was known as Task Force 58 under Spruance. While Halsey was in command, the nomenclature changed to Third Fleet and Task Force 38.

In early 1944, the US war planners identified the Marianas Islands, particularly Saipan, Guam, and Tinian, as the next targets for assault. When their occupation was completed, these islands would serve as bases for long-range Boeing B-29 Superfortress bombers that could ravage Japanese cities and industrial targets in the home islands. The war would be brought to the enemy's doorstep, while the Marianas could also serve as a staging area for further island-hopping amphibious operations toward Japan itself.

During the Marianas operations, Spruance's Task Force 58 was responsible for providing naval air and bombardment support for the ground troops on the islands, as well as protecting the transports and supply vessels clustered offshore. Spruance was free to engage the Imperial Japanese Fleet if the opportunity to inflict significant damage on enemy warships presented itself. In mid-June, the Japanese came out to fight and the resulting Battle of the Philippine Sea was a significant American victory. Three Japanese aircraft carriers were sunk and more than 600 enemy planes shot down. The aerial action was so one-sided that a US pilot nicknamed the encounter the 'Great Marianas Turkey Shoot'.

Spruance was later criticised for opting not to pursue the retiring Japanese ships that had survived the Battle of the Philippine Sea. He considered his primary task still to be the protection of the landing beaches and environs. Despite the extensive controversy that resulted from a possibly missed opportunity, producing even a letter from Nimitz that reflected his disappointment, Chief of Naval Operations Admiral Ernest J King was squarely in Spruance's corner. King

During ceremonies at Pearl Harbor in November 1945, Spruance takes command in the Pacific from Admiral Chester Nimitz. (Public Domain)

defended Spruance's decision to stay in Marianas waters and wrote approvingly: "Spruance, you did a damn fine job there. No matter what other people tell you, your decision was correct."

Last land battles

The last major land engagements of World War Two in the Pacific were the battles of Iwo Jima and Okinawa. Marines landed at Iwo Jima in February 1945 and fought tenacious Japanese defenders for more than a month before securing the island. The landings at Okinawa took place on April 1, 1945 and that island was secured in June. Spruance was responsible for naval support during both difficult campaigns and the ships offshore endured harrowing assaults by Japanese kamikaze suicide planes. The losses were particularly heavy off Okinawa, where waves of kamikazes struck, but the ships of the Fifth Fleet remained at their posts throughout. More than 4,000 American naval personnel were killed.

For much of the Pacific War, Admiral Spruance directed the operations of Task Force 58 from the cruiser *Indianapolis*, which was later lost to a Japanese submarine attack. Off Okinawa, *Indianapolis* was struck by a kamikaze and forced to withdraw from action. Spruance transferred his flag to the elderly battleship USS *New Mexico*, commissioned in 1918 and then a part of the battleship bombardment force.

On May 12, 1945, *New Mexico* was approaching a berth at the Hagushi Bay anchorage when a pair of kamikazes appeared seemingly out of nowhere just as the sun was setting. One enemy plane crashed into the old battleship, while the other missed but unleashed its bomb accurately. Explosions and fires erupted aboard the ship and 54 sailors were killed while more than 100 were wounded. Amid the chaos, members of Spruance's staff searched for the admiral. Soon enough, they found the 58-year-old officer helping a crew busily playing water from a hose on a fire that had erupted amidships. In that moment, Spruance displayed his true character and willingness to risk his own life in time of peril. Those who witnessed his extraordinary bravery carried that memory with them for the rest of their lives.

After the Japanese surrender in September 1945, Spruance followed Nimitz as commander of the Pacific Fleet. He then served as president of the Naval War College in Newport, Rhode Island. He retired from active duty on July 1, 1948 and was appointed ambassador to the Philippines by President Harry Truman, serving from 1952-1955. Afterwards, he lived quietly with his wife, Margaret Dean, in Pebble Beach, California. Spruance never smoked and seldom drank spirits. He loved his pet schnauzer and regularly took long walks, some eight miles or more in a single day. An avid gardener, he was often seen working among the flowers while wearing old clothes that would offer no hint of his extraordinary contribution to victory in the Pacific.

Spruance displayed a talent for getting along with others who were often difficult to deal with, including the irascible King, tough and aggressive Halsey and Admiral Richmond Kelly Turner, commander

Contrails from fighter planes lace the sky above Task Force 58 during the Battle of the Philippine Sea. (Public Domain)

of numerous amphibious operations who was known for his caustic temper. Nimitz and Spruance also became close friends, so much so that they were buried beside one another at the Gold Gate Cemetery in San Bruno, California. Admirals Turner and Charles Lockwood and their spouses were also buried nearby.

Spruance died on December 13, 1969 at the age of 83. After a lifetime of devotion to duty, he was an obvious choice for promotion to the rank of five-star fleet admiral, just as Bull Halsey had been. However, the promotion was blocked by Georgia Congressman Carl Vinson in a clear case of partisan politics. Amid an outcry, Congress nevertheless voted to raise Spruance's pay to that of full admiral for life. It was an unprecedented and fitting tribute.

Spruance flew his flag in command of Task Force 16 from the aircraft carrier *Enterprise* during the Battle of Midway. (Public Domain)

This bust of Admiral Spruance resides at the Naval War College in Newport, Rhode Island. (Creative Commons Leonard J Francisci via Wikipedia)

ADMIRAL BERTRAM RAMSAY

In was indeed a miracle. When British prime minister Winston Churchill rose to his feet to address the House of Commons on June 4, 1940, he delivered a stirring call to arms and resistance against the Nazis. He was able to do so because of the tremendous success of Operation Dynamo, the evacuation of 338,226 soldiers of the British Expeditionary Force and their French allies at the embattled English Channel port of Dunkirk.

And the success of Dynamo was largely attributed to the dedication and organisational skills of one man – Vice Admiral Bertram Ramsey. A scant two years earlier, Ramsay had been side-lined. He had refused a posting in China and it appeared that he was headed towards an obscure retirement from the Royal Navy after 40 years of service. But Churchill had been prescient. He realised that as war clouds gathered in Europe, there would be a need for veteran senior officers throughout the British armed forces and prevailed on Ramsay in August 1939 to become engaged once again.

Ramsay was 57 years old and posted as commander of Royal Navy facilities and personnel at the port of Dover. During the early months of World War Two, he was concerned with coastal defence and preparedness, but his focus changed sharply after May 10, 1940 when the Germans shattered the uneasy peace of the 'Phoney War' on the Western Front and launched Fall Gelb – Case Yellow – the invasion of France and the Low Countries. Within days, panzer spearheads crashed through French defences and turned northward toward the Channel ports, threatening to cut off thousands of British, French and Belgian troops that

Admiral Bertram Ramsay was the architect of Operation Dynamo, the Miracle of Dunkirk. (Public Domain)

Ramsay during preparations for the D-Day landings in 1944. (Public Domain)

Below: Ramsay stands second from left during a meeting of D-Day commanders. (Public Domain)

had moved towards the apparent main thrust of the German offensive.

As the panzers drove swiftly toward the coast, the Allied armies either retreated under tremendous pressure or surrendered. While the debacle unfolded, British military commanders understood the gravity of the situation and made contingency plans for an evacuation of troops to safety in Britain. Pragmatic observers realised that extricating the bulk of the soldiers defending a collapsing perimeter was a forlorn hope. They predicted that around 45,000 soldiers might be saved from German captivity.

From his command bunker chiselled into the famous white cliffs and deep beneath Dover Castle, Ramsay peered across the expanse of the Channel. At night, he could see the glow of fires as the battle raged in coastal France. In his position at Dover, responsibility for any evacuation effort fell to Ramsay and in the end, he proved more than equal to the task.

A military man

Bertram Ramsay was the son of a brigadier general of the British Army. Two of his brothers opted to follow their father into that branch of the service. But Bertram, the youngest born in London on January 20, 1883, charted another course in the service of his country. Educated at Royal Colchester Grammar School, he joined the Royal Navy as a cadet in 1898 at the age of 15.

Ramsay attended the Royal Naval College, Dartmouth, graduating in 1899 and then served aboard the cruiser HMS *Crescent*, co-operating well with army detachments in Somalia and receiving promotion to lieutenant in 1904, then joining the crew of the famous battleship HMS *Dreadnought*. He graduated from the Royal Navy War College in 1913.

During World War One, Ramsay initially commanded the small monitor M25 on the Dover Patrol. He was offered the post of flag lieutenant for the Grand Fleet's cruiser command but declined as he believed the post was prestigious but an impediment to receiving his own shipboard command. Had he taken the flag lieutenant post, he would have been assigned to HMS *Defence*, which was sunk at the epic Battle of Jutland in May 1916. In the spring of 1918, he was given command of the destroyer HMS *Broke* and he participated in the second raid on the German base at Ostend and in the Zeebrugge raid, being mentioned in despatches for conspicuous gallantry.

After the war, Ramsay served as a staff officer to Admiral of the Fleet John Jellicoe and was promoted captain in 1923. He commanded the light cruiser HMS *Danae* and then spent two years as an instructor at the War College. He became chief of staff to Admiral Arthur Waistell at the China Station and then taught at the Imperial Defence College before taking command of the battleship HMS *Royal Sovereign* in 1933.

By 1935, Ramsay was chief of staff of the home fleet, serving under his friend Admiral Roger Backhouse. The two differed on their command structure theories, Backhouse advocating a strong central control while Ramsay favoured decentralised operations with individual captains at sea directing and responding to conditions in a more immediate fashion. Their disagreements became heated and after only four months, Ramsay requested a transfer. The next three years were spent in a virtual wilderness of inactivity as he declined the

During an inspection of D-Day beaches in France, Ramsay watches Allied aircraft fly overhead. To the right, with pipe, is Air Chief Marshal Arthur Tedder. (Public Domain)

opportunity to return to China and worked on plans to reinvigorate the Dover Patrol. However, by the autumn of 1938, he was among those rear admirals that were targeted for retirement. His career, it seemed, was over. Soon enough, though, Churchill called him.

Challenge accepted

The evacuation of Allied troops from Dunkirk had been unthinkable until the rapid thrust of German forces to the Channel in May 1940. Realising that the defeat and capture of more than 400,000 troops would constitute the worst defeat in the British military history and leave the British Isles themselves terribly vulnerable to invasion without adequate troops to defend, Churchill approached Ramsay to put an evacuation plan together.

On May 20, the admiral held his first organisational meeting and the effort was codenamed Operation Dynamo since the conference room was located adjacent to the dynamo room that constantly whirred while supplying electric power to the command bunker and headquarters facilities. In the days that followed, the gallant defenders of both Boulogne and Calais bought time before surrendering to overwhelming German pressure. This left only Dunkirk as a suitable evacuation port and even as Ramsay and company worked feverishly, British General Alan Brooke, commander of the BEF II Corps and future Chief of the Imperial General Staff, wrote a diary entry that was more like an epitaph for the entire BEF.

Ramsay briefs Winston Churchill on the day's action at Dover in August 1940. (Public Domain)

"Nothing but a miracle can save the BEF now and the end cannot be very far off. It is a fortnight since the German advance started," Brooke wrote, "and the success they have achieved is nothing short of phenomenal. There is no doubt that they are most wonderful soldiers."

Still, Ramsay looked the situation over realistically and developed the blueprint for that miracle. He issued orders to marshal as many ships of the Royal Navy as possible that were capable of carrying at least 1,000 men. The British Broadcasting Corporation (BBC) had already aired a directive to civilians stating: "The Admiralty have made an order requesting all owners of self-propelled pleasure craft between 30 feet and 100 feet in length to send all particulars to the Admiralty within 14 days from today if they have not already been offered or requisitioned."

Such was the impetus for an assemblage of the 'little ships', piloted by civilian volunteers who were to participate in the upcoming epic sealift, rescuing so many Allied soldiers from the jaws of the German vice. The Admiralty authorised Operation Dynamo at 6.57pm on May 26, 1940 and Ramsay was a tower of strength throughout its execution. He had organised the conglomeration of warships and civilian rescue vessels as best he could and demonstrated coolness and command presence in the process, relying on capable officers near the scene to make crucial decisions. Such reliance was in keeping with the principle

During the Sicily campaign, Ramsay (far right) confers with British ground commanders on the island of Malta. To Ramsay's immediate right is General Bernard Montgomery. (Public Domain)

of command that had got him in hot water with Admiral Backhouse a few years earlier. But it worked.

One of the key players at Dunkirk was Captain William George Tennant, an Admiralty officer who volunteered his services and identified not only the east beaches for evacuation points, but also the east mole, where deeper draft vessels could tie up and soldiers evacuate quickly since the port facilities had been severely damaged. Tennant arrived at Dunkirk on the evening of May 27 and observed: "The sight of Dunkirk gave one a rather hollow feeling in the pit of the stomach. The Boche had been going for it pretty hard – there was not a pane of glass left anywhere and most of it was still unswept in the centre of the streets."

The evacuation process occurred under relentless attacks from Luftwaffe dive bombers, which sank or damaged dozens of small craft and Royal Navy warships. German fighters strafed the ships and the beaches, while the RAF flew 4,822 sorties to stave off as many of the attackers as possible. Some boats were lost to torpedoes fired from swift German E-boats and only one of three possible evacuation routes was in service until a second could be cleared of treacherous mines.

During the tough days of Operation Market Garden in September 1944, Ramsay meets Montgomery at the latter's headquarters. (Public Domain)

The first load of rescued soldiers, 7,669 of them, reached safety in England on the evening of May 27. As the numbers steadily grew, logistical concerns were handled adroitly. The ports of Dover, Ramsgate and Margate were particularly busy and, to keep them from being overwhelmed, transportation for soldiers to inland destinations was arranged. In the meantime, thousands had to be fed and wounded men cared for. It was a herculean effort and Ramsay and his close associates went many hours without sleep. On May 28, an astounding 11,847 soldiers were evacuated from the East Mole, while another 5,930 were taken off the eastern beaches.

Although the numbers were rapidly exceeding the expectations of some Admiralty officers, the Royal Navy took a dreadful pounding. On May 29 alone, the destroyers *Wakeful, Grafton* and *Grenade* were sunk, while six others were damaged and six merchant ships participating in Dynamo were lost. Among the casualties were several of the newest destroyers in the navy and the remainder were abruptly withdrawn to minimise further losses. However, when Admiral Frederic Wake-Walker arrived on May 30 to take command of all ships operating off the French coastline, he discovered that the modern destroyers had been withdrawn and went directly to Ramsay with his concern. Ramsay went personally to Admiralty and soon, seven of the newest destroyers were back in service at Dunkirk.

May 30 was a productive day despite the interference of the Luftwaffe and 58,823 BEF and French soldiers were evacuated. The following day 68,014 soldiers were brought to safety. Operations concluded June 1-4 and, as French officials voiced concerns

Soldiers of the British Expeditionary Force await evacuation at Dunkirk during Operation Dynamo, May 1940. (Public Domain)

regarding the number of their soldiers evacuated in comparison to the British, every effort was made to increase the rate of French evacuation as well. On the last day 26,175 soldiers, most of them French, were rescued.

Operation Dynamo was a colossal achievement, succeeding well beyond the hopes of those involved and Ramsay's professional conduct was largely responsible. He had not presided over a victory per se, but had shown his mettle in 'glorious defeat'.

Churchill was ebullient when he rose to speak on June 4, but did his best to contain his enthusiasm in consideration of those lost and the long road that lay ahead in the fight against the Nazis. He warned: "We must be very careful not to assign to this deliverance the attributes of a victory. Wars are not won by evacuations." He went on state boldly: "We shall fight in France, we shall fight on the seas and oceans, we shall fight with growing confidence and growing strength in the air, we shall defend our island, whatever the cost may be. We shall fight on the beaches, we shall fight on the landing grounds, we shall fight in the fields and in the streets, we shall fight in the hills. We shall never surrender."

Bertram Ramsay went on to serve as deputy commander of naval operations for North Africa and the Mediterranean under Admiral Andrew Cunningham. He was responsible for most of the planning for support of the invasion of Sicily. Later, he was named to lead Operation Neptune, the naval component of the D-Day landings of June 6, 1944. He managed to convince both Churchill and King George VI to remain in Britain rather than observe the landings in Normandy from the deck of the cruiser HMS *Belfast*. In itself, that was no small feat.

By 1945, Ramsay had come full circle, from the brink of obscure retirement to the pinnacle of Royal Navy command. Tragically, though, he lost his life in a plane crash while flying from Paris to Brussels for a meeting on January 2. He did not live to see the ultimate victory but without question made tremendous contributions to it. His finest hour had occurred in the dark days of 1940, transforming stark defeat into hope and glory.

While awaiting evacuation at Dunkirk, a British soldier points his rifle skyward and takes a shot at a strafing Luftwaffe fighter plane. (Public Domain)

Snatched from the jaws of death or German captivity, British soldiers rescued from Dunkirk during Operation Dynamo arrive at Dover on May 31, 1940. (Public Domain)

ADMIRAL JOHN TOVEY

The opportunity, it appeared, had slipped through the grasp of the Royal Navy. Every available asset had been marshalled to hunt down and sink the Nazi super battleship *Bismarck*. The German behemoth of more than 50,000 tons and mounting huge 15-inch main batteries had been wounded but not brought to heel.

Admiral John Tovey, commander of the Home Fleet, had done his mightiest, but *Bismarck* was approaching the cover of U-boats and Luftwaffe aircraft that would ensure her bid to reach the French port of Brest was successful. Tovey was unmoved and silent. The shadow of a smile crossed his face, a smile that concedes defeat after a hard-fought contest.

For days, Tovey, flying his flag aboard the battleship HMS *King George V*, and scores of other Royal Navy officers and crew had chased *Bismarck*. A last, desperate torpedo attack by antiquated Fairey Swordfish planes off the deck of the aircraft carrier HMS *Ark Royal* appeared to have achieved no hits. The game was up.

But then, a strange message from Captain Charles Larcom aboard the cruiser HMS *Sheffield* arrived. Remarkably, it indicated that *Bismarck* had changed course, moving in a circle.

Tovey dismissed the alert as a common error mistaking a ship's bow for its stern, and the foul weather made the error more likely. He remarked sullenly: "I fear Larcom has joined the reciprocal club."

Seconds later, though, the message was repeated. True enough, a Fleet Air Arm torpedo had struck home, jamming *Bismarck*'s steering gear. So, there it was. The pride of the Nazi Kriegsmarine could only await its fate. Within hours, *King George V*, the elderly battleship *Rodney*, and a host of Royal Navy warships had found their quarry at last, pummelling *Bismarck*, which sank after taking incredible punishment.

May 27, 1941, was the date of Tovey's triumph and it was the supreme moment of a naval career spanning 46 years.

Admiral John Tovey persevered until the German super battleship *Bismarck* was sunk. (Public Domain)

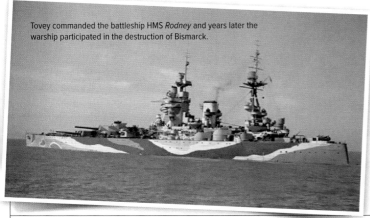

Tovey commanded the battleship HMS *Rodney* and years later the warship participated in the destruction of Bismarck.

Tovey on the quarterdeck of HMS *King George V* with Winston Churchill and Labour politician Sir Stafford Cripps. (Public Domain)

A soldier's son

Tovey was 56 years old when the *Bismarck* chase, one of the most famous actions in naval history, concluded. He was born March 7, 1885, at Borley Hill, Rochester, Kent, the youngest of 11 children. His father, Colonel Hamilton Tovey, was an officer of the Royal Engineers.

At the age of 14, young John entered Brittania, the Royal Naval Academy, Dartmouth and he went to sea as a midshipman in the spring of 1901. Postings to various warships and the North American and West Indies stations followed commissioning and led to mixed appraisals of the budding officer's talent, one calling him 'zealous and diligent' while another commented, 'painstaking and steady but stupid'.

As his career progressed, Tovey grew in stature, acquiring a reputation for candour and moral courage. With the outbreak of World War One, he was aboard the scout cruiser *Amphion*, which participated in the sinking of a German minelayer. In early 1916, Lieutenant Commander Tovey, in charge of the destroyer HMS *Jackal*, assisted with the dispatch of the German cruiser *Blucher*. He displayed tremendous courage in the epic Battle of Jutland on May 31, 1916, while in command of the destroyer HMS *Onslow*. Mention in Despatches was later upgraded to the Distinguished Service Order.

Between the world wars, Tovey commanded the 8th Destroyer Flotilla, then spent five years on shore duty with appointment as naval assistant to the Second Sea Lord. He took command of HMS *Rodney* in the spring of 1932 and two years later was appointed Commodore, Royal Naval Barracks, Chatham. He was promoted rear admiral as naval aide to King George V in the summer of 1935.

Tovey enjoyed the time at Chatham and a gleam came to his eye when he told a favourite story. On the morning of his promotion to admiral, he walked past a young sailor who failed to salute. Tovey called the man to attention and asked why. The unnerved rating replied: "I'm terribly sorry, sir. I didn't notice." Tovey called attention to his sleeve and with a noticeable rise in his voice demanded, "Don't you know what these stripes mean?" The response was quick and innocent. "But of course sir – the lowest form of admiral."

Again to war

Appointed Rear Admiral (Destroyers) in the Mediterranean in 1937, Tovey was promoted vice admiral two years later and in June 1940, with the war on, he was made second in command of the Mediterranean Fleet under Admiral Andrew Cunningham. Tovey was responsible for all light forces in the theatre, including nine cruisers and 25 destroyers. A couple of minor scrapes with the Italian fleet ensued and the sinking of one Italian destroyer had come at the expenditure of too much ammunition as far as Admiral Cunningham was concerned.

The battleship HMS *King George V*, Tovey's flagship during the Bismarck chase, at-sea in 1941. (Public Domain)

In November 1940, promotion to the rank of acting admiral and command of the Home Fleet at its Scapa Flow anchorage in the Orkney Islands of Scotland came. Tovey found himself subsequently at odds from time to time with Winston Churchill and First Sea Lord Admiral Dudley Pound. Although he was encouraged to maintain headquarters ashore, he was well aware of the difficulties sailors endured while at sea and determined that a seagoing commander would engender stronger support from staff and ratings.

Six months after taking Home Fleet command, Tovey found his destiny in the Atlantic, confronting *Bismarck*. As the distance between the hunters and the hunted closed, he retired to his cabin, offered a prayer and penned a message to the crew of *King George V*. It read: "To KGV. The sinking of the *Bismarck* may have an effect on the war as a whole out of all proportion to the loss to the enemy of one battleship. May God be with you and grant you victory. JT 26/5/41"

At 8.34am the following morning, *Bismarck* was finally in sight. *Rodney* opened fire moments later and then an orange flash seen to ripple across the length of *Bismarck*. The German was returning fire and an officer on the bridge of *King George V* dutifully announced that the enemy shells were due to arrive in 55 seconds. Tovey barked: "For heaven's sake, shut up!"

Controversy persists to this day as to whether British shells and torpedoes finished off *Bismarck* or whether the German crew scuttled the battleship when the situation became obviously hopeless. In the intervening time, a slightly frustrated Tovey quipped: "Somebody get me my darts! Let's see if we can sink her with those."

After the sea fight was over, a message from Churchill was received. "We cannot visualise the situation from your signals," it rattled. "*Bismarck* must be sunk at all costs and if to do this it is necessary for *King George V* to remain on the scene, then she must do so, even if it subsequently means towing *King George V*."

The message related an awareness that the British battleship was low on fuel, but it was rather ridiculous. If *King George V* had run out of fuel, German U-boats and aircraft would no doubt have sunk her. Tovey labelled the message 'the stupidest and most ill-considered signal ever made'.

In the aftermath of the *Bismarck* chase, Tovey defended two subordinates, Admiral Frederic Wake-Walker, commander of the cruisers *Norfolk* and *Suffolk*, and Captain John Leach of the battleship *Prince of Wales*, whom Pound wanted to court martial for 'lack of fighting spirit' during the early Battle of the Denmark Strait. The battlecruiser *Hood* had been sunk by *Bismarck* and the heavy cruiser *Prinz Eugen* and *Prince of Wales* was damaged. Tovey asserted that the two officers had handled their ships in exemplary fashion and threatened to resign if the charges were brought. He concluded afterwards: "I heard no more about it."

Tovey remained in command of the Home Fleet for the designated two-and-one-half year term and was promoted full admiral on October 30, 1942. He argued with Pound, who was dying of a malignant brain tumour, over the conduct of the Atlantic convoys en route to Russia. He decried Pound's order for Convoy PQ17 to scatter and the subsequent slaughter of the merchant ships, calling it 'sheer bloody murder'. Probably unaware of Pound's illness at the time of the controversial disposition of PQ17, Tovey nevertheless later wrote a caustic appraisal of Pound's performance. "He was neither a great tactician nor a great strategist, but unfortunately he believed he was."

Through much of the exchange, it later came to light, Pound had acted as Churchill's mouthpiece. The prime minister and the victor of

Tovey entertains a Soviet liaison officer aboard *King George V*. (Public Domain)

the *Bismarck* chase maintained a tenuous relationship and despite being labelled an 'obstructionist' by Churchill, Tovey responsibly discharged his duties with the Home Fleet and then as Commander-in-Chief, the Nore. He was promoted to admiral of the fleet in October 1943 and made significant contributions to the logistical preparations for the Normandy landings of June 6, 1944. He was appointed First and Principal Aide-de-Camp to King George VI in January 1945.

Tovey retired from the Royal Navy in early 1946 and was raised to the peerage as 1st Baron Tovey of Langton Matravers, Dorset. He served in the House of Lords and worked with numerous charities in later years, caring for his disabled wife until her death in 1970. He died the following year at age 85, his place in history secured with the vanquishing of *Bismarck*, a dreaded symbol of a dark enemy.

The German battleship *Bismarck* in home waters prior to her fatal encounter with the Royal Navy. (Creative Commons Bundesarchiv Bild via Wikipedia)

ADMIRAL BRUCE FRASER

The Nazi Kreigsmarine battlecruiser *Scharnhorst* was a menace to Allied merchant shipping and when the opportunity came to confront the enemy surface raider, Admiral Bruce Fraser was ready. The Admiralty had received reports that *Scharnhorst* was preparing to sortie in December 1943 and Fraser formulated a plan that might lure the German warship into a decisive surface action and dispatch the enemy once and for all.

Fraser, commander of the Royal Navy Home Fleet, set sail from the anchorage at Akureyri, Iceland, on December 23, his flag flying aboard the battleship HMS *Duke of York*. The primary mission of *Duke of York* and the remaining ships of his Force 2, including the light cruiser HMS *Jamaica*, the British destroyers *Savage, Scorpion*, and *Saumarez* and the Norwegian destroyer *Stord*, was to escort Murmansk-bound convoy JW55B.

Fraser knew that an empty convoy, RA55A, bound for Britain, was also at sea and vulnerable. He alerted Admiral Robert Burnett, at Kola Inlet near Murmansk, to prepare his Force 1, the light cruisers HMS *Belfast* and *Sheffield* and the heavy cruiser *Norfolk*, to prepare for battle. Fraser hoped that the potential targets of two convoys would be enough to entice *Scharnhorst* towards them while the Royal Navy warships cut off the Germans' retreat to the safety of the Norwegian fjords. The two British flotillas would then close and sink *Scharnhorst*.

During a conference at sea aboard *Duke of York*, Fraser listened intently to various reports and then rose to his feet, thrusting both hands into his jacket pockets and lifting his heels in anticipation of an action to come. He commented: "Should we encounter *Scharnhorst*, I have decided first to close with the enemy and open fire with starshell at a range of about 12,000 yards. I intend to form the escorting destroyers into subdivisions and when the right moment comes to release them for torpedo attack." He quickly turned to Captain John Hughes-Hallett and added: "Finally, I will keep you and your *Jamaica*

Admiral Bruce Fraser was the victor of the Battle of the North Cape in 1943. (Public Domain)

with me. You will, however, have freedom of action and may of course open the distance between us if I go into action with *Duke of York*."

Scharnhorst had indeed weighed anchor from Altenfjord in Norway on Christmas Day, her crew throwing all holiday decorations into the sea and consuming a specially prepared but hurried dinner. Escorted by five Kriegsmarine destroyers, the battlecruiser commander, Admiral Erich Bey, went on the hunt for the convoys. Meanwhile, Fraser detached four destroyers from RA55A to increase his own strength while Burnett and Force 1 steadily pounded southwest through vile weather and towering wavetops.

At roughly 8.30am on December 26, 1943, Boxing Day in Britain, Burnett's radar picked up *Scharnhorst* sailing alone after Bey had dispatched his destroyers to search for convoy prey in a wider area of open sea. Burnett's *Belfast*, *Sheffield* and *Norfolk* opened fire, drawing blood with six- and eight-inch shells. *Scharnhorst* was hit twice and blinded when her radar was knocked out.

Bey turned away but, like a bloodhound, Burnett picked up the scent again around noon and another exchange occurred. At the same time, Fraser was a move ahead of the German commander, racing across the windswept Barents Sea near the North Cape. *Duke of York's* radar picked up *Scharnhorst* at 4.17pm and once within range, the battleship's 14-inch guns barked. *Scharnhorst* was cornered and the ensuing fight ended a few hours later. As the German battlecruiser slid beneath the waves, only 36 of her complement of 1,932 sailors survived to be plucked from the icy water.

The victory in the Battle of the North Cape was the highlight of the long naval career of Admiral Bruce Fraser, an admired officer of the Royal Navy known for his good humour but a matter-of-fact gentleman just the same. His communique to the Admiralty was a masterpiece of brevity: "Scharnhorst sunk."

Army and navy

Bruce Austen Fraser was born in Acton, West London, on February 5, 1888, the son of a 64-year-old retired officer of the British Army. Educated at Bradfield College, Berkshire, Fraser decided to pursue a naval career and embarked as a midshipman aboard the training ship HMS *Britannia* in 1902. After completing his midshipman cruise, he spent months at sea aboard battleships of the Royal Navy.

Fraser attended HMS *Excellent*, the Royal Navy Gunnery School at Whale Island, Portsmouth, in 1911 and returned two years later as an instructor, authoring the earliest edition of the *Royal Navy Director Firing Handbook*. He served in the Middle East

Fraser signs surrender documents in Tokyo Bay on behalf of the United Kingdom, September 2, 1945. (Public Domain)

Fraser escorts King George VI while greeting officers aboard the battleship HMS Duke of York. (Public Domain)

the critical years prior to the outbreak of World War Two. His decision to arm the King George V-class battleships, including *Duke of York*, with 14-inch main batteries paid off with the destruction of both *Scharnhorst* and the famed Nazi battleship *Bismarck*.

After a year as deputy commander of the Home Fleet, Fraser succeeded Admiral John Tovey as commander in mid-1943. When the victory in the Battle of the North Cape was won, Fraser addressed his staff officers: "Gentlemen, the battle against *Scharnhorst* has ended in victory for us. I hope that if any of you are ever called upon to lead a ship into action against an opponent many times superior, you will command your ship as gallantly as *Scharnhorst* was commanded today."

Fraser managed himself with skill not only while in battle, but also during exchanges with other officers and political leaders when differences emerged. During World War Two, he visited Britain's Soviet allies in Murmansk and with the horrible memories of Baku still fresh, he greeted his hosts warmly. He also managed to deal with Winston Churchill effectively. Although their disagreements were heated and devolved into shouting matches at times, Fraser was patient and unruffled. In one exchange, Churchill at last conceded: "Fraser, you are a mule, but you are right."

Always placing the good of the Royal Navy above his own, Fraser nobly declined Churchill's offer as First Sea Lord when Admiral Sir Dudley Pound fell ill in the autumn of 1943. Fraser earnestly believed that his lack of combat experience might inhibit his acceptance by the fleet and endorsed Admiral Andrew Cunningham, telling Churchill: "I believe I have the confidence of my own fleet. Cunningham has that of the whole navy."

In August 1944, Admiral Fraser was named commander of the Royal Navy Eastern Fleet headquartered in Ceylon. In December he was elevated to command of the Royal Navy Pacific Fleet at Sydney, Australia. In this role he supervised the transition of British sea power from an Atlantic focus. In the circumstances, he played his role with diplomatic aplomb. The US Navy had surpassed the strength of the Royal Navy during the war years, and the Pacific War was decidedly an American show.

Despite the wrangling and mistrust that were bound to occur among allies, one group of whom were newly arriving in substantial numbers, Fraser was determined to win the Yanks over with goodwill while his command proved its mettle amid what combat was left against the Japanese. He succeeded handsomely.

during World War One and was promoted to lieutenant commander in March 1916. He was present at Scapa Flow during the surrender of the German High Seas Fleet in 1918 and prevented the battleship SMS *Baden* from being intentionally scuttled.

As his career progressed, Fraser acquired the nickname 'Tubby' for his stocky build. He was outwardly reserved and succinct when speaking to groups. However, those who knew him considered him an excellent conversationalist and an affable sort. Even as he progressed in rank and responsibility, Fraser was never pretentious. He was the proverbial man of action rather than gab.

Captivity and command

Promoted to commander in June 1919, Fraser was ordered to the Black Sea during the unrest of the Russian Civil War. While in the city of Baku, his small contingent of sailors was caught up in a Bolshevik attack and taken prisoner. Agonising months in Russian captivity followed, but Fraser was released in November 1920 with the few other survivors of the ordeal.

By 1924, Captain Fraser was Fleet Gunnery Officer of the Mediterranean Fleet. He returned to Britain and duty with the Admiralty and commanded the aircraft carrier HMS *Glorious* in the mid-1930s. Promoted to rear admiral in the spring of 1938, he was named Third Sea Lord and Controller of the Navy. With the purse strings, he was instrumental in the construction of warships during

Fraser pours the rum into the Christmas pudding aboard the battleship HMS *Duke of York*, November 1943. (Public Domain)

Fraser accepts the surrender of Japanese forces at Hong Kong, 1945. (Public Domain)

Fraser stands with other representatives of the Allied powers aboard the battleship USS *Missouri* in Tokyo Bay. (Public Domain)

The crew of a 14-inch main gun aboard the battleship HMS *Duke of York* poses after the Battle of the North Cape. (Public Domain)

"It was quite clear that in the intensive, efficient and hard striking type of war that the US fleet was fighting, nothing but the inclusion of a big British force would be noticeable and nothing but the best would be tolerated," Fraser later assessed. After an invitation to lunch with American Admiral Raymond A Spruance, commander of the Fifth Fleet, Fraser commented on the meeting and said that his counterpart was a 'great commander – but very austere. He gave me lunch – I think we had a couple of lettuces or something'.

While Fraser's command contributed gallantly, especially during the gruelling fight off the island of Okinawa in the spring of 1945, Fraser actually won the affection of the Americans. He enjoyed visits from US Navy officers in the late afternoon. Alcohol was prohibited aboard American ships, but Admiral Chester Nimitz, Commander-in-Chief Pacific Ocean Areas, warmed to his British friend thoroughly, admitting that he would call on Fraser '…partly on official business, partly because I like him, and mostly to get a Scotch and soda before dinner…'.

During the surrender ceremonies in Tokyo Bay on September 2, 1945, Fraser signed the documents as the chief representative of the British government. He was subsequently named First and Principal naval aide to King George VI and in September 1946, he was raised to the peerage as Baron Fraser of North Cape of Molesey in the County of Surrey. In February 1948, he was promoted Admiral of the Fleet and that September he became First Sea Lord and Chief of the Naval Staff.

Fraser remained true to his convictions during the establishment of NATO, backing the prevailing international perspective that an American admiral should be named Supreme Allied Commander Atlantic while a howl of dissent went up among Royal Navy officers. It was, in fact, a pragmatic stance expected from such an experienced officer.

After retirement in December 1951, Fraser lived quietly for 30 years and died in a London nursing home on February 12, 1981. He was 93 and had never married. Newspapers around the world carried brief reports of his passing, and eight admirals attended his funeral at HMS *Excellent*.

Little is written or actually documented of Fraser's last years. But it was just as well that his quiet end brought silent symmetry to a life of adventure proven in heroic deeds and not words only.

The German battlecruiser *Scharnhorst* was sunk by British forces under Admiral Bruce Fraser in the Battle of the North Cape. (Creative Commons Bundesarchiv Bild via Wikipedia)

ADMIRAL CHUICHI NAGUMO

The First Air Fleet of the Imperial Japanese Navy was the most powerful fighting force of its kind in the world. Centred on six fleet aircraft carriers, the striking force, or Kido Butai, could launch hundreds of fighters, level bombers, dive bombers and torpedo bombers in a single blow.

And its destructive power was on full display with the attack on Pearl Harbor and other military installations on the Hawaiian island of Oahu, December 7, 1941. The strike crippled the US Pacific Fleet, sinking or damaging eight battleships and many other vessels and disabling American air power in the area as well.

At the head of the Kido Butai was Admiral Chuichi Nagumo, appointed to the commander's post on April 10, 1941. Some observers questioned the appointment, made largely due to Nagumo's seniority. He had little appreciation for carrier-based air power, they said, and was of the old school with emphasis on heavy warships and fleet surface action. Further, Nagumo was opposed to the attack on Pearl Harbor as it was sponsored by Admiral Isoroku Yamamoto, Commander-in-Chief of the combined fleet.

Perhaps these detractors were at least partially correct. As Nagumo wielded the fighting fist of the Imperial Japanese Navy, he made two crucial decisions that shaped the future of World War Two in the Pacific and ultimately contributed to Japan's defeat.

Rising in the navy

Chuichi Nagumo was born March 25, 1887, in Yonezawa, Yamagata Prefecture, northern Japan. He attended the naval academy at Eta Jima, graduating in 1908 and ranking 36th among 191 peers. He served aboard cruisers and received promotion to ensign in 1910 before completing the torpedo and naval artillery schools.

Young Nagumo was promoted steadily through the World War One years and took his first command aboard the destroyer *Kisaragi* on December 15, 1917. A specialist in torpedo and destroyer tactics, he graduated the Naval War College in 1920, received promotion to lieutenant commander and became a general staff officer by the mid-1920s. Elevated to commander in 1924, he travelled to the United States and Western Europe to study foreign naval warfare tactics and weaponry.

Service in China and then as an instructor at the naval academy led to promotion to captain and sea duty with cruisers and as commanding officer of the 11th Destroyer Division. He was promoted rear admiral in late 1935, leading the 8th Cruiser Division in support of Japanese Army troops then fighting in China. As commander of the Torpedo School, he became well known for his hawkish political stance, which boosted his career and facilitated promotion to vice-admiral in 1939. When he was given command of the Kido Butai, Nagumo was presiding over the Naval War College.

Nagumo was 54 years old and possibly set in his ways when the great air arm of the Imperial Japanese Navy became his responsibility. He was already known as a risk-averse officer who displayed caution during war games. Nevertheless, he was an advocate for expansion of the empire and was surrounded by highly motivated and capable lieutenants.

Off to war

Still concerned about the great risk involved in war with the US, Nagumo remarked to an official: "I feel that I have undertaken a heavy responsibility. If I had only been more firm and refused. Now we have left home waters and I am beginning to wonder if the operation will work."

He led the Kido Butai to sea in late November 1941 – target Pearl Harbor. The force consisted of the six aircraft carriers *Akagi, Kaga, Shokaku, Zuikaku, Soryu* and *Hiryu,* their hangar decks crowded with combat aircraft. The carriers would sail a northerly route toward Hawaii to avoid commercial shipping lanes and maintain radio silence to minimise the chance of discovery.

At a distance of roughly 230 miles from the island of Oahu, the carriers turned into the wind and launched their planes in two waves on the morning of December 7. The attackers achieved complete surprise and executed the plans devised by Lieutenant Commander Minoru Genda and under the mission leadership of Lieutenant Commander Mitsuo Fuchida near flawlessly. When the planes returned to the carriers, only 29 of their number had been shot down in the raid and Nagumo was confronted with the first of his major decisions.

Those staff officers and returning air commanders clustered around the admiral recommended the launching of a third wave of strike aircraft against Pearl Harbor. Rich targets remained untouched, including the vast oil reserves that would fuel a resurgent US Navy, the machine shops and repair facilities that would be vital to resurrecting the American offensive naval power and the submarine base, which would service the weapons that provided immediate capability of the Americans to hit back.

Nagumo weighed his options. His carrier airmen had already won a great victory. The whereabouts of the American aircraft carriers was

Nagumo shows the strain of command in this photo from World War Two. (Public Domain)

Left: Admiral Chuichi Nagumo led the Japanese First Air Fleet at Pearl Harbor and Midway. (Public Domain)

Below: Nagumo poses with staff officers on the island of Saipan in early 1944. (Public Domain)

The aircraft carrier *Akagi*, Nagumo's flagship, under way in the Indian Ocean. *Akagi* was sunk during the Battle of Midway. (Public Domain)

Hawaii had been reading Japanese radio traffic and determined that the next target for the Imperial Navy was indeed Midway. Armed with this knowledge, Admiral Chester Nimitz, Commander-in-Chief Pacific Fleet, ordered the aircraft carriers *Yorktown, Enterprise* and *Hornet,* under Admirals Frank Jack Fletcher and Raymond A Spruance, to lie in ambush and hit the Japanese when the opportunity was available.

For the Japanese, the Midway plan unfolded as expected at first. Nagumo's combat air patrol and shipboard antiaircraft guns shot down dozens of attacking American planes launched from Midway and though Nagumo was shaken by near-misses and a flaming US plane that almost crashed into the bridge of his flagship Akagi, his command was unscathed.

On the morning of June 4, Nagumo made his second fateful decision. He launched a massive air attack against Midway. The Japanese planes swept in, destroying installations on the atoll and attempting to render the airstrip unusable for future attacks against the invasion force. Although his planes had wrought considerable destruction, the commander of the Midway strike made his way to the bridge of Akagi upon his return and recommended a follow-up raid to put the Midway facilities out of action for good.

Nagumo concurred, but while aircraft were being refuelled and re-armed with bombs for the next Midway assault, the situation changed dramatically. An alarming report was received. An American aircraft carrier was sighted by a search plane from the cruiser *Tone* and the prospect of attack by US carrier planes became real while the carrier presented a priority target if it could be sunk.

Hastily, Nagumo ordered a change from bombs to torpedoes, more suitable for an attack on the American carrier. Time was of the essence and while the bombs were removed and stacked for securing later, fuel lines stretched across the decks of the carriers.

Just at the critical moment, American planes appeared overhead. Torpedo bombers were blown out of the sky, but the US dive bombers hit three of Nagumo's carriers. *Akagi, Kaga* and *Soryu* became flaming pyres. *Hiryu* was sunk in another raid hours later. The Japanese striking sword had been shattered.

Nagumo survived the ordeal at Midway, transferring his flag to a nearby cruiser. Perhaps better planning would have prevented his carriers from such vulnerability on that fateful morning.

In the wake of the devastating defeat at Midway, Japan was obliged to fight a defensive war until its surrender in 1945. Nagumo went on to training and district commands and committed suicide on Saipan in the Marianas on July 6, 1944, as American troops battled to wrest control of the island.

unknown and they might launch a retaliatory strike against his own force at any time. The seas were rough and the pilots and aircrew tired. He believed the risk of a third wave was too high and opted to retire. And so, the question remains. Had a third strike been delivered, would the US Pacific Fleet have recovered as rapidly and contested further Japanese expansion in the region as effectively? Within a year, Admiral Yamamoto had openly criticised the decision to retire without launching a third wave while the opportunity presented itself.

Still, the attack on Pearl Harbor was hailed as a major victory. Nagumo was congratulated and while Japanese troops advanced on the ground in Malaya and the Philippines, he launched a devastating foray into the Indian Ocean in early 1942. Nagumo's carrier planes executed devastating raids on the port of Darwin, Australia and then pounded other targets while chasing the British Royal Navy westward to safe haven in East African waters. In the meantime, Japanese planes sank the aircraft carrier HMS *Hermes,* two cruisers and two destroyers.

Just as the Indian Ocean raid was concluding in April 1942, the Americans were planning an electrifying response to the Japanese aggression at Pearl Harbor that had plunged the unprepared nation into World War Two. On the 18th, American bombers flew from the deck of the aircraft carrier USS *Hornet* under the command of Lieutenant Colonel Jimmy Doolittle. They bombed the Japanese capital of Tokyo and industrial targets in other nearby cities. Although little damage was done, it was a psychological blow to the Imperial General Staff and the fateful decision was made to extend the defensive perimeter of the Japanese Empire further across the Pacific.

A primary target was Midway Atoll, just 1,300 miles west-northwest of Hawaii. Japanese seizure of Midway would place Hawaii under the threat of invasion and facilitate air operations against US installations in the area as well. Admiral Yamamoto conceived a complicated plan to capture Midway. And if the Americans chose to risk their aircraft carriers in an attempt to interfere with the landings, the overwhelming Japanese strength would destroy them.

Nagumo was handed the responsibility of softening up ground defences at Midway in support of the landings while also neutralising the American air forces stationed there. While the Kido Butai was still a powerful force when the Midway operation was launched, Nagumo was without two of his fleet carriers. *Shokaku and Zuikaku* had been damaged in early May during the Battle of the Coral Sea, and both had lost many planes and valuable aircrew. Neither would be present during the Midway engagement.

Still, the balance of power appeared heavily in favour of the Japanese. The Americans did possess one key advantage. Code-breakers in

Right: Nagumo as a young lieutenant in the Imperial Japanese Navy. (Public Domain)

Below: A Mitsubishi Zero fighter takes off from the aircraft carrier *Akagi* on December 7, 1941, en route to Pearl Harbor. (Public Domain)

ADMIRAL ERICH RAEDER

When Adolf Hitler revealed his plans to invade Poland in September 1939, Grand Admiral Erich Raeder, chief of the Kriegsmarine, the Nazi navy, was taken aback. His plans for the growth and combat potential of the fleet would not be achieved for some time and he was hoping that war would be delayed until 1944.

Regardless, when war became inevitable, Raeder was committed. He was also willing to express his opinion on a variety of strategic topics. In early 1940, for example, Raeder was aware that German industry needed the iron ore and other resources then being imported from Scandinavia, while ingress and egress from ports on the Baltic Sea were critical to future operations. Therefore, he proposed to Hitler the invasion of Norway and Denmark. These operations were completed successfully in April 1940 as the British military expedition to oppose the conquest of Norway was thoroughly defeated.

Raeder was concerned with the prospects for victory in the proposed invasion of Great Britain later that year and expressed the firm opinion that the Luftwaffe would have to gain control of the skies over the English Channel in order for landing barges and German warships to operate safely. He generally opposed the effort, codenamed Operation Sea Lion, and it was shelved when the Royal Air Force won the Battle of Britain. Again, in early 1941, Raeder opposed Operation Barbarossa, the Fuhrer's invasion of the Soviet Union, which ultimately led to disaster. However, he did support the German declaration of war against the United States on December 11, 1941.

The apparent lacklustre performance of the German cruisers and destroyers sent to intercept a convoy bound for the Soviet Union in the Battle of the Barents Sea, December 31, 1942, was the final breach in relations between Raeder and Hitler. The admiral was shunted away from command of the Kriegsmarine and replaced by Admiral Karl Donitz, leader of the U-boat arm of the fleet. Raeder resigned in January 1943.

High seas, high stakes

Erich Raeder was born on April 24, 1876, in Schleswig-Holstein, the son of a stern schoolmaster. The son held fast to his father's principles through his own career, often appearing detached from others and without charm. He joined the Imperial Navy in 1894 and saw the growth of the German fleet under the command of Admiral Alfred von Tirpitz, who committed to a building programme that would hopefully yield at least parity with the British Royal Navy, perhaps

Grand Admiral Erich Raeder led the Nazi Kriegsmarine from the mid-1930s until 1943. (Creative Commons Bundesarchiv Archiv Bild via Wikipedia)

deterring British interference with plans for the expansion of the burgeoning German Empire.

Raeder gained a reputation for hard work and discipline and rose steadily in the ranks of the navy. He spoke fluent Russian and was sent to Asia as an observer during the Russo-Japanese War of 1904-1905. He was a fervent supporter of the effort to construct battleships that would compete for dominance with the Royal Navy and became captain of the personal yacht of Kaiser Wilhelm II before World War One.

During the Great War, Raeder participated in the Battle of the Dogger Bank in 1915 and the epic Battle of Jutland the following year. At the time of Jutland, he was serving as Admiral Franz von Hipper's chief of staff and was extensively involved in the planning of the cruiser deception that was intended to lure the Royal Navy grand fleet into a decisive surface battle with the German high seas fleet. In the autumn of 1918, he was a key figure in the suppression of a mutiny within the fleet and in 1922, he was promoted rear admiral in the interwar navy, limited in size and scope by the terms of the Versailles Treaty. In 1928, he was promoted to full admiral and made head of Naval Command.

Raeder did not personally agree with some of the Nazi Party's policies but was an enthusiastic supporter of Hitler's efforts to rebuild the German armed forces. In 1936, he was elevated to the new rank of general admiral as Commander-in-Chief of the Kriegsmarine. Three years later, Hitler raised him to the rank of grand admiral. With the onset of World War Two, the Kriegsmarine was not prepared to take on the Royal Navy and relied on its surface raiders and U-boats to take a heavy toll in Allied merchant shipping.

In 1945, Raeder was captured by soldiers of the Soviet Red Army. He was charged with war crimes, including conspiracy, crimes against humanity and planning, initiating and waging wars of aggression. Convicted and sentenced to life in prison, he was released in 1955 due to failing health. He published his memoir, Mein Leben, two years later and died at age 84 on November 6, 1960.

Right: Raeder meets with Hitler in 1943. Raeder was later convicted of war crimes. (Creative Commons Bundesarchiv Bild via Wikipedia)

Below: The German destroyer *Friedrich Eckoldt* takes a fatal hit during the Battle of the Barents Sea. (Creative Commons Irwin J Kappes via Wikipedia)

Raeder walks with German president Paul von Hindenburg during ceremonies in 1931. (Creative Commons Bundesarchiv Bild via Wikipedia)

ADMIRAL HUSBAND E KIMMEL

Early on December 7, 1941, a disturbance rocked the entrance to Pearl Harbor as the destroyer USS *Ward* sank a Japanese midget submarine with gunfire and depth charges. The skipper of the *Ward* flashed a report of the encounter, but it seemed to generate no appreciable response. These were the first shots of World War Two in the Pacific.

Minutes later, a messenger was pedalling a bicycle toward one of Pearl Harbor's gates. He carried a war warning from General George C Marshall, Army Chief of Staff in Washington, to the US naval commander at Pearl Harbor, Admiral Husband E Kimmel and his Army counterpart, General Walter C Short, in command of the Hawaii Department. Atmospheric interference had temporarily shut down military channels and the civilian RCA line had been used to transmit the warning.

Marshall's message was too late. Japanese bombers, torpedo planes and fighters were turning to make their runs toward sleepy Sunday morning targets and the United States was suddenly and violently at war. In the wake of Pearl Harbor, Admiral Kimmel and General Short were found culpable for the American unpreparedness and guilty of dereliction of duty by the Roberts Commission, the most influential of several official inquiries into the disaster. Kimmel and Short had failed to ensure the security of the fleet and the military installations on the island of Oahu.

Kimmel had taken command of the Pacific Fleet in February 1941 and immediately assessed the situation. He faced several challenges, including the fact that supply was complicated with ships transiting the Pacific from the West Coast to deliver them. Any ship of the Pacific Fleet that required extensive repair or overhaul had to sail to the West Coast as well. The confines of Pearl Harbor presented security issues. Smaller ships had to be clustered together and a surprise air attack would find these targets easy marks. Still, Kimmel considered his defensive preparations adequate.

Just days after assuming command, Kimmel wrote to Admiral Harold R Stark, Chief of Naval Operations: "I feel that a surprise attack (submarine, air or combined) on Pearl Harbor is a possibility and we are taking immediate practical steps to minimise the damage inflicted and to ensure that the attacking force will pay."

Dedicated navy man

Admiral Husband E Kimmel, commander of the Pacific Fleet, was a veteran of nearly 40 years' service with the US Navy. A 1904 graduate of the Naval Academy at Annapolis, Maryland, he was born in Henderson, Kentucky, on February 26, 1882. He sailed with the famed Great White Fleet, circling the globe from 1907 to 1909 and served with occupation forces at Veracruz, Mexico in 1914. He served briefly on the staff of Franklin D Roosevelt, then Assistant Secretary of the Navy. During World War One, Kimmel was a squadron gunnery officer with

Admiral Husband E Kimmel was responsible for defences at Pearl Harbor on December 7, 1941. (Public Domain)

Battleship Division Nine. He served aboard several battleships and destroyers during the interwar years and was promoted rear admiral in 1937. Kimmel had developed a reputation for diligence and hard work, although his attention to minor details that should have been left to subordinates has been criticised.

Kimmel was well aware of the possibility of a Japanese attack in the days leading up to the disaster of December 7, 1941. Clearly, he and General Short had received only a portion of the available intelligence regarding Japanese intentions. Marshall and other officers and government officials in Washington DC shared classified information selectively to prevent the Japanese from discovering that their diplomatic code had been compromised. Further, orders from Washington seemed vague at times.

On that terrible morning, Admiral Kimmel watched the debacle at Pearl Harbor unfold from his office window at the submarine base. His intelligence officer, Commander Edwin T Layton, remembered: "As he watched the disaster across the harbour unfold with terrible fury, a spent .50-calibre machine gun bullet crashed through the glass. It brushed the admiral before it clanged to the floor. It cut his white jacket and raised a welt on his chest. 'It would have been merciful had it killed me,' Kimmel murmured."

Admiral Kimmel was relieved of command 10 days after the attack. He was reduced in rank from four-star full admiral to two-star rear admiral, retired from the navy on February 28, 1942 and received a long-sought public hearing on the terrible events at Pearl Harbor during a congressional inquiry in 1945. He was never formally court-martialled. For the rest of his life, Kimmel sought to clear his name. He died at age 86 on May 14, 1968.

After the admiral's death, family members took up his cause, but three US presidents declined to restore him to full admiral rank. In the spring of 1999, the US Senate passed a non-binding resolution exonerating both Kimmel and Short by a narrow 52-47 vote. To date, no further action has been taken and Admiral Husband Kimmel remains, perhaps, a scapegoat in the great tragedy that brought the United States into World War Two.

Right: Kimmel was found guilty of dereliction of duty in the aftermath of the Pearl Harbor attack. (Public Domain)

Below: Following a catastrophic explosion, the battleship USS *Arizona* burns furiously on December 7, 1941. (Public Domain)

Kimmel confers with staff officers at Pearl Harbor in the summer of 1941. (Public Domain)

ADMIRAL ANDREW CUNNINGHAM

The Fairey Swordfish was antiquated. A biplane constructed of wood and canvas that was reminiscent of the Great War, it was slow and lumbering with a torpedo slung beneath its fuselage. Nevertheless, the Swordfish executed one of the most daring air raids of World War Two on the night of November 11, 1940, as 21 daring pilots and aircrew swept into the anchorage of the Italian Fleet at Taranto and put three enemy battleships out of action.

When the raid was over, Admiral Andrew Cunningham, commander of the Royal Navy Mediterranean Fleet, informed the Admiralty: "Manoeuvre well executed." It was a dazzling success and Cunningham further commented: "Taranto, and the night of 11-12 November 1940, should be remembered forever as having shown once and for all that in the Fleet Air Arm, the Navy has its most devastating weapon."

The Italian battleship *Littorio* lies seriously damaged, its bow underwater, after the Fleet Air Arm attack on Taranto, November 11, 1940.

This portrait of Admiral Cunningham was commissioned by the Ministry of Information in 1943. (Public Domain)

Andrew Cunningham commanded Royal Navy forces in the Mediterranean and excelled as First Sea Lord during World War Two. (Public Domain)

The success at Taranto was characteristic of Cunningham's wartime service in the Mediterranean and then as Admiral of the Fleet, First Sea Lord and Chief of the Naval Staff. Cunningham displayed tremendous skill in the Mediterranean as the Royal Navy was heavily outnumbered in the region by the navy of fascist Italy, the Regia Marina. When hostilities started, he recognised the threat posed by the Italians, but his first duty was to remove the possibility of Axis seizure of French naval forces at Alexandria, Egypt. Cunningham skilfully negotiated the co-operation of the French under Admiral René-Émile Godfroy and avoided a shooting incident such as occurred elsewhere.

Focusing subsequently on the Italians, the Fleet Air Arm executed the Taranto Raid, Operation Judgement, brilliantly. Then, in March 1941, the Italian Fleet came out to fight, attempting to ravage the merchant convoys then supplying the British and Commonwealth troops fighting in Greece. During the Battle of Cape Matapan, March 27-29, Cunningham's warships inflicted a stinging defeat on the Regia Marina, sinking three cruisers and two destroyers. The victory wrested control of the Eastern Mediterranean permanently from the Italians.

However, the British expedition to Greece was in grave trouble. The German invasion to prop up the Italian ground forces, followed by the airborne assault on the island of Crete, compelled the British to withdraw. It was Cunningham's persistence in the face of heavy Luftwaffe air attack that allowed the evacuation of 16,500 soldiers from Crete. The Royal Navy remained in the area as long as possible and suffered the loss of three cruisers and six destroyers sunk, while 15 other ships were damaged. It was a courageous display of co-operation with the beleaguered army.

After rendering such tremendous

Cunningham stands behind prime minister Winston Churchill at the 1945 Yalta Conference. (Public Domain)

service, Cunningham was destined for even greater responsibility – and he delivered.

Rise to high command

Andrew Cunningham was the son of an educator, born January 7, 1883, in Rathmines, Ireland. He attended school in Dublin and Edinburgh and then the Naval Preparatory School, Stubbington House, Hampshire. He entered the Royal Naval College, Dartmouth in 1897 and finished 10th in a class of 64 the following spring. Cunningham served on the Cape of Good Hope Station during the Second Boer War and experienced combat on land with the Naval Brigade. He was promoted lieutenant in 1904 and received his first command, a torpedo boat, four years later.

During World War One, Cunningham commanded the destroyer HMS *Scorpion*, receiving the Distinguished Service Order (DSO) and promotion to the rank of commander for heroism during the Dardanelles campaign. After commanding Scorpion for seven years, he transferred to the destroyer HMS *Termagant* in the spring of 1918, receiving a bar to his DSO for his performance with the anti-submarine Dover Patrol.

Between the world wars, Cunningham served in the Baltic Sea during the Russian Civil War and with the North American and West Indies Squadrons. By 1930, he was in command of the battleship HMS *Rodney* and within months was appointed commodore of the Royal Navy Barracks at Chatham. After serving as an aide-de-camp to King George V, he was promoted to admiral and given command of destroyers in the Mediterranean.

Promoted vice-admiral in 1936, Cunningham led effective training exercises in the Atlantic and Mediterranean and in two years he was appointed Deputy Chief of the Naval Staff. Cunningham then commanded all naval forces in the Mediterranean, including Operation Torch, the Allied landings in North Africa on November 8, 1942. His surface and submarine assets harried Axis supply convoys to North Africa, hastening the victory there. He was promoted Admiral of the Fleet in 1943 and commanded the Allied naval forces during the invasions of Sicily and Italy.

As First Sea Lord Admiral Dudley Pound was dying of a malignant brain tumour, Cunningham was named First Sea Lord in his place. He participated in strategic conferences and in the future direction of the war in Europe and the Pacific.

Upon retirement in 1953, Cunningham was raised to the peerage as Viscount Cunningham of Hyndhope. He remained active, holding high office in the Church of Scotland, among other endeavours. He served as Lord High Steward for the coronation of Queen Elizabeth II in 1953 and died a decade later at the age of 80.

Cunningham's enduring legacy as one of the most successful naval officers of World War Two remains.

ADMIRAL MARC MITSCHER

It was an amazing moment in an unlikely career when Secretary of the Navy James V Forrestal summoned Admiral Marc Mitscher to his office in Washington DC on Sunday, November 18, 1945. World War Two was over and Mitscher had been praised for his service in command of the fast aircraft carriers of Task Force 38/58 during the Pacific campaigns of 1944-1945.

Forrestal, like Mitscher, was a soft-spoken man of few words, but he was pleased to see the 58-year-old veteran of the great Carrier War. The two men discussed the future of the US Navy in the Atomic Age and the threat of the Soviet Union during the burgeoning days of the Cold War. Then, Forrestal offered Mitscher the post of Chief of Naval Operations, succeeding Fleet Admiral Ernest J King.

Mitscher was taken aback but prepared with a response in keeping with his mild manner. "No, thank you, Mr. Secretary. I'd want to make too many changes around here." The conversation was remarkable not for its result, but the fact that it had taken place at all. Admiral Mitscher had barely made it through the US Naval Academy at Annapolis, Maryland, 35 years earlier.

Mitscher had never been the academic sort and he disdained the rigours of academy life. He had taken the entrance examination for Annapolis and accepted an appointment from his congressman to please his father, then agent for the Osage Indian Tribe in Oklahoma. Marc was 17 when he entered the naval academy in 1904, but was forced to resign two years later due to an accumulation of demerits, lacklustre grades and general rebelliousness. His father was furious and told young Marc to stay at Annapolis while he prevailed on his congressman friend again for another appointment. Though he still found trouble from time to time, Mitscher managed to graduate from the naval academy in 1910, 107th in a class of 130.

Career and carriers

Marc Mitscher was born on January 26, 1887 in Hillsboro, Wisconsin and grew up on the Osage reservation in northern Oklahoma, spending some of his school years in Washington DC and returning for the summers to ride horses and play baseball and football with the Native American children.

After graduating from Annapolis, Mitscher served in numerous shipboard postings and nearly got thrown out of the navy for missing the last launch back to his ship from the port of Chimbote, Peru. He was intrigued by the idea of flying and sought a transfer to the fledgling aeronautics branch of the navy. After being told he should learn seamanship first, a transfer was finally approved in September 1915. From there, he earned his wings as Naval Aviator No. 33. He saw no combat in World War One but participated in the first attempt to cross the Atlantic Ocean west to east by air in 1919. Three Curtiss flying boats took off and only one succeeded. The plane flown by Mitscher and Lieutenant Patrick N L Bellinger failed to complete the air voyage, but all the Americans were hailed as heroes.

Mitscher commanded several naval air stations in the 1920s and 1930s and also headed the air department of the USS *Langley,* the navy's first aircraft carrier. He was executive officer aboard

Admiral Marc Mitscher commanded the US Navy's fast carriers during World War Two in the Pacific. (Public Domain)

the carrier *Saratoga* and in August 1941 took command of the brand new carrier USS *Hornet.* As *Hornet* was readied for sea at Norfolk, Virginia, the Japanese attacked Pearl Harbor.

In February 1942, Mitscher was promoted rear admiral and two months later *Hornet* was taking the famed Doolittle Raiders near the Japanese home islands for their spectacular attack on Tokyo. Mitscher commanded *Hornet* at the pivotal Battle of Midway in June 1942 and spent months recovering his health after such demanding work. By early 1943, he was ordered to Guadalcanal in the Solomon Islands to command the air group there. Spectacular results were achieved as Mitscher's fighter pilots shot down 472 Japanese planes and his bombers sank 17 enemy ships during his six-month tour of duty.

Mitscher left Guadalcanal a sick man. Malaria turned his skin pale yellow and his weight dropped to just over eight stone. Again, he recovered physically and grew restless for the sea. When the time came, he was the perfect choice to command the fast carrier spearheads of the 3rd and 5th Fleets, depending on which senior admiral was in charge at the time – Admiral William F 'Bull' Halsey as 3rd Fleet and Task Force 38 and Admiral Raymond Spruance as 5th Fleet and Task Force 58.

Mitscher skilfully commanded the fleet carriers at the great battles of the Philippine Sea and Leyte Gulf and numerous other operations across the Pacific. During action off Okinawa, his flagship, the carrier USS *Bunker Hill,* was hit by two Japanese kamikaze suicide planes, forcing his transfer to *Enterprise.* Then, *Enterprise* was hit and he transferred again to the carrier USS *Randolph.*

By the time Admiral Mitscher's duties were concluded in the Pacific, Admiral Chester Nimitz, Commander-in-Chief Pacific Ocean Areas, commented: "It is doubtful if any officer has made more important contributions than he towards extinction of the enemy fleet."

Mitscher was promoted full admiral in January 1946 and suffered a major heart attack a year later. He died at age 60 on February 3, 1947, a pioneer naval aviator and the prototype carrier commander.

Right: Mitscher sits on the bridge of a US Navy aircraft carrier. (Public Domain)

Below: Mitscher and Lieutenant Colonel James Doolittle with a group of army fliers on the deck of the carrier USS Hornet, April 1942. (Public Domain)

Mitscher at the controls of an aircraft as a young naval aviator. (Public Domain)

SUMMATION

The commanders of World War II, Allied and Axis, determined the outcome of the greatest conflict of the 20th century, and indeed all of human history. Their bold decisions, triumphs, and failures charted the course of the great conflict and left a legacy of resolve, determination, and command brilliance at time punctuated with failure, frustration, and lost opportunity. Their lives and times are fascinating, and their influence on modern history remains incalculable. From the battlefields of Europe to the scorching deserts of North Africa, the expanse of the Atlantic and the Pacific, to dozens of otherwise nondescript island outposts and the continent of Asia, World War II was truly a global conflict, and these men discharged duties – for better or worse – that shaped the future.

General Dwight Eisenhower, Supreme Allied Commander in Western Europe, and Deputy Supreme Commander Air Chief Marshal Arthur Tedder confer after the German signing of surrender documents on May 7, 1945. (Public Domain)